D1558184

What is Special about the Human Brain?

OXFORD PSYCHOLOGY SERIES

Editors

Mark D'Esposito   Daniel Schacter
Jon Driver   Anne Treisman
Trevor Robbins   Lawrence Weiskrantz

What is Special about the Human Brain?

Richard Passingham

Professor of Cognitive Neuroscience,

University of Oxford, UK

OXFORD

UNIVERSITY PRESS

OXFORD
UNIVERSITY PRESS

Great Clarendon Street, Oxford OX2 6DP

Oxford University Press is a department of the University of Oxford.
It furthers the University's objective of excellence in research, scholarship,
and education by publishing worldwide in

Oxford New York

Auckland Cape Town Dar es Salaam Hong Kong Karachi
Kuala Lumpur Madrid Melbourne Mexico City Nairobi
New Delhi Shanghai Taipei Toronto

With offices in

Argentina Austria Brazil Chile Czech Republic France Greece
Guatemala Hungary Italy Japan Poland Portugal Singapore
South Korea Switzerland Thailand Turkey Ukraine Vietnam

Oxford is a registered trade mark of Oxford University Press
in the UK and in certain other countries

Published in the United States
by Oxford University Press Inc., New York

© Oxford University Press 2008

The moral rights of the author has been asserted

Database right Oxford University Press (maker)

First published 2008

British Library Cataloguing in Publication Data

Data available

Library of Congress Cataloging in Publication Data

Data available

Typeset by Cepha Imaging Private Ltd., Bangalore, India
Printed in Great Britain
on acid-free paper by
Biddles Ltd., King's Lynn, Norfolk

ISBN 978–0–19–923013–6

10 9 8 7 6 5 4 3 2 1

For my wife, Clare

When psychologist Irene Pepperberg turned to leave her parrot, Alex, in a vet's office for surgery, Alex called out, 'Come here. I love you. I'm sorry. Wanna go back'.

Irene Pepperberg, personal communication

Preface

Background

When neuroscientists become old, they try to solve the problem of consciousness. This book is more ambitious yet. It tackles the soul. For Descartes (1644) it was the soul that distinguished humans from animals. He believed that it interacted with the brain via the pineal gland. Later, the distinguished British anatomist Richard Owen (1858) continued the defence of the unique status of humans by pointing to a structure in the human brain called the hippocampus minor. The absurdity was that this was a mere groove on the inside of temporal lobe (Gross 1993); and anyway Thomas Huxley (1895) had no trouble in demonstrating that it could also be detected in the brains of apes.

But this strange history should not deter us from the task of trying to account for the mental gap between humans and our primate relatives. The topic remains one of the most important in science. It is not enough to understand the universe, the world or the animal kingdom: we need to understand ourselves. Humans are unlike any other animal in dominating the earth and adapting to any environment, even the moon. So this book continues the search for specializations in the human brain that make this possible.

This book depends on advances in functional brain imaging. These mean that we can measure activity in the brains of human subjects while they perform complex cognitive tasks. This became practical in the 1980s using Positron Emission Tomography (PET), and in the 1990s using Functional Magnetic Brain Imaging (fMRI). So we can now study the neural basis of abilities such as speech that are unique to humans. We easily forget what a revolution this has been.

The book

A word of explanation. This is not a book about the evolution of our hominid ancestors or about the genomes of modern humans and apes.

Nor is it a comparative study of primates, since that would require information on a wide variety of species. Most of the evidence reviewed here comes from studies of macaque monkeys, chimpanzees and humans (see front cover). The reason is that laboratory experiments have been mainly restricted to these primates, and indeed neurophysiological experiments have been almost entirely limited to macaques. There is no implication that macaques, chimpanzees and humans form an 'evolutionary series'. Each has continued to evolve since diverging from the ancestors that they share in common.

There is, however, a downside to the concentration on macaque monkeys. This is that it has led to pressures to 'emphasize the similarities and downplay the differences' between humans and the 'monkey model' (Preuss 2004) . Having worked with macaque monkeys all my professional life I am not immune to these pressures. And the success of biomedical science suggests that this is not always a bad thing. Nonetheless, in this book it is *differences* that I am after. In this respect it differs from an earlier book (Passingham 1982) in which I stressed the overall similarities. It is not that I have changed my mind: I still believe that the fundamental design of the human brain is the same as in other primates and that it operates according to the same principles. But we fail to understand what is special about people if we only stress the similarities.

Much of the anatomical information that is currently available is exhaustively reviewed in the volume on the primate brain edited by Kaas and Preuss (2007). An edited volume has the advantage that each contribution can be very detailed and up to date, since it is written by an expert on that specific topic. But there are also advantages in a book that is written by a single author. It can focus on one theme, here on the anatomical and functional specializations of the human brain. It can be personal in representing one individual's search for these specializations. And it can be written at a level which is accessible to neuroscientists who are not specialists in either comparative brain anatomy or functional brain imaging.

One final word of caution. Studies using fMRI with monkeys are in their infancy (Orban *et al.* 2004; Nakahara *et al.* 2007) and developments in the method may make it possible one day to use it with chimpanzees.

Also there are rapid advances in the delineation of anatomical areas of the human cortex from MRI scans (Eickhoff *et al.* 2005*a*; Amunts *et al.* 2007; Walters *et al.* 2007). And there are corresponding advances in charting the binding of receptors in different brain areas (Zilles *et al.* 2002; Scheperjans *et al.* 2005*b*; Eickhoff *et al.* 2007).

So why write the book now? The reason is that I am old and impatient.

Terms used in the book

I should defend some of the terms that I use. First, when I refer to 'monkeys' it is usually to macaque monkeys. The reason is that it is on these animals that most of the neurophysiological and neuropsychological experiments have been performed. Second, I use the term 'chimpanzees' to refer both to the common chimpanzee (*Pan troglodytes*) and to bonobos or 'pygmy chimpanzees' (*Pan paniscus*). Third, I use the ugly word 'humans'. This is shorter than 'human beings' and less offensive than 'man' or 'mankind'. Finally, I use the word 'subjects' when referring to those taking part in an experiment. This has the convenience that it can be applied to animals as well as humans. When used for humans there is no implication that the people were rounded up and then treated like animals. I have not used the strange term 'participants' just to keep PC editors at bay.

Activations in imaging studies

One last note. Where there is uncertainty as to the correct location of the activations in imaging studies, I have used the coordinates that are given in the tables so as to establish for myself where the peaks most probably lay. To do this I have consulted the pattern of gyri and sulci as available on MRIcro. This means that my own description of the locations do not always fit those given by the authors. My training has taught to me to be obsessional about anatomical accuracy. I hope that the authors will forgive me for my presumption.

Acknowledgements

My interest in this topic began long ago when I was a graduate student working under the supervision of George Ettlinger. A memorial volume in honour of him was edited by David Milner who was a graduate student with George at the same time as me (Comparative Neuropsychology 1998, Oxford University Press). George worked with macaque monkeys and chimpanzees and he also studied both healthy human subjects and neurological patients. So I came to work with macaque monkeys and also to write comparative papers on non-human primates and humans. The comparative work was later summarized in my first book *The Human Primate* (1982).

Since then, my interest has been reawakened by the chance to work with human subjects using functional brain imaging. I am indebted to Richard Frackowiak for introducing me to imaging in 1988. I also thank all my graduate students, postdocs and collaborators for keeping me in the business since then.

This work has led to many conversations with colleagues that have helped in the formulation of my ideas. I particularly thank Chris Frith, Matthew Rushworth and Hakwan Lau.

It is a problem that no one person can be a specialist in all the subjects covered here. I have tried to protect myself by showing chapters to others who know more about the material in those chapters. I am particularly indebted to Chris Frith who has read most of the chapters. Particular chapters have been read by Jim Rilling, Katerina Semendeferi, Alan Cowey, Cathy Price, Matthew Rushworth, Hakwan Lau, Marian Dawkins, Marc Hauser and Lisa Parr. I am especially grateful to those anonymous referees who commented very critically on an earlier draft of three chapters. I found these comments very helpful and have revised the book extensively as a consequence.

Sara Bengtsson plotted the data for Fig. 2.1 and Kathryn McDonald the data for Fig. 2.2. Joyce Bennett drew the brain diagrams that I use in this book. Anita Butterworth took the photograph that appears on the front cover. Dave Woodward gave technical help in compiling the final endnote file of references. I thank them all.

Contents

Chapter 1

The mental gap

It is plausible that evolution could have created the human skeleton, but it is hard to credit that it created the human mind. Yet, in six or seven million years evolution came up with *Homo sapiens*, a creature unlike anything the world had ever known. The mental gap between man and ape is immense, and yet evolution bridged that gap in so short a space of time. Since the brain is the organ of the mind, it is natural to assume that during the evolution of our hominid ancestors there were changes in the brain that can account for this gap. This book is a search for those changes. Chapter 1 starts that search by evaluating the nature of the gap between the human mind and that of chimpanzees, our nearest living relatives.

Consciousness

The traditional view in philosophy was that only human beings are conscious. There are two ways in which this term is used. First, it refers to perceptual awareness; for example, the subjective impression that objects are arrayed in front of one. The second use of the term refers to reflective awareness, the fact that we are aware of our thoughts and can comment on them. Philosophers would be more precise in their terminology, but the above distinction will serve us here.

Awareness of external stimuli

There is experimental evidence for perceptual awareness. If the primary visual cortex is damaged on one side, the patients become unable to see stimuli that are presented in the half of the visual field that is represented by the damaged cortex. They have a 'hemianopia', that is they are unaware of stimuli in that half-field. Yet, some of these patients can guess correctly the location of the stimulus, its orientation and its direction of movement (Weiskrantz 1986, 1997).

To find out whether the subjects are aware of the stimuli on trials when they guess, Weiskrantz (1997) introduced a 'commentary key' with patient GY. For every judgement that GY made, for example, about the direction of movement of a slow-moving stimulus, he was also required to press the commentary key to say whether he was visually aware of the stimulus that had just been presented. Even though on most trials GY guessed the direction correctly, he indicated on the commentary key that he was unaware of having *seen* anything. Thus, we can distinguish experimentally between judgements that a subject makes on the basis of perceptual awareness and judgements that a subject can make without being aware. Weiskrantz (1986) coined the term 'blindsight' to refer to the ability to make accurate visual judgements in the absence of awareness.

Yet a macaque monkey with a bilateral lesion of primary visual cortex can pick up small items of food from the floor (Humphrey 1974) and reach relatively accurately for visual targets on a panel (Weiskrantz *et al.* 1977). One's first impression is that these animals cannot be 'blind' in the way in which GY is blind, and this might lead us to suppose that there must be important differences between the cortical visual system in humans and other primates.

We need a way of finding out if the monkeys are indeed blind. So, Cowey and Stoerig (1995, 1997) presented macaque monkeys with a light on some trials and no light on others. The animals were taught to press a panel in trials on which no light appeared: thus a press on the panel indicated that the animal had not detected a light. The primary visual cortex was then surgically removed on one side. The animals now pressed the panel every time a stimulus was presented in the half field represented by the damaged cortex. This indicates that they had failed to detect a light. And it was not that they perceived a light but it appeared dim, since they gave the same response however bright the stimulus that was presented.

In a follow-up experiment, Stoerig *et al.* (2002) directly compared reaching and perceptual judgements. They showed that after removal of the primary visual cortex the animal could reach for a target, but that when it was tested for detection of that target, it pressed the panel, evidence that it had failed to see it. These data strongly suggest that normal monkeys are visually aware in the same way as human subjects, and that it is necessary for stimuli to be processed through the primary visual cortex for the subject to be aware of them.

Bodily awareness

Perceptual awareness is not restricted to awareness of visual or auditory stimuli. We are also aware of our bodies, that is, of the location and movements of our limbs. Information about our bodies is provided by touch and 'body sense', i.e. proprioception. Paillard *et al.* (1983) described a patient who had a right-sided anaesthesia due to a lesion in her somatic cortex. Though she reported that she did not feel touch to her right arm, she could point to where she was touched, even though she was blindfolded. As in the case of blindsight, it was possible to dissociate awareness and behaviour.

Awareness of body sense (proprioception) can also be disturbed in humans by brain lesions. There is a report of a patient with a lesion in the parietal lobe who had an impairment in maintaining a representation of the exact position of the affected arm (Wolpert *et al.* 1998). A temporary inactivation of cortical function can be caused by infusing sodium amytal into the blood supply, and infusions into the right hemisphere can cause patients to deny that their left arm is paretic (Carpenter *et al.* 1995), and even to claim that it belongs to someone else (Meador *et al.* 2000). Even healthy subjects can be fooled into feeling that a rubber arm is their own arm if they see the hand of the rubber arm being touched at the same time as they feel a touch to their own hand while it is out of sight (Botvinick and Cohen 1998). This illusory change in awareness is associated with activity in the parietal and premotor cortex (Ehrsson *et al.* 2004).

There is no reason to treat perceptual awareness of body sense differently from awareness of external stimuli. Again we need a way of asking animals to report. So rats have been trained to press different levers depending on whether they were standing up or grooming at the time that the choice was presented (Beninger *et al.* 1974; Morgan and Nicholas 1979). The rats could do this, and this shows that they must have been using information about the action they were performing. It does not, of course, prove conclusively that this information reached awareness. However, if it is accepted that animals can be aware of external sensory information, and it is accepted that they must also process internal information, it is not clear why they should be aware of one and not the other.

The strongest evidence that an animal can be aware of its own body comes from the studies of mirror recognition in chimpanzees (Tomasello and Call 1997). There are two strands of evidence. The first is anecdotal: chimpanzees will use mirrors to inspect themselves; for example, exploring their mouths in the reflection (Eddy *et al.* 1996). However, an experimental paradigm has also been devised to test mirror recognition (Gallup 1970). While the animal is anaesthetized, the experimenter places a mark on its forehead that the animal can neither smell nor feel. When the animal has come round, one then measures the number of times that it touches the mark when viewing itself in a mirror. Great apes touch the mark when they see it in their reflection (Tomasello and Call 1997; de Veer *et al.* 2003). This means that they can notice the match between their own movements and those that they see in the mirror. This strongly suggests that they are aware of their own movements.

Mental imagery

We are aware not only of sensory information but also of mental images. In pioneering experiments, Kosslyn (1994) asked subjects to imagine a letter such as an F. To prove that they could do it, he presented a grid of squares with a cross and asked whether the cross would lie on the F as imagined on this grid. The subject could do this, and this must mean that they could indeed summon up an image of the letter F.

We cannot instruct other primates to imagine stimuli in the same way. However, we can give chimpanzees a task to perform on which they can only succeed if they are able to recall detailed visual representations. There have been two attempts. The first experiment was on the chimpanzee Sarah. She had been taught to use plastic symbols, and had learned, for example, that a blue triangle meant apple (Premack 1976). In the critical experiment she was presented with the blue triangle and then required to describe it by choosing between a series of alternatives: a red or green circle, a circle or square, a square with a stem or a square without a stem. She picked red, circle and stem, effectively describing an apple (Premack 1976; Premack and Premack 2003).

It is tempting to accept the interpretation that the blue triangle evoked a stored representation of an apple, and that that representation was in terms of the visual properties of an apple. But the experiment is not conclusive because Sarah had previously been required to describe a picture of an apple in the same way. She could simply have remembered her pattern of choices for the picture and repeated them for the blue triangle. A rigorous test would have involved testing many symbols for one trial each, and without first testing pictures.

The logic of the second experiment was similar. Here the chimpanzees Sherman and Austin were studied (Savage-Rumbaugh *et al.* 1980). Both had been taught to press keys on which different symbols were displayed, and had learned to request items in this way (Savage-Rumbaugh 1986). In the crucial experiment, the chimpanzees were first required to sort pictures of foods into one tray and pictures of tools into another. Then the same task was repeated, except that the chimpanzees were required to sort the *symbols* for the same foods and tools. One trial was given for each symbol so as to preclude learning by trial and error. The chimpanzees passed this test. The experiment clearly demonstrates that when the chimpanzees looked at a symbol it evoked a representation of the relevant item. But it does not prove that the animals visualized the item. The sorting was between food and non-food rather than according to the visual properties of the item with which the symbol was associated.

While these experiments show that the animals can retrieve stored representations from long-term memory, they do not prove that the animals are aware of those representations in the same way that a human subject can be aware of an image of the letter F. But this does not mean that we are justified in simply *assuming* that the animals are not aware. Chapter 3 reviews evidence that the same visual areas are activated when human subjects see or imagine a shape or object. Given that monkeys are aware of what they see, we cannot rule out the possibility that they also experience visual imagery.

Recollection

The issue may be more tractable in the case of memory. Inoue and Matsuzawa (2007) presented 5 numerals on a screen for 210 milliseconds, and these were then replaced with white squares. The task was to press the numerals in ascending order after they had been replaced by the squares. Human subjects were tested together with a young chimpanzee, Ayumu. The chimpanzee could perform at 80% correct whereas the human subjects could only achieve 20%. It is true that Ayumu had more practice, but it is unlikely that the adult human subjects would have succeeded however much they practiced. The authors suggest that Ayumu coped because he had eidetic imagery, in other words he could visualize the numerals in their absence.

This opens up the possibility that chimpanzees might also be able to visualize past events in their life. Humans can recollect such events, sometimes in vivid detail. We know this because they can be asked to describe their memories. But this is not possible with animals, and so we need other ways to establish whether animals can retrieve such memories, in other words whether they experience 'episodic memories'. Clayton *et al.* (2003) have suggested criteria that need to be satisfied for demonstrating episodic memory. These are that the subjects can recollect what happened, where it happened and when it happened, and can integrate the information into a flexible representation. They tested this ability, not in primates, but in captive scrub-jays (*Aphelocoma californica*) (Clayton *et al.* 2001, 2003). These birds were chosen because they cache food. The question was whether the jays could remember when they had cached it, as well as what they had cached and where they had done so.

If the scrub jays had cached perishable foods, for example mealworms and crickets, the birds preferentially recovered the mealworms after a short retention interval, when the mealworms would still be fresh. On the other hand, they recovered the crickets after longer retention intervals, when the mealworms would no longer be fresh. And they recovered peanuts, their least preferred food, at the longest interval, when the crickets would no longer be fresh. The series of experiments described by Clayton *et al.* (2003) demonstrates that the birds encode information in memory about 'what, when and where', and can integrate this information to guide food-retrieval. With due scientific caution, the authors suggest the term 'episodic-like' to describe these memories.

However, Suddendorf and Busby (2003) have argued that these experiments do not show that the birds actually *recollect* the episode. The crucial distinction is between 'knowing' that you have seen something before and being able to 'recollect' it, in the sense of recreating in awareness the original episode. We know that human subjects can draw this distinction when they remember items with which they have been presented (Henson *et al.* 1999).

Hampton (2001, 2005) has tried to produce evidence that macaque monkeys are aware when they can and cannot remember. The monkeys were shown pictures, and later given a choice as to whether to proceed to a recognition test or not. The monkeys were more accurate on those tests that they chose to take than on tests that were given when they had no such choice. The argument is that at the time of the choice the monkeys knew how well they remembered the items. But the experiment cannot distinguish between two possibilities: first, that the animals simply had a measure of the strength of the memory; second, that they retained some of the visual detail of the memory (Hampton 2005). Though the second explanation is the more interesting, the data do no discriminate between the two possibilities.

Attempts to establish episodic memory in chimpanzees have pointed to data on two chimpanzees, Kanzi and Panzee, that had been trained to use symbols on a keyboard (Menzel 2005). Kanzi was shown different foods being placed in 17 areas within a 20-hectare forest. Four months later he was taken out by someone who did not know where the food had been hidden, and he was able to press the relevant symbol for a particular food on the keyboard and take the human companion to the appropriate location, even if the journey took as much as 30 minutes.

Panzee was tested by showing her 26 food and 7 non-food items being hidden within an outdoor enclosure, with the distances to the objects ranging up to 8 m (Menzel 2005). After 24 or even 48 h, Panzee could successfully recruit someone to find the food, even though that person had no other information about where the food was. She did this by pointing with her finger extended, giving low vocalizations and gesturing 'hide'. At the same time she could specify what the object was by pressing on a symbol on her keyboard.

What the experiments on Kanzi and Panzee certainly demonstrate is that they have very impressive memory for where things have been hidden and what they were. But unlike the studies of scrub jays, they do no tell us about their memory of when the items were hidden. Nonetheless, these experiments are consistent with chimpanzees also having an 'episodic-like memory'.

The term 'episodic memory' was introduced by Tulving (1983). The original idea was that the human mind is unique in being able to travel back in time (Tulving 2005). However, there is a danger that whenever animals appear to be capable of human performance, one says that it is only a matter of appearance and that there might be fundamental differences. Take visual awareness. For a long time philosophers tended to assume that this was unique to humans; but the experiments of Cowey and Stoerig (1995, 1997) suggest that it is not. The problem with saying that the monkeys just 'appear' to be visually aware is that it may prove impossible to falsify the claim that awareness is unique to humans. Chapter 3 suggests that the issue of whether animals experience episodic memories may be tackled by considering the brain mechanisms that are known to support it.

Inner speech and reflective awareness

There is, however, one respect in which humans are clearly unique. Not only do we speak but we are also aware of inner speech. This is not to say that we are aware of all our thinking. Much of it occurs automatically and without awareness (Velmans 1991; Jackendoff 1997), but we can become aware when, for example, mentally rehearsing telephone numbers or deliberating.

We do so by using the 'phonological' or 'articulatory loop'(Baddeley 2003). If we are asked to read a series of letters and to remember them for a brief period, we sometimes make mistakes by producing a letter that sounds the same as one of the letters that we read (Conrad 1972, 1973). The reason is that when we read the letters we convert them into an auditory code in short-term memory, hence the occasional confusions. The phenomenon can also be demonstrated by 'articulatory suppression'. If subjects are asked to remember a series of numbers, but at the same time to repeatedly say a word such as 'the', they remember fewer numbers correctly (Baddeley 1986). The reason is that there is interference between the two articulatory codes.

We are also often aware of 'hearing' ourselves think and, indeed, much of our inner life consists of a running commentary. Jackendoff (1997, 2007) has suggested that humans can become aware of their thoughts via the phonological images that are associated with them. This provides something new to pay attention to; it then allows us to reflect on what we are thinking. No other sort of imagery allows one to do this. It cannot, for example, be done using visual imagery. Whether or not other primates experience visual imagery, it is certain that phonological imagery is unique to humans. It follows that only human can reflect in this way on their own thought processes, i.e. on their mind. It is in this sense that humans are conscious in a way that other animals are not.

This is a bold claim. It specifically links 'meta-cognition', that is, the ability to reflect on one's own thoughts, to language. How could it be tested? One way would be to see if monkeys without language can reflect on their mental states. There are two claims that they can do so. First, as described in an earlier section, Hampton (2005) has reported that macaque monkeys can make judgements about the strength of their memory. Second, Terrace and colleagues (Kornell *et al.* 2007) taught macaque monkeys to report their confidence in their perceptual judgements by choosing between two icons. It paid to press one if they were confident that they were correct and to press the other if they were not. Having been taught to use the icons in a perceptual task, the same monkeys could then use them reliably on a memory task. But we must be clear what has and what has not been demonstrated. First, the monkeys are simply using the strength of their internal representation: they are not describing it. Second, as admitted by Kornell *et al.* (2007), the experiment does not show that the monkeys are aware of their metacognitive judgements.

An alternative approach would be to study people without language. The problem with this approach is that adult patients with aphasia have learned to reflect on their own thoughts before the insult, and deaf subjects will have learned a sign language that they can use for the same purpose. There is, however, one enticing piece of evidence. Gazzaniga and colleagues (Cooney and Gazzaniga 2003, Roser and Gazzaniga 2007) cite observations of patients with section of the cerebral commissures. If a word such as 'laugh' or 'walk' is presented to the right hemisphere, the patient may obey the command but when asked why, they will produce some confabulation. The suggestion is that it is the left hemisphere, i.e. the 'language hemisphere', that produces the fake interpretation. In other words it is the language hemisphere that comments. The obvious experiment would be to see if one can study meta-cognition in patients with section of the commissures. The test would be to compare the abilities of the dominant and non-dominant hemisphere to make judgements about their own internal processing.

Willed action

The traditional view was that animals lacked awareness, and should therefore be regarded as machines (Descartes 1644). Many philosophers held that humans differed in that they are aware of the idea of the action before they act. This was the ideomotor theory of action as espoused, for example, by William James (1890) who coined the term 'willed action'. The more neuroscience learns about the mechanisms of the human brain, the more acute becomes the problem of reconciling a causal account of our behaviour with our subjective impression that we are free to do as we wish. This question is one for professional philosophers to debate (Honderich 1993; Dennett 2003; Searle 2007). Here it is enough to ask whether there is experimental evidence that humans are free in a sense in which their nearest living relatives are not.

Spontaneous actions

We often act spontaneously, that is unprompted. In the laboratory this ability can be studied by asking subjects to raise their forefinger whenever they want (Libet *et al.* 1983*a*; Jahanshahi *et al.* 1995). The actions are said to be 'free' in the sense that they are not made in response to some external stimulus: it is we who decide. But the distinction between actions that are or are not prompted by an external cue is one that can also be made with animals. Macaque monkeys have been trained either to press a button when they want (self-initiated) or to press it when a light comes on (externally-triggered) (Okano and Tanji 1987).

A philosopher might object that there is an important difference, and this is that humans are aware of their intention before they perform a self-initiated action. The assumption has been that this must be so if the action is to be free. In a classic experiment, Libet *et al.* (1983*a*) therefore asked human subjects to judge the time at which they were first aware that they had formed the intention to act and they could do this reliably. There was much concern when Libet *et al.* (1983*a*) reported that human subjects only became aware of their intention between 150 and 350 ms *after* one could detect electrophysiological evidence of preparatory activity in the brain. This finding has proved to be replicable (Haggard and Eimer 1999). It is clear that we are not aware of the earliest neural changes that occur before a simple action such as pressing a finger spontaneously.

The implications of these studies are not catastrophic and for three reasons. First, few people now take the dualist position that consciousness interacts with the physical events in the brain. Second, there are other possible roles for awareness, such as enabling us to claim ownership of our actions (Wegner 2002, 2003). But thirdly, and most importantly, the fact that decisions can be taken without awareness does not mean that they are not 'free'. When I return your serve at tennis I may not be aware of preparing to do so, but that does not mean that I was forced to return your serve.

Deliberation and planning

In everyday life we do not need to be aware of initiating simple finger movements. They are not something to which we need to attend. But the case is quite different when we are choosing between several alternative strategies and must deliberate, or where we are planning a complex series of actions. However, animals can also freely choose between alternative actions or plan a simple set of moves. For example, macaque monkeys have been given a free choice between two panels (Barraclough *et al.* 2004). The task was modelled on the matching-pennies task. The animal would make its choice, and would then be given feedback as to whether the target it had selected was also the one that had been selected by the computer. Thus, in advance, the monkey did not know which target was correct, and its choice was free.

Macaque monkeys have also been trained to use a manipulandum to move a cursor in a visual maze (Mushiake *et al.* 2001). Mazes were presented on a computer screen, and on any one trial, a goal position was presented. The monkeys could move the cursor to that goal from the start position, and learned to do so by choosing the shortest route. This involved the selection of particular intermediate locations. If the shortest route was blocked off, the monkeys quickly adapted and selected a new route, which took them to their goals in the shortest number of steps. Thus, when obstacles were placed in their way, they could choose novel paths.

In these cases, the planning is for the immediate future, i.e. the next few seconds. But humans can plan into the distant future, days, months or even years ahead. Tulving (2001) links the ability to do so to episodic memory and calls it 'mental time travel'. So can animals plan for events hours ahead? Tulving (2005) has suggested a way of finding out. The essence of planning is that one takes steps now for a future situation in which one will be in a different motivational state (Clayton *et al.* 2003). So Tulving (2005) proposed the 'spoon test'. The idea is that a child carries a spoon to a party because they can think about the party in the future and plan for their needs, such as eating ice-cream.

The proposal led Mulcahy and Call (2006) to try the test on bonobos and orang-utans. The animals learned to open an apparatus to obtain grapes using a particular tool, and were then given the chance to save the tools when they left the testing room. They then waited in a waiting room from which they could see the apparatus. They later returned to the room. The finding was that when they originally left the room, they were more likely to take with them suitable than unsuitable tools, and when they returned they were more likely to bring suitable tools with them. An essential control condition was included in which the apes returned to the room with the apparatus no longer there. They were less likely to return with the tool, suggesting that it was not that they had simply learned to associate the tool with grapes.

In these experiments the need was in the future, but the animals were constantly reminded of that need because they could see the apparatus that was associated with the particular tools. The same objection does not apply to two experiments on scrub-jays (*Aphelocoma californica*) (Raby *et al.* 2007). The scrub-jays were given the opportunity to cache food either in a place in which they had previously been hungry or in a place in which they had not. The result was that they tended to cache the food where they had been hungry in the past. But were they simply caching in response to stimuli associated with hunger? To rule this out, a second experiment was run in which the birds were fed pet-food in one compartment and peanuts in another. When given the chance to cache food in these compartments, they cached more of the other food in each compartment. The authors explain this by saying that the birds prefer to have a choice of foods, and were thus caching so as to provide that choice in the future.

But does this involve 'mental time travel'? Like nest building, caching leads to the fulfilment of a future need. A bird's nest will provide a warm and safe environment for the eggs when they are laid. However, we do not have to suppose that in building it the bird 'imagines' the future state of the nest with eggs in it. Raby *et al.* (2007) make the point by saying that their results do not prove that the scrub-jay 'projects itself into tomorrow morning's situation'.

Nonetheless, because the experiments on apes and scrub jays do not demand such an explanation does not mean that that explanation is wrong. The experiments do not rule out the possibility that the animal can imagine events in the future. After all people can imagine breakfast tomorrow by using visual imagery, and we argued in an earlier section that other animals may experience such imagery. Chimpanzees have been described carrying stones so as to use on nuts elsewhere (Mercader *et al.* 2002), and it could be that in doing so they imagine nuts. We will probably never know.

What is clear, however, is that visual imagery is inefficient for long-term planning. There are three advantages of using phonological imagery. The first is that it is motoric, and planning a sequence of moves is best done by rehearsing the moves using motor imagery. Jeannerod (1994, 2006) specifically relates motor imagery to motor preparation. The same brain areas are activated when human subjects prepare for movements (Pochon *et al.* 2001; Toni *et al.* 2002) as when they imagine them (Gerardin *et al.* 2000).

The second advantage of linguistic imagery is that it allows the representation of a proposition. For example, a proposition can explicitly specify the causal link between a possible action and its consequences. Propositions can refer either to current, future or even hypothetical states of the world.

But there is a final advantage. Consider Charles Darwin when he was deliberating as to whether to get married. He famously drew up two lists, one on why he should and one on why he should not marry, and each list included consequences far into his old age (Desmond and Moore 1991). He then totted up the points in favour and against. Darwin drew up these lists on paper and the advantage is that this clarifies the issues by drawing attention to each of the points. But he could have drawn up the list in his head using phonological imagery, and this too would have clarified his thoughts in the same way.

Language

Speech

The capacity for inner speech follows from the ability to speak. Humans are the only species that naturally develops speech. Parrots (*Psiticus*) and mynah birds (*Gracula*) can copy human speech if exposed to it, but they do not use speech in their natural habitat. Chimpanzees do not speak and attempts to teach them to do so have met with almost no success. The chimpanzee, Viki, brought up in the home of Cathy and Keith Hayes, could be taught only to utter a breathy 'ahhh' and to produce poorly articulated versions of four words, including 'mama' and 'cup' (Hayes 1951). Chapter 5 will point to the brain specializations that they lack.

Symbols

The fact that chimpanzees cannot speak does not mean that they are necessarily unable to understand human speech. The chimpanzee

Kanzi was exposed to human speech from birth, and spontaneously learned the meaning of many words (Savage-Rumbaugh and Lewin 1994). He was tested by playing a word to him over headphones and requiring him to pick out one of three photographs. Over three sessions Kanzi performed at 93% correct. In all, he has learned the meaning of more than 150 words.

This ability is not confined to chimpanzees. Kaminski *et al.* (2004) tested a dog, Rico, which appeared to have learned the meaning of many words. At any one time, 10 items were arrayed in one room, and the owner, who was in another room, told Rico to retrieve one of them. It turned out that Rico's vocabulary extended to over 200 words. Furthermore, Rico learned the referent of new items very rapidly. If a novel item was included in the array for which Rico did not know the word, he retrieved that item when he heard the new name, and he could then pick out that item in future.

The ability to learn words has also been demonstrated in parrots. At the last count, the grey parrot, Alex, learned to say the words for more than 50 different objects, as well as 7 colours, 5 shapes and numbers up to 6 (Pepperberg 2002). The testers were careful to test his knowledge by presenting new cases, and they report data for the first trial for each new case. Success on the first trial cannot be explained by rote learning as the result of feedback.

Of course, symbols do not need to be auditory. The chimpanzee, Kanzi, has also been trained to press keys on a keyboard to make requests. Each key has a design or 'lexigram' on it, and the keyboard has 256 such lexigrams (Savage-Rumbaugh and Lewin 1994). The keyboard was first used with other chimpanzees, Lana, Sherman and Austin (Savage-Rumbaugh 1986). However, the fact that a chimpanzee can press the appropriate lexigram for say 'apple' to request an apple does not in itself demonstrate that the chimpanzee understands that the lexigram *means* apple.

In an experiment already described, Savage-Rumbaugh *et al.* (1980) tried to find out. They required Lana, Sherman and Austin to sort objects or lexigram symbols into piles depending on whether they referred to foods or tools. The analysis concentrated on data for the first trial, so as to preclude learning by trial and error. Lana failed, indicated that she had indeed simply learned to use the lexigrams by rote, without recognizing that the symbols had referents. However, Sherman and Austin were successful, indicating that they were able to retrieve the referents of the symbols.

Other chimpanzees have been taught versions of manual sign language. The first was Washoe, taught by Alan and Beatrice Gardner (1969). Her ability to name was tested in a blind test in which she was presented with slides and her signs were interpreted by someone who could not see the slides. During the tests Washoe was given no feedback about whether she was or was not signing correctly. Thirty-two pictures were shown, each of them four times, and Washoe gave the correct sign on 92 out of the 128 trials (Gardner and Gardner 1985).

We have talked up to now as if these results show that chimpanzees in the laboratory can learn that words or signs have *referents*. But the sceptic might urge the more cautious conclusion that they can learn the link between signs and their associated items, without the implication that they understand that the symbols have *meaning*. The difference is that between A being associated with X and A meaning or referring to X. Words convey meaning in a language because, by using the word A, one person can induce the mental state X in another.

However, a distinction should be drawn between the *mechanism* by which words are learned and the *purpose* to which they are put in a language. The learning of words involves an associative mechanism by which a word such as 'snake' leads to the retrieval of a representation of a snake, and there is no a priori reason to suppose that this mechanism is any different in Kanzi or a young child. However, the child also comes to speak the word so as to communicate 'snake' to its mother; for example, in pointing to a snake in a picture book. In communicating, the child induces the mental retrieval of that representation in its mother.

So, to be convinced that Kanzi understands that words have referents we need evidence that he too uses symbols to communicate in this way with others. One could offer the evidence that Kanzi makes requests on his portable keyboard when he is out with his trainers, travelling in the forest (Savage-Rumbaugh and Lewin 1994). But the sceptic could still argue that Kanzi is just using the lexigrams to get things done, i.e. to affect behaviour. He knows that if he presses a particular lexigram his human companions will fulfil his request.

Here the parrot, Alex, was more impressive. He also makes requests as in 'come here', 'wanna go X' and 'want Y' (Pepperberg 2002). But he also used words to answer questions. For example, when presented with a set of coloured shapes he could answer the question 'what material is green and three-cornered?' or 'how many blue wood?'. Alex used words to identify, request, refuse and categorize. It is this flexibility that makes his achievements impressive.

Neither chimpanzee nor parrot comment spontaneously in the way that young children do. Tomasello (1999, 2003) points out that children spend much of their time spontaneously naming and commenting; as, for example, in showing objects to their mothers. When they do this, they are directing the attention of their mothers to an outside object, and the result is shared attention to the referent. Tomasello and Carpenter (2005) specifically tested whether chimpanzees will make declarative gestures, pointing to an object or toy that the experimenter has not noticed, and unlike human infants the chimpanzees failed to do so.

It is clear that humans are specialized to communicate with spoken language. Furthermore, while enculturated chimpanzees can learn the meaning of words, young children acquire vocabulary at an extraordinary rate (Bloom 2000; Houston-Price *et al.* 2005). The fact that there is a rudimentary ability in chimpanzees should not blind us to the enormous difference between chimpanzee and child. After all, a typical graduate has a vocabulary of 60 000 words (Premack 2004).

Grammar

There is more to language than names. The comprehension and production of language also requires the capacity to acquire the rules of grammar. So Savage-Rumbaugh and colleagues tested the comparative ability of Kanzi and a two and a half-year-old child called Alia. They required them to respond to 660 novel sentences played over headphones and video-taped what they did (Savage-Rumbaugh and Lewin 1994). Examples were 'put the tomato in the melon' or 'tickle Liz with the umbrella'. Overall, Kanzi correctly carried out 72% and Alia 66% of the requests.

There are two problems in interpreting these data. First, the sentences could be correctly interpreted without understanding all the words used. For example, the sentence 'put some pine needles in the back pack' can be understood without knowing the meaning of 'some' or the use of 'in' and 'the' (Premack and Premack 2003). Kanzi would presumably have responded in the same way had he heard 'put pine needles back pack'. The same argument can, of course, be applied to Alia. However, Premack and Premack (2003) cite work by Shady in which it was shown that infants may be sensitive to function words before they can use them. They were found to listen less long if nonsense words, rather than the correct function words, were inserted into sentences. As these authors suggest, the same test could be applied to a chimpanzee such as Kanzi.

The second problem is that the sense of a sentence could often be gleaned from the context. It would not be possible to put the melon in the tomato or to tickle the umbrella with Liz. What is needed is an analysis of the critical sentences such as 'put the coke in the lemonade' where either of two responses is possible. A formal demonstration could be set up by training Kanzi on a series of sentences such as 'dog bites cat' and 'cat bites dog', with Kanzi being required to pick the appropriate picture. His understanding of the rule could then be tested by testing for words not used in the training series, and assessing performance on the first trial of each sentence.

Sign language also has ways of distinguishing the subject and object of a sentence. Gardner and Gardner (1975) reported that Washoe tended to prefer certain orders in her signs; for example, putting the gesture for 'you' first when signing to companions. However, Terrace *et al.* (1979) re-analysed films of Washoe, and found that she was often prompted by her companions. For example, she once signed 'baby in my drink', but in asking 'where is the baby' her companions were unwittingly prompting the first sign. Terrace *et al.* (1979) therefore trained another chimpanzee, Nim, to use gestural language. Since a complete corpus was collected of Nim's productions, it was possible to analyse the order of the signs. Terrace concluded that, though Nim preferred certain orders, there was no evidence that Nim appreciated that order carried meaning.

Before accepting that conclusion, it is necessary to carry out critical tests. Fouts *et al.* (1978) tested another chimpanzee called Ally in which he was asked, for example, to put the box in the bag or to sign whether the box was in the bag or the bag in the box. Ally was trained on one set of objects and locations, and then tested on another set, and he performed well on the transfer tests. However, the experiment was not decisive because Ally was asked questions of the form 'where is X' and this could have prompted him to gesture 'X' first.

This objection does not apply to an experiment by Muncer and Ettlinger (1981) where no such prompts were given to a chimpanzee called Jane. She performed above chance on the first trial of transfer trials, but she only knew a small number of signs, and thus it was not possible to generate transfer trials that were novel in all respects. Nonetheless, it seems likely that chimpanzees can at least master the rule 'agent first, focus last', a rule that may have been mastered early in the historical development of language (Jackendoff 1999).

Even if it were conclusively shown that chimpanzees can distinguish 'cat bites dog' from 'dog bites cat', this would not be enough to convince most linguistics that the animals possessed language. Language consists of a variety of abilities; for example, the ability to combine words and phrases in ever new ways (Pinker 1994; Hauser *et al.* 2002), the use of morphological markers and mastery of the rules of agreement Pinker and Jackendoff (2005). It is true that Kanzi has a rudimentary ability to understand symbols and Alex could imitate what he heard, but what is unique to humans is the full set of abilities, understanding symbols, imitating what one hears, acquiring symbols at a very rapid rate, spontaneously using symbols to comment, modifying them according to tense and combining them to say ever new things.

Understanding mental states

The aim of communication in language is to affect the mental states of others. But that pre-supposes that we know what those states are. We cannot directly observe the thoughts of others; and yet we interpret their actions in terms of their thoughts and beliefs. The term 'theory of mind' was coined for this understanding (Premack and Woodruff 1978; Baron-Cohen 1995), but here we adopt the more general term 'mentalizing', as suggested by Frith and Frith (2006). There are several abilities involved in mentalizing and they need to be distinguished.

Seeing

The first is the ability to understand seeing. Several studies have been conducted to establish whether chimpanzees follow gaze (Tomasello and Call 1997). But there is a problem in interpretation: if the animals do follow gaze, it may simply be that they are turning in the general direction and then looking out for an interesting object. But Tomasello *et al.* (1999; Tomasello and Carpenter 2005) established that chimpanzees will go behind a barrier if they see a human experimenter looking there rather than elsewhere. Furthermore, they will continue to follow the direction of gaze even if a distracting object is presented. If they find nothing, they will look back at the experimenter to check where he or she is looking (Tomasello and Carpenter 2005).

But do they understand 'seeing'? To find out, Povinelli and colleagues (Povinelli and Eddy 1996, Povinelli and O Neill 2000) had the good idea of asking whether chimpanzees would continue to make a begging gesture towards humans who were blindfolded; and they found that they did. However, more recently Tomasello and Carpenter (2005) have reported that two out of the three young chimpanzees that they tested were more likely to beg if the experimenter had their eyes open rather than closed. Furthermore, the chimpanzees gestured more frequently if the head and eyes were directed forwards rather than turned to one side.

There are two problems with these experiments. First, a chimpanzee might fail not because it did not understand seeing but because it could not inhibit begging (Hauser 2003). Second, the chimpanzees are interacting with a person. So, Hare *et al.* (2000, 2001) set up experiments in which a subordinate chimpanzee competed with a dominant chimpanzee for food. The subordinate watched while a piece of food was placed behind one of two opaque barriers. In one condition the dominant animal could not see the baiting and in another it could.

The subordinate animals were more likely to go for the food if the dominant animal either could not see the baiting (Hare *et al.* 2000) or had not seen it (Hare *et al.* 2001). Here there is no need for the subordinate chimpanzee to inhibit reaching.

Melis *et al.* (2006) also tested whether chimpanzees would deliberately go for food by a route that was hidden from the view of the experimenter. The chimpanzees did not have to be taught to do this, they did so even on the initial trials. Again the chimpanzees did not have to inhibit reaching.

So do these experiments prove that chimpanzees understand 'seeing'? The ability to do so, if it exists, must depend on the subjective experience that the chimpanzees have of the consequences of shutting and opening their eyes. So how could we show that they can generalize this experience to others? Povinelli and Vonk (2006) suggest that chimpanzees be taught that they can see out of a bucket with a transparent front and not through one with an opaque front. The critical test would then be whether they gestured towards a person wearing the one with the transparent front in preference to a person wearing the opaque one. My only complaint about this proposed test is that chimpanzees are very familiar with opening and closing their eyes, and no amount of training will make them as familiar with the properties of the buckets.

I argue below that being able to reflect on the mental states of others demands the ability to reflect on one's own mental states. But seeing is not an internal state in the same sense as 'believing' or 'hoping'. If I report that I see X, I am not introspecting on an internal state: I am reporting on something that appears as if on an external cinema screen—*pace* Dennett (1991). Given that other primates appear to be perceptually aware in the same way, it would be foolish to simply dismiss the possibility that they can attribute the same experience to others. My bent is to go further. I am persuaded by Tomasello and Call (2006), who list 12 observations and then argue that the sceptic would have to produce a different *ad hoc* explanation for each one of them. Just as I concluded earlier that other primates are perceptually aware, I am happy to risk the provisional conclusion that chimpanzees also understand seeing.

Joint attention

Human infants not only follow gaze, but also engage in joint attention, that is they look at objects such as toys and then look back to the adult's face. When chimpanzees were tested by Tomasello and Carpenter (2005) they did not show this pattern (Carpenter *et al.* 1998). Okamoto *et al.* (2002) carried out a series of formal tests to see whether an infant chimpanzee would use pointing or gaze as cues to look at one object rather than another. The chimpanzee did so, even using the direction of the eyes as a cue when the person's head was oriented else-where. But these authors do not report that the chimpanzee then looked back at the person.

The reason that this could matter is that Tomasello (1999) has argued that joint attention promotes the learning of language. Houston-Price *et al.* (2006) carried out an experiment in which infants of 15 months were presented with pictures of two objects and heard the names 'shoofy' and 'gopper'. The infants attached the label to the object towards which a female actor looked. Thus, joint attention serves to make disambiguate the potential referent.

Yet, the chimpanzee Kanzi has spontaneously learned the meaning of many words, and the parrot Alex learned to say many words. Pepperberg and McLaughlin (1996) specifically compared the ability of two parrots to learn words, either when the trainer engaged in full interaction with them or only in limited interaction. The finding was that the birds only learned to say the words in the case of full interaction, and the authors suggest that this shows the importance of joint attention. But the experiment did not specifically manipulate where the trainer was looking, nor did the paper report whether the parrot looked back at the person.

Both Kanzi and these parrots have been brought up in human environments, i.e. they are 'enculturated' (Tomasello 1999). Tomasello and Carpenter (2005) admit the possibility that interaction with humans might *teach* chimpanzees to engage in joint attention. This possibility could be tested by finding out whether Kanzi looks up from an object to his human companion. But it is not just a matter of enculturation. Dogs are better than chimpanzees at reading human signs such as pointing gestures (Hare and Tomasello 2005). These authors suggest that domestication has led to pressures for social skills. In the same way, from an early age young children share experiences for the sake of it.

Joint intentions

Not only do human share experiences, they also share intentions. They have adapted to varied and challenging environments by cooperating. Tomasello and Carpenter (2007) have argued that this has led to a distinctively human pattern of shared intentionality. This is not to say that chimpanzees have no understanding of intentioms. Like children (Carpenter *et al.* 1998) they will copy actions that are intentional, but not those that are accidental (Tomasello and Carpenter 2005). They are more impatient and frustrated if the experimenter fails to give them food deliberately than if an accident prevents the transfer (Call *et al.* 2004).

Tomasello and Carpenter (2005) argue that chimpanzees cannot understand what they call 'communicative intentions'. They set up an experiment in which the experimenter either marked one of two cups, or pointed to it to indicate where a piece of fruit was to be found. The chimpanzees could understand what was implied by the marker, a piece of sponge, but not by the pointing. Tomasello and Carpenter (2005) argue that they did not take the test to be a collaborative game. But, as already mentioned, dogs can use pointing gestures to locate food (Hare and Tomasello 2005). They are much more likely to engage in joint games.

One could, of course, encourage chimpanzees to collaborate. Tomasello and Carpenter (2005) did so by testing for role reversal: the experimenter placed an object on or in a base, then gave the base to the chimpanzee and held out the object. Though two of the three chimpanzees tested held out the base, they did not look at the experimenter, unlike the human infants that were tested on the same task. Similarly, when a social game with an adult was interrupted, the chimpanzees did not look at the experimenter to start the game again (Warneken *et al.* 2006).

It could be that the reason was that they were not cooperating or playing with a chimpanzee partner. Povinelli and O'Neill (2000) gave two chimpanzees experience in pulling in a heavy box, and specifically trained them to cooperate in so doing, each one pulling on one of the two ropes that were attached to the box. The test was to see whether a trained chimpanzee would gesture towards a naïve chimpanzee to encourage it to help. They did not do this, but the trained chimpanzee did repeatedly look at the naïve animal.

The problem could be that the chimpanzees were being tested in the laboratory and on novel tasks. In some areas in the wild, chimpanzees cooperate in hunting red colobus monkeys (*Procolobus badius*) (Mitani and Watts 1999). Research is now needed to find out to what extent the animals solicit help and to what extent they look at others for information during the hunt. However, whatever the outcome, there is no doubt that chimpanzees are quite outclassed by children who constantly engage in cooperative games that require them to communicate their intentions to others.

Beliefs and other mental states

Given that our ancestors became specialized for cooperation and communicating intentions, there was a premium on being able to both understand and influence the mental states of others. This pre-supposes that the subject is aware of and can reflect on their own mental states. I argued in an earlier section that humans are unique in being able to do this, and Chapter 9 looks for the brain specializations that underlie this ability.

The ability to reflect on the mental states of others has been tested in the case of children through the understanding of 'false belief'. For example, on the 'Sally Anne' task (Wimmer and Perner 1983; Baron-Cohen *et al.* 1985), the child knows that Sally has seen a toy being hidden but that while she is out of the room, the toy has been moved. If the child understands what Sally has 'seen' and 'believes', it will appreciate that the Sally would look in the original hiding place, and not in the new place where the child knows the toy actually to lie. Children can do this around the age of four.

There are many problems with this task. For example, the child has to understand the story and has to realize that it is being asked where Sally would look *first*. But most important of all, it has to be able to inhibit a prepotent response based on their own knowledge (Carlson and Moses 2001). It is probably for this reason that young children perform better on a version of the Sally Anne task in which they are encouraged to put a sticker on the correct location (Hauser 2003). Placing a sticker is a deliberate and novel act: the children do not have to inhibit reaching. One can also devise a test that does not involve reaching. One example is the 'Smarties' test (Sullivan and Winner 1993). Here the child is directly shown that there is a pencil in a pack of Smarties or 'M and Ms', and then asked what another child would think was in the pack. Children succeed on this test one year earlier than on the Sally Anne test.

Nonetheless, it is easier to devise a version of the Sally Anne test for chimpanzees. In an experiment by Call and Tomasello (1999) both chimpanzees and children were tested. One of the experimenters, the 'communicator', watched a reward being hidden in one of two boxes, and then left the room. The boxes were then transposed, and the communicator came back to mark the box where they had seen the reward put. The children ignored the mark and chose the other box because they could infer that the reward must be in the other box. The chimpanzees failed the test, though control tests showed that the chimpanzees could follow the mark to find food and could ignore it if they knew the mark to be incorrect. But the test required the complex inference that the reward must be in the unmarked box, because the mark indicated where the adult had seen the food and the boxes had now been moved. It may be that chimpanzees fail because they could not make this inference.

So a more direct test was devised by Hare *et al.* (2001). As in their experiments described in a previous section, a subordinate chimpanzee competed with a dominant animal for food. In the crucial condition, the dominant animal saw the baiting and the food was then switched to the other location. On half the trials the dominant animals were permitted to see the switch and on half they were not; on all trials the subordinate animal saw the switch. So on half the trials the dominant animal was misinformed. On these trials the subordinate animals were more likely to go for the food in its new location.

But does this mean that the subordinate chimpanzees infer knowledge on the part of the dominant chimpanzee? Povinelli and Vonk (2003, 2006) argue that the subordinate chimpanzee simply learns to use the *behaviour* of the dominant chimpanzee in deciding where to look for the food. If the dominant animal is present for the switch, it will look at the new location, and the subordinate chimpanzee learns to avoid it. On the other half of the trials, the dominant animal is not present for the switch, the subordinate chimpanzee learns to go for the food in the new location. I have argued earlier that we should not rule out the possibility that the subordinate chimpanzee understands what the dominant chimpanzee can *see*. But it is going beyond the data to suggest that it can understand what the dominant animal *knows*.

One could reply, of course, that human infants are also unable to understand beliefs. Here we need to introduce the distinction between implicit and explicit understanding. The distinction can be made with reference to experiments on young children by Onishi and Baillargeon (2005) and Garnham and Perner (2001). In both experiments, eye movements were monitored and a comparison was made of the time that the children spent looking at each of two boxes.

Onishi and Baillargeon (2005) showed an actor placing a piece of watermelon in one of two boxes and the food then being moved when the actor was behind an opaque screen. Infants as young as 15 and a half months were surprised and looked longer if the actor reached for the box to which the food had been moved. Garnham and Perner (2001) studied older children with a mean age of just over 3 years. The authors told stories about Alan and his football. They report that the children looked longer at the box where Alan would believe the football to be. While for obvious reasons it would not be possible to try this experiment with chimpanzees, it would in principle be possible to try the experiment with the watermelon.

So do the children have an explicit understanding? One can find out either by asking them to point to the appropriate box or to say which it is. In the experiment by Garnham and Perner (2001), the children did not point to or name the correct box. Two experiments back up this finding. In one, 3-year-old children looked at the right location but reached for the wrong one (Clements and Perner 1994). In the other, 3-year-olds again looked towards the right location, but bet on the other location (Ruffman *et al.* 2001).

So how can we find out if chimpanzees can achieve an explicit understanding? One could, of course, maintain that they can never do this because they lack speech and are therefore unable to give a verbal account; but this is too restrictive. If correct pointing is accepted as evidence of an explicit understanding in children, why could it not be accepted as evidence in chimpanzees? However, the problem would be to get the chimpanzee to understand the question. The same difficulty arises if the chimpanzees are given the opportunity to answer by pressing lexigrams on a keyboard.

Perhaps we should not even require pointing. Consider the understanding that young children have of solidity (Hauser 2003). Pioneering experiments by Spelke (1988) show that infants are surprised if a toy appears to go through a solid surface. Yet 2-year-olds wrongly search for the object below the shelf (Hood *et al.* 2000). Here again there is a dissociation between an implicit and an explicit understanding. So perhaps we could test an explicit understanding in other primates by studying where they search.

There are no such problems in determining whether children can achieve an explicit understanding. They end up by telling us where Sally would think the food to be. Karmiloff-Smith (1992) has proposed that an explicit understanding is reached via 'representational re-description'. By this she means the process in child development via which information is progressively recoded so as to make information increasingly available to awareness. Inner speech fosters such an understanding because it is one way in which we can become aware of our thoughts.

Povinelli and colleagues take a strong line (Povinelli 2000; Povinelli *et al.* 2000; Subiaul *et al.* 2007). They argue that chimpanzees never achieve that awareness. The claim is that chimpanzees do not have an explicit understanding either of the physical or mental world. People differ in explaining events in terms of underlying causes. This involves developing theories; for example, theories about solidity or gravity or psychological motivation. The representational re-description in language promotes such an understanding

Conclusions

The purpose of this chapter is to evaluate the mental gap between humans and their nearest living relatives. Sixty years ago the conclusion would have been clear-cut. Humans were judged to be unique in being conscious, able to engage in willed action, communicating in language, making tools and passing on cultural traditions. At that time there was little experimental evidence and little to challenge the traditional assumptions. In the last fifty years some of these have turned out to be incorrect. As early as the 1960s, it was found that humans were not unique in using or modifying tools or in having traditions of tool use (van Lawick-Goodall 1968). Then it was found that chimpanzees could be taught to use manual signs (Gardner and Gardner 1969). Little by little the differences appear to have been whittled away.

One reason is that the capacities of chimpanzees have turned out to be greater than expected if they are reared in human environments, as in the case of Kanzi. We cannot draw conclusions about species differences on the basis of comparisons between chimpanzees reared in impoverished laboratory conditions and infants brought up in the rich environment of a home. In this comparison two factors differ: species and rearing. So we need to compare the child with the enculturated chimpanzee.

In searching for differences between humans and chimpanzees we have as often found similarities. Chimpanzees have turned out to have abilities that we had not suspected. There can be two reactions to this. The first is to suggest that the same apparent performance in chimpanzees and children may actually reflect quite different abilities (Povinelli *et al.* 2000; Povinelli and Vonk 2003). For example, 'episodic-like' memory in animals may not be genuine episodic memory. But what if future research showed that, just as the hippocampus is involved in episodic retrieval in humans, so it is in 'episodic-like' memory in monkeys? In that case one might appeal to parsimony. Of course, the sceptic could still argue that this does not constitute proof, but in that case one might wonder whether their hypothesis is falsifiable. We return to the issue in Chapter 3.

The second reaction accepts that chimpanzees may have some of the same abilities but points out that chimpanzees do extremely badly what human infants do extremely well. This point is documented by Premack (2007). In evaluating the mental gap, we are always looking for abilities that are unique to humans, but this should not lead us to overlook major quantitative differences. Consider the fact that Kanzi has learned to understand some individual words of spoken English. Kanzi's performance is nonetheless very poor compared with human infants who pick up the meaning of words at an astonishing rate (Bloom 2000). Or consider the vast superiority of humans in general intelligence as measured by tests of reasoning. Gillan *et al.* (1981) report that with an enormous amount of practice the chimpanzee Sarah could succeed on a very simple test of analogical reasoning. But her performance would be quite outstripped by children.

The distinction is often referred to by contrasting quantitative with qualitative differences. I find this unhelpful. Of course, if an ability is unique to humans it is appropriate to call that a qualitative difference. But surely quantitative differences can be so extreme that we would want to mark that by some indication that it is not just more of the same. Take intelligence as an example. Someone with an IQ of 130 is cleverer than someone with an IQ of 50, and the scale is quantitative. But there are whole realms of understanding that are available to the one person but not to the other. Or consider the scale of 'innovation' and 'behavioural flexibility' that has been developed by Reader and colleagues (Lefebvre *et al.* 2004) for comparing cognition in animals in their natural environment. Human would be at one extreme on this scale. Is that a qualitative difference or a quantitative difference?

The issue matters because, as we shall see in the next chapter, there is a tendency to argue that mere differences in brain size cannot account for qualitative differences in the abilities of humans and chimpanzees. A large network of computers, such as that run by Google, can do things that a single PC cannot. The implication is that the distinction between qualitative and quantitative differences breaks down at the extremes.

It is time to summarize what we have found. I list below the main findings on the nature of the mental gap.

1. Humans are unique in experiencing phonological imagery and this allows them to attend to and reflect on their own thoughts. It is not certain whether other primates experience visual imagery, but even if they do, imagery is not helpful in reflecting on one's own thoughts. We can rephrase Descartes' Cogito. I am aware of my own thinking, therefore I am human.

2. Humans can deliberate and engage in mental trial and error. This can involve planning into the distant future. Visual imagery can be used for representing future actions, but it is cumbersome. Phonological imagery allows attention to the different reasons for actions.

3. Humans are unique in naturally learning to speak, and children also spontaneously comment to others on what they see around them. They spontaneously pick up the rules of grammar, and there is as yet no conclusive proof that a chimpanzee can learn even the simple rule that word order carries meaning. Children are hungry for language in a way that chimpanzees are not.

4. Humans have adapted by cooperating and this means that they can share intentions. This can be seen, for example, in the play of children.

5. Humans can reflect not only on their own mental states but also on those of others. This facilitates the learning of language in which saying X puts X in the mind of the other person. It is true that chimpanzees may understand seeing, but this does not mean that they can either reflect on their own internal states or on those of other chimpanzees.

6. Humans can achieve an explicit understanding of both the physical and mental world. This understanding is promoted by being inculcated via teaching in a language. People can formulate theories on the causal structure of the world.

The above is a list, and lists are by their nature unsatisfactory. One wants to know how the list is structured. Is one item fundamental, such that the others follow from that? It will be clear that I have put more stress on the phonological loop than is typical. Others might stress the ability to mentalize and share intentions as a pre-requisites for language (Tomasello 1999; Frith 2007; Tomasello and Carpenter 2007). However, I am not trying to give an account of the order in which the various abilities developed in our hominid ancestors. The aim of this chapter was simply to evaluate the mental gap. The next chapter suggests a metric to calibrate the size of that gap.

Chapter 2

The anatomy of the brain

The previous chapter evaluated the mental gap between humans and their nearest living relatives. This chapter documents the brain gap. Subsequent chapters investigate the consequences for behaviour of the anatomical specializations of the human brain.

Brain size

The front cover presents photos of the human brain alongside the chimpanzee and macaque brain. The obvious comment is that the gap in absolute size between the human and the chimpanzee brain is very much larger than that between the chimpanzee and the macaque brain.

The problem with this is that absolute brain size tends to be larger the bigger the animal, and humans are bigger than chimpanzees. This relation between brain and body size holds across a wide range of vertebrates (Jerison 1973). So the issue becomes whether the human brain differs significantly from the size that would be expected for a primate with our body size. This can be answered by plotting the values for brain and body size on a logarithmic scale, and fitting the regression or 'best fit' line. This is illustrated in Fig. 2.1 where the line is fitted to data provided by Stephan *et al.* (1981) for monkeys and apes. It turns out our brain is over three times as big as predicted for a simian primate our size (Passingham 1973, 1982; Rilling 2006). To be more precise, if data are combined from comparative studies using actual brain slices and MRI sections, the human brain is 3.5 times bigger than expected for an ape our size, and 4.8 times the size of a monkey of equivalent size (MacLeod *et al.* 2003).

We need some metric so as to evaluate this gap. So Fig. 2.2 plots the size of the brain relative to the size of the medulla, part of the brainstem. The justification for this comparison was initially presented

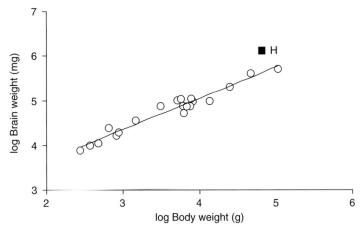

Fig. 2.1 Brain weight (mg) plotted against body weight (g) on a log–log scale for monkeys and apes. Only one value is given for any one genus. The value for the human brain (H) is over three times as big as predicted from the regression or 'best fit' line through the values for monkeys and apes. Data from Stephan *et al.* (1981).

by Passingham (1975*a*). The rationale for using it is that there is a very close relation between body size and medulla size, and the same relation holds across a wide range of body sizes from insectivores to prosimians to monkeys and apes and even humans (Passingham 1975*b*; Barton 2007). It turns out that on the index of brain to medulla size, the gap between the human brain and that of the chimpanzee is larger than the gap between the chimpanzee and a shrew (*Sorex minutus*), a tiny, insect-eating mammal. This is an astonishing fact.

Why are size differences of this magnitude so often downplayed? The assumption is that something other than mere differences in brain size must underlie the mental gap between humans and our nearest living relatives; but we are in danger of operating a double standard. A chimpanzee is not just a clever shrew. In the wild, chimpanzees use and make tools and have complex social relationships, and in captivity they can learn the meanings of words. Though there are many differences between the brains of chimpanzees and shrews, we feel no embarrassment in appealing to differences in brain size as one of the critical factors. Why then are we so resistant to the idea that, in part at least, the mental gap between humans and chimpanzees might be similarly explained?

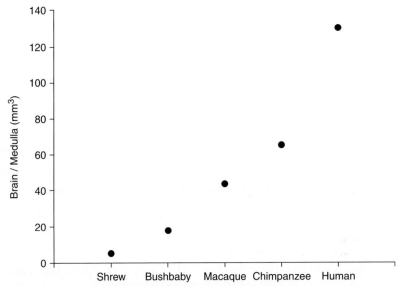

Fig. 2.2 The size of the brain relative to the size of the medulla in the brain stem. Shown for a shrew (*Sorex minutus*), bushbaby (*Galago demidovii*), macaque monkey (*Macaca mulatta*), chimpanzee (*Pan troglodytes*) and human. Data from Stephan *et al.* (1981).

Neocortex size

So far we have argued as if the sole difference between the brains of human, chimpanzee and shrew was in overall brain size. But the brain could be bigger, not because it ballooned as a whole, but because a particular part was selectively increased. So we need to consider the relative proportions of parts of the brain. The comparison between the chimpanzee and the shrew is not fully fair because the neocortex with its underlying white matter forms just 12% of the brain in the shrew but as much as 76% in the chimpanzee.

So we need to establish whether the neocortex forms a bigger proportion of the brain in humans than in other primates. Rilling and Insel (1999) have fitted a regression line to the data on neocortical grey matter and underlying white matter in monkeys and apes. They then used this line to predict the value of neocortex that would be expected for a monkey or ape with as large a brain (minus the neocortex) as humans. Their calculation was that the human neocortex is 35% larger than predicted: this is equivalent to an extra 254 cc of neocortex. This difference may not be large, but it does suggest that in human evolution there were selection pressures, not only for brain size as a whole, but also specifically for the size of the neocortex.

These increases would be achieved by genetic changes in the control of developmental processes. The longer the period of symmetric division of the progenitor cells, the more the cells produced (Huttner and Kosodo 2005). So, if we compare macaques and humans, an increase in only a few days in the length of this division can account for the vast difference in the number of neocortical cells (Rakic 1995; Rakic and Kornack 2007). The reason is that mitotic cell division creates cells at an exponential rate. Though humans share with chimpanzees roughly 99% of coding DNA (Chen and Li 2001; Chen *et al.* 2001), the crucial differences may be in transcriptional control and gene expression. It is known, for example, that the transcription factor BF-1 influences the number of cortical cells (Rakic and Kornack 2007). The continuance of symmetric division also depends on the ASPM protein (Fish *et al.* 2006), and we know that neurone numbers are affected because mutations in ASPM are the most common cause of microcephaly in humans (Bond *et al.* 2003).

Prefrontal cortex

The processing capacity of the neocortex is determined not just by its overall size but also by the relative size of its various component parts. The neocortex can be divided into primary sensory, primary motor and association areas. The term 'association' is a loose one taken over from the empiricist philosophy of John Locke (1689), who accounted for human understanding in terms of the association of ideas. The term 'association areas' has been kept on simply to refer to areas that are not primary sensory or motor. It has long been known from the effects of lesions in macaque monkeys that it is the association areas that are most critical for learning, memory and decision-making (Mishkin 1972; Ungerleider and Mishkin 1982; Goldman-Rakic 1987). So as to help the reader, Fig. 2.3 labels these areas on a lateral view of the human neocortex.

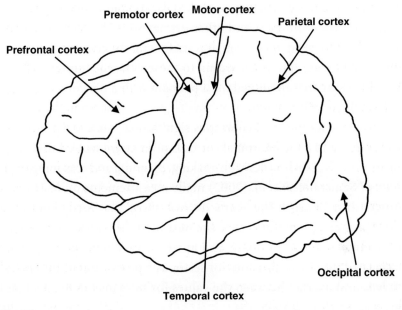

Fig. 2.3

Of the areas of the human neocortex, it is the prefrontal cortex that is most frequently said to be disproportionately enlarged. However, we should be careful about terminology. The correct use of the term 'frontal lobes' is to refer to the whole lobe, including motor cortex, the premotor areas in front of it and the prefrontal cortex in front of that (Fig. 2.3). Psychologists sometimes use the term 'frontal lobes' loosely when what they mean is the prefrontal cortex. This is defined by its cell or cyto-architecture: unlike motor and premotor cortex, it has a well-developed fourth cortical layer packed with small granule cells. Thus it is often referred to as the 'granular frontal cortex'. It lies in front of the premotor cortex (Fig. 2.3). The border can, therefore, only be detected by analysing the architecture of the cell layers. MRI scans do not currently have a sufficiently good spatial resolution to distinguish the layers, except in exceptional cases (Walters *et al.* 2007). We are, therefore, fortunate that Korbinian Brodmann, who can be regarded as the father of cyto-architecture, published data on the size of the granular frontal cortex in humans and other primates (1912, 1913). Since the data were published in German, it is useful that the relevant figures are given by Elston (2007). According to these data, the human value is roughly twice that predicted for a primate with a neocortex our size (Passingham 1973).

If true, the finding is of enormous significance, since as described in Chapters 7 and 8 the prefrontal cortex is intimately involved in higher-order processes such as decision-making, planning and reasoning. So is it true? Semendeferi *et al.* (2002) made measurements on MRI scans (2002) but because the scans do not show the border between prefrontal and premotor cortex, she measured the cortex rostral to the precentral sulcus in human and ape brains. When these authors calculated the size of this anterior sector as a proportion of the cortex, they found overlap between the values for humans (28.8–33%) and great apes (25.5–29.7%).

One's immediate thought is that it is the measurements taken with MRI that are unreliable. But, remarkably, for the human brain the values of anterior sector as given by Semendeferi *et al.* (2002), and the prefrontal cortex as given by Brodmann (1913), agree. The lower limit for Semendeferi *et al.* (2002) is 28.8%, which compares with the values of 27.9% and 29%, which are given by Brodmann (1913) for two human brains.

So the disagreement is not about the human prefrontal cortex. Instead it turns out that the disagreement is over chimpanzees. Semendeferi *et al.* (2002) suggest that the anterior sector forms between 25.5 and 29.7% of the cortex in chimpanzees, whereas Brodmann's figure for the granular frontal cortex is 16.9% (Brodmann 1913). There is independent evidence that suggests that the figures given for the anterior sector by Semendeferi *et al.* (2002) are not a good guide as to the size of the prefrontal cortex in the chimpanzee. The cyto-architecture of the chimpanzee brain was studied by Bailey *et al.* (1950), and their map shows that in this brain the premotor cortex extends far beyond the precentral sulcus. Much of this cortex is classified as FC, that is as dysgranular cortex, and this would not have been included by Brodmann (1913) in his measure of the granular frontal cortex.

Avants *et al.* (2006) took a different approach. They took MRI scans of chimpanzee brain and warped them so as to fit them to human MRIs. The procedure allows one to compute how much the chimpanzee scans have to be deformed in order to fit the human ones, and this provides an estimate of the degree of difference between the brains. The authors conclude that the prefrontal cortex is roughly twice as large in relative terms in the human compared with the chimpanzee brain. However, they do not say how they judged whether cortex was prefrontal as opposed to premotor cortex.

Fortunately there is another way of resolving the issue. Semendeferi *et al.* (2001) carried out a cyto-architectonic study of the frontal polar cortex. Brodmann (1909) assigned numbers to the different areas, and he labelled the frontal polar cortex as area 10. It can be regarded as the top of the information processing hierarchy of the brain. In the human brain, area 10 forms a significant part of the prefrontal cortex (Petrides and Pandya 1999). Semendeferi *et al.* (2001) report that area 10 forms roughly twice as much of the total brain volume in the human as in the chimpanzee. This is consistent with the belief that there has been a disproportionate increase in prefrontal cortex in the human brain. It is also consistent with Brodmann's data for the prefrontal cortex as a whole (Brodmann 1913). His figures show that, relative to the neocortex, the prefrontal cortex is roughly twice as large in the human as in the chimpanzee brain (Brodmann 1913).

Posterior association areas

The obvious question is whether there has also been a proportionate increase in the association areas within the human temporal and parietal lobes. Unfortunately, there are no data for the parietal lobes on their own. Semendeferi and Damasio (2000) give values for the parietal cortex together with the occipital lobe in humans and other primates.

However, Rilling *et al.* (2002) have taken measurements of the superior temporal gyrus and of the temporal lobe as a whole. Apart from the primary auditory area, all of this is association cortex. It turns out that the human temporal lobe is 23% larger than predicted for an ape with as large a brain. However, the data are not quite as expected. There is a trend in other primates for the temporal lobe to form *less* of the brain as brain size increases (Rilling and Seligman 2002). The finding that the human temporal lobe is larger than expected reflects a slight reversal of this trend.

Differentiation of areas

It would be short-sighted to stop the search at this point. After all, there might be neocortical areas that are unique to the human brain. As Preuss (2001) recommended, one should expect and search for specializations in evolution. For example, Preuss and Goldman-Rakic (1991b) compared the cyto-architecture of the prefrontal cortex in the bushbaby and rhesus macaque. Using Walker's (1940) numbering system, they identified the prefrontal area 46 as distinct from areas 8 and 45 in the macaque brain, whereas in the bushbaby they could only identify a posterior area corresponding to 8 and 45. They suggest that in the evolution of the macaque brain, area 46 differentiated out of this posterior region.

There are several factors that determine the number of specialized areas. One is the particular adaptation of the species. For example, there are more visual areas in the squirrel than in the mouse (Krubitzer and Hunt 2007), and the squirrel depends on vision for leaping from branch to branch during the day. Another factor is the size of the neocortex. There is a close relation between the area of the neocortex and the number of sensory areas and this can be shown to be true not only for visual areas but also for somatic areas (Krubitzer and Huffman 2000; Finlay and Brodsky 2007). As the size of the neocortex increases, there is a tendency for new specialized areas to differentiate out.

One reason may be that, as the neocortex increases in size, there is a penalty. With the change in the number of neurones, it becomes increasingly difficult to maintain the connections of each neurone with the same percentage of related neurones (Ringo 1991; Kaas 2000; Kaas and Preuss 2002). One way of coping with this problem of design would be to increase the number of processing areas so that these areas are smaller and local connections are maintained within them.

Given the vast expansion of the human neocortex relative to body size, we might therefore expect to see new areas differentiating out. Also, during the evolution of the human brain there were selection

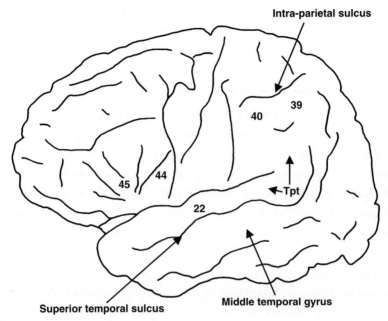

Fig. 2.4

pressures for the development of speech and language, as well as for the ability to adapt to novel environments by tool making and planning. So we should be on the lookout for the development of new areas or sub-areas. The following sections consider candidates in the parietal, temporal and frontal lobes. Figure 2.4 labels the areas.

Parietal cortex

The first candidates lie in the parietal lobes. Brodmann (1909) identi-fied two areas in the human inferior parietal lobe, and he gave these new numbers, 39 and 40, because he could not identify them in a monkey brain (*Cercopithecus*). These areas lie below the intra-parietal sulcus (Fig. 2.4). But more recent cyto-architectural analyses point to a similarity between the areas in the inferior parietal cortex in the monkey and human brain. Three subregions, PF, PFG and PG, have been identified in the macaque monkey brain (Pandya and Seltzer 1982; Geyer *et al.* 2005; Gregoriou *et al.* 2006). The lettering system (von Bonin and Bailey 1947) is an alternative to Brodmann's numbering system. Eidelberg and Galaburda (1984) carried out a cyto-architectural study of the human inferior parietal cortex and identified the same three areas.

More recent cyto-architectural studies of the human inferior parietal cortex have used automated methods to distinguish the cyto-architectural boundaries. A number of other areas or sub-areas have been identified in this way in the human brain (Caspers *et al.* 2006). Unfortunately the authors do not compare their results with those reported by Geyer *et al.* (2005), who used the same automated methods for the macaque brain. These authors comment that more work needs to be done to examine the opercular areas in the macaque monkey. Nonetheless the increase in size of the human parietal cortex does appear to have led to further sub-areas differentiating out.

We can, however, be certain of one difference between the human and macaque inferior parietal cortex. An area called Tpt (temporo-parietal) has been identified in the human brain (Galaburda and Sanides 1980). It extends from the back of the superior temporal cortex into the inferior parietal lobe on the angular gyrus (Fig. 2.4). The same area can be identified in the macaque brain, but here it is restricted to the superior temporal cortex (Galaburda and Pandya 1983). In the human brain, electrical stimulation of the angular gyrus disrupts language (Ojemann 1994), and there is also activation in the angular gyrus when subjects carry out a task involving the detection of phonemes (Simon *et al.* 2002).

So is the extension of Tpt into the parietal lobe of the human brain related to our specialization for language? We should hold fire until a cyto-architectural analysis of parietal cortex has been conducted of the chimpanzee brain. The speculation would be strengthened if Tpt is restricted to the temporal lobe in the chimpanzee.

Wernicke's area

In the human brain, the posterior part of the left superior temporal cortex is traditionally referred to as 'Wernicke's area' (Fig. 5.1). It is so-called because it was identified as a language area by Wernicke (1874).

The area lies outside the 'core' auditory cortex, which can be reliably identified in the macaque, chimpanzee and human brains (Hackett *et al.* 2001).

The primary auditory cortex sends connections to the belt and parabelt regions that lie beside it, as well as area Tpt that lies more posteriorly (Galaburda and Pandya 1983). In the chimpanzee and human brains, one can identify the 'planum temporale', which lies on the superior temporal plane. It may include part of the cortex that has been identified as parabelt in the macaque monkey brain (Sweet *et al.* 2005). Hackett (2007) states that the planum temporale is greatly expanded in the chimpanzee and human brains, but no quantitative data are presented that would allow us to see if this area is disproportionately expanded in the human brain.

The initial identification of Wernicke's area was based on patients with lesions. But these lesions are rarely restricted to one area, and they also include the white matter. Penfield and Roberts (1959) and Ojemann (1994) therefore tried to chart Wernicke's area by stimulating the cortex during surgery and measuring the interference with language. This led both groups to widen the limits of Wernicke's area so as to include the superior temporal sulcus and the middle temporal gyrus below it (Fig. 2.4). The claim is supported by the finding that cell activity can be recorded in the middle temporal gyrus when patients listen to speech during surgery (Creutzfeldt *et al.* 1989).

Yet in the macaque monkey the tissue below the superior temporal sulcus is visual association cortex. Lesions of it cause a severe impairment in the ability to identify complex visual stimuli (Gaffan *et al.* 1986). Yet they have no effect on the ability to discriminate sounds (Dewson *et al.* 1969). Furthermore, in the monkey brain this area receives visual (Desimone and Ungerleider 1989) but not auditory input (Pandya and Yeterian 1985).

There are three ways of trying to explain the discrepancy. The first is to maintain that the superior temporal sulcus is not homologous in the human and macaque brain. One could point to the fact that the motion area MT/V5 lies in the depths of the superior temporal sulcus in the macaque brain, but well below it in the human brain (Peuskens *et al.* 2005).

The term MT/V5 is used here because this area was first identified in the middle of the temporal lobe (MT) of the owl monkey (*Aotus trivergatus*) (Allman and Kaas 1971) and as V5 in the superior temporal sulcus of the macaque (Zeki 1971, 1983).

The second explanation accepts that the superior temporal sulcus is homologous, but suggests that it has become opened up and the tissue in it expanded so as to include tissue on the middle temporal gyrus. Since there are auditory inputs to the upper bank of the superior temporal sulcus (Seltzer and Pandya 1994), the result could be that there are auditory inputs to the middle temporal gyrus in the human brain.

Both of these explanations assume that there has been re-organization in the human brain, and the most likely reason would be that this was due to the expansion of multi-sensory tissue as the result of the specialization for language. One could try to avoid this conclusion by a third line of argument. Chapter 3 will review imaging data that indicate that activation in the middle temporal gyrus can be related to the analysis of the *semantics* of words rather than their auditory properties.

The issue could be resolved by identifying where area MT/V5 lies in the chimpanzee brain. This could be done by using the high-resolution MRI methods employed by Walters *et al.* (2007) to identify this area in the human brain. If MT/V5 lies in the superior temporal sulcus in the chimpanzee brain, that would point to a re-organization in the human brain. If, on the other hand, MT/V5 lies below this sulcus in the chimpanzee brain, this would argue against such a major re-organization.

Broca's area

The other language area is Broca's area, first identified as being the area that was damaged in patient 'Tan' who had a very severe non-fluent aphasia (Broca 1861). But, though the term is widely used in textbooks of neurology, authors are not consistent in the way in which they use it. It is most commonly used to designate the cyto-architectonic area identified by Brodmann (1909) as area 44 (Fig. 2.4). This area very roughly corresponds to 'pars opercularis' as identified by the pattern of sulci. But an MRI scan of Tan's brain shows that the lesion was very extensive. In other words, it was not restricted to pars opercularis and it undercut the deep white matter underlying it (Dronkers *et al.* 2007). Damasio and Damasio (1989) present a scan of a patient who suffered a stroke that was relatively restricted to pars opercularis. Initially, the patient had laboured speech, but then showed an excellent recovery. Mohr *et al.* (1978) reviewed a series of such cases, and again reported good recovery.

For this reason, the term 'Broca's area' is sometimes used to include not only area 44 but also the tissue immediately in front of it. Brodmann (1909) labelled this area 45. This very roughly corresponds to 'pars triangularis' as identified by the pattern of sulci. Damasio and Damasio (1989) present a scan of a patient who suffered an infarct that included both areas 44 and 45, and in this case speech was severely impaired and recovery very limited. However, as in Tan's brain, the infarct also included most of the deep white matter underlying both areas. The lesions that produce Broca's aphasia usually extend along the frontal operculum and include infarction of the white matter (Alexander *et al.* 1990). The result is that connections from posterior regions to the more anterior prefrontal cortex are severely disrupted.

The problem is that strokes lead to the loss of the blood supply not only to the cortical cells but also to the axonal fibres in white matter. It is for this reason that Chapter 5 appeals to imaging studies of speech and language. The advantage of imaging is that the peaks are localized in the grey matter. There is the further advantage that peaks can be restricted to specific cyto-architectonic areas.

Brodmann (1909) did not identify an area 44 in the monkey brain (*Cercopithecus*), and this has led to the widespread belief that area 44 is unique to the human brain. The issue has been re-examined by Petrides *et al.* (2005). In the human brain there is a transition from premotor cortex (area 6) with no layer IV populated with granule cells, to area 44 with a disrupted granular layer, to area 45 with a prominent and contin-uous granular layer (Petrides and Pandya 1995). A similar transition can be demonstrated in the macaque brain, i.e. an agranular inferior premo-tor cortex (area 6), then a dysgranular area, and finally a granular area of inferior prefrontal cortex in front of that (Petrides *et al.* 2005). These divisions should be reliable since they are based on quantitative data.

These authors propose that the dysgranular area is the homologue of area 44 in the human brain. In favour of this suggestion, electrical stimulation of this area evokes mouth movements (Petrides *et al.* 2005).

It could be objected that in the human brain, area 44 lies in front of the precentral sulcus, whereas the proposed homologue of this area lies in the fundus of the arcuate sulcus in the macaque brain. Yet, these sulci are often assumed to be homologous. However, Sherwood *et al.* (2003) had no trouble identifying area 44 in the chimpanzee brain—it lies in the anterior bank of the precentral sulcus and on the convexity cortex in front of it, just as in the human brain (Amunts *et al.* 1999). In both the chimpanzee and human brains there is considerable variability, and in some brains, area 44 extends into the fundus of the precentral sulcus. It is in the fundus of the arcuate sulcus that Petrides *et al.* (2005) identify area 44 in the macaque brain.

Though area 44 has now been identified in the brains of squirrel monkeys (*Saimiri sciureus)* (Simonyan and Jurgens 2002), macaque monkeys, chimpanzees and humans, no data are available that would allow a comparison of its relative size in the different species.

Anatomical connections

In previous sections, areas were identified on the basis of their cyto-architecture. The reader may wonder why cyto-architecture should be taken to be so important. One reason is that anatomical connections run to and from areas that are distinct in their cyto-architecture (Young 1993). Passingham *et al.* (2002) have proposed that each cyto-architectonic area has a unique pattern of inputs and outputs. They illustrate this principle by taking different regions within the prefrontal and premotor cortex. By applying multidimensional scaling techniques to the data on connections, they show that no two areas have the identical set of inputs and outputs. The authors then go on to suggest that it is the unique pattern of connections that is the main determinant of the functions of an area. They call this pattern its 'connectional fingerprint'.

But can we show that these fingerprints relate to function? Passingham *et al.* (2002) have tried to answer this question by plotting the degree to which cells in related areas respond to different stimuli and to different situations. This allows them to plot 'functional finger-prints'. As an illustration, the paper presents these for five different motor or premotor areas. Multidimensional methods now exist by which it would be possible to take the further step and directly test the proposal that these functional patterns directly relate to the connectional patterns.

If these proposals are correct, we should expect that a new area would also be distinguished by a new pattern of inputs and outputs. We have, for example, already mentioned that prefrontal area 46 can be identified in the macaque brain but not the bushbaby brain (Preuss and Goldman-Rakic 1991b). So these authors plotted the anatomical connections of the prefrontal cortex of the bushbaby (Preuss and Goldman-Rakic 1991a). As expected, they failed to find the pattern of connections that is typical of area 46 in macaques.

So we now need to apply the same methods to the human brain. But there is a problem. Studies of connections in animals make use of the fact that tracers can be injected into specific regions, and these are transported along the axons of the cells. The sites to which these tracers travel can be identified either in post-mortem brain sections or by using MRI scans to visualize the transport of contrast agents *in vivo* (Saleem *et al.* 2002). As Crick and Jones (1993) sadly reflected, such methods are not available for the study of the human brain because it is not ethical to inject tracers into the living brain for purely scientific purposes.

This leaves three methods. The first is to inject tracers into brains post-mortem. In this way Tardif and Clarke (2001) have studied the intrinsic connectivity of auditory areas in the human brain. But in post-mortem brains, tracers take a very long time to move along the axon and only move very short distances. This method cannot, as yet, be used to study the long-distance connections between cortical areas.

The second method is to study the degeneration of the terminals of axons when a lesion damages the cell bodies of origin. By using a silver stain it is possible to visualize the degeneration of the axon terminals in the brain post-mortem. It was in this way that Clarke (1994) was able to demonstrate projections from an anterior part of the prestriate cortex back to earlier visual areas in the human brain. But the method has the drawback that one has to find brains with very restricted lesions, and this means reviewing a large number of brains. More importantly, small infarcts will include not just the cortex but also the white matter, and therefore fibres running under the area will also degenerate. It was for this reason that the method of injecting tracers was developed for use with animals, since the tracers are only taken up by cells and not by the underlying white matter.

There is, however, a more recently developed method, and this is 'Diffusion Tensor Imaging' (DTI). This makes use of the fact that water in brain preferentially diffuses in the direction of white-matter fibres, and the magnetic resonance signal can be sensitized to detect the coherent diffusion of water in one direction rather than another (Conturo *et al.* 1999). It is possible in this way to visualize the orientation of the large white-matter bundles. The method has been validated by charting 10 long, association, white-matter pathways using both diffusion imaging and tracer methods in the macaque monkey brain (Schmahmann *et al.* 2007). The results are impressively similar for the two methods.

Specific pathways

This allows us to use diffusion imaging to directly compare these pathways in human and macaque brains. This has been done for the projections from different parts of the temporal and parietal cortex to different sub-areas with the prefrontal cortex (Croxson *et al.* 2005). The authors divide the prefrontal cortex into a number of sub-areas that are taken to be homologous in the human and macaque brain. They then present histograms that show the connection probability with each prefrontal sub-area. The over-riding finding is that the cortico-cortical connections are very similar in the two species. One hopes that there will be many such comparative studies in the future. In particular one looks forward to studies of regions such as the frontal polar cortex that are poorly developed in monkeys.

One obvious place to search for new connections is the language areas, given that the human brain is specialized for language. It is commonly believed that the projections to Broca's area run in the arcuate fasciculus, with their origin in the posterior part of the superior temporal gyrus (Geschwind 1979), but this claim was not based on experimental studies. Experiments using tracers in the macaque brain show clearly that the fibres of the arcuate fasciculus terminate in a posterior part of the superior prefrontal cortex (Petrides and Pandya 2006). It is true that there are fibres that run from the superior temporal cortex to the ventral prefrontal cortex, but these are contained in the extreme capsule (Croxson *et al.* 2005).

So what of the human brain? DTI imaging suggests that area 44 receives projections from the inferior parietal cortex as in the macaque brain, whereas the ventrolateral prefrontal cortex, including area 45, receives projections from the superior temporal cortex (Croxson *et al.* 2005). DTI has also been used by Anwander *et al.* (2006) to study the connections of areas 44 and 45. They identified seed voxels in the white matter under area 45 or 44. The overall pattern of connections of the two areas was distinct enough to allow them to be distinguished on the basis of the pattern. However, the method was not optimal for idenfying the detailed connections of each of these neighbouring areas.

For this reason, Rilling *et al.* (in press) took seed voxels in the inferior parietal cortex, superior temporal cortex and middle temporal cortex. They then used probabilistic tract tracing to trace fibres from these seed voxels to a region of interest that included the white matter at the level of the precentral sulcus or in the case of the macaque monkey the arcuate sulcus. In this animal, fibres from the superior temporal cortex and anterior parietal cortex appeared to terminate in the depths of the arcuate sulcus. In the chimpanzee, there were connections from the superior temporal gyrus to the inferior frontal area 47, and strong connections from the anterior parietal cortex to the ventral premotor cortex and inferior limb of the precentral sulcus. The main difference for the human brain is that the projections from the middle temporal gyrus were stronger, and the terminations in the inferior frontal gyrus were more widespread.

Size of pathways

What matters is not just the origin and termination of pathways but also the size of the pathways. So are there particular connections that are better developed in the human brain? The fibres run in the white matter, and we can measure the volume of the white-matter bundles.

This has been done, for example, for the prefrontal white matter. As the size of the neocortex increases, so there is a disproportionate increase in the volume of the prefrontal white matter (Schoenemann et al. 2005). This follows the general rule that white matter expands more than neocortical grey matter (Barton and Harvey 2000). It is not clear whether this reflects a compensation for brain size or a genuine increase in connectivity. There is no agreement on whether the prefrontal white matter is more extensive than predicted in the human brain: it depends what comparisons are made (Schoenemann et al. 2005; Sherwood et al. 2005b). Schenker et al. (2005) have tried to resolve the issue by distinguishing between the long association fibres in the core of the white matter and the shorter fibres that connect neighbouring regions within the gyri of the frontal lobes. They find that it is the latter that are more extensive than predicted. This finding is supported by the observation that there are more gyri in the human prefrontal cortex than expected for a brain our size (Rilling and Insel 1999; Rilling 2006). The formation of gyri is related to pattern of the local connections.

The same authors also measured the white matter in the temporal lobe. They calculate that the gyral white matter of the temporal lobe is also greater than predicted in the human brain. In an earlier analysis using the same data for non-human primates, Rilling and Seligman (2002) report that the increase is 22%.

These calculations relate to the white matter as a whole, but it is more pertinent to see whether particular bundles within the white matter have been disproportionately enlarged. The place to start looking is the language system. As mentioned above, Rilling et al. (in press) used DTI to chart connections from the temporal lobe to the inferior frontal cortex in the human, chimpanzee and macaque monkey brains. There were two findings of note. The first was that the projection from the middle temporal gyrus was heavier in the human than chimpanzee brain. The second was that, in the human but not chimpanzee brain, the projection was heavier in the left than the right hemisphere. This parallels the findings of Paus et al. (1999) who studied the maturation of white matter in children and adolescents. These authors reported that with age there was a change in the white-matter density for the arcuate fasciculus/extreme capsule, but mainly in the left hemisphere. This change may reflect increases in the diameter or myelination of the fibres, but in either case it probably leads to faster transmission of information.

Microstructure

The previous section considered the extrinsic connections of particular cyto-architectonic areas, but the functions of an area are also determined by its intrinsic connections. Different areas differ in the thickness of the layers, and therefore in the number of pyramidal, stellate and other cell types. And different cell types have different arrays of dendrites onto which other cells connect (Lund *et al.* 1993). Even if we take one cell type, for example, the pyramidal cell, one finds increases in the size and complexity of the dendritic tree and the number of spines on the dendrites as one progresses along the ventral visual stream from the primary visual cortex to the infero-temporal cortex (Elston 2003, 2007). This has consequences for the intrinsic connectivity, since it is on these spines that axons terminate. Elston (2003) argues that it is the differences in intrinsic connectivity that accounts for the fact that there is 'set' activity in the infero-temporal cortex, that is persistent activity rather than the phasic activity that is characteristic of the primary visual cortex.

So we should be alert for differences in microstructure between the brains of humans and their nearest living relatives. Preuss (2001) and DeFelipe *et al.* (2007) point out that one can find differences between the structure of the cortex in different mammals such as the sea cow (*Dugong dugon*), platypus (*Ornithorynchus anatinus*) or mole (*Talpa europea*). If there are specializations in microstructure in other mammals, we should not be surprised if we find specializations in the microstructure of the human brain.

Architecture of neocortex

The neocortex is divided into six layers. Layer IV is the 'granular' layer because it contains 'granule' or 'stellate' cells. Layers II and III above are therefore referred to as 'supra-granular layers'. These are proportionately thicker in primates than in smaller mammals such as the mouse, rat or cat (Marin-Padilla 1992; Hill and Walsh 2005; DeFelipe *et al.* 2007). This has consequences for function as the large pyramidal cells in layer V send an apical dendrite up through these layers into layer I, making synaptic contacts on the way.

The supra-granular layers are proportionately best developed in the human brain (Marin-Padilla 1992; DeFelipe *et al.* 2007). We now need measurements in a series of non-human primates so that we can see whether these layers are thicker than would be predicted for a primate with as extensive a neocortex. When we consider the consequences of a large brain size, we need to take into account the increase in processing power that could result from the associated change in microstructure.

Pyramidal cells

There are also changes in the morphology of pyramidal cells as brain size increases. Elston *et al.* (2001, 2006; Elston 2007) have compared the pyramidal cells in the prefrontal, occipital and temporal cortex. They measured the complexity of the branching pattern of the dendrites and the density of the spines on the dendrites of pyramidal cells in layer III. These measurements were taken in the human brain and in the brains of macaques and other monkeys.

There were two findings. First, the total number of spines in the basal dendritic arbor of the average pyramidal cell was greater in prefrontal than temporal or occipital cortex. This reflects the greater diversity of inputs to prefrontal cortex. The second finding was that the maximum spine density was higher in the human prefrontal cortex than in macaques, baboons (*Papio*), vervet monkeys (*Cercopithecus*) and marmosets (*Callithrix*). Furthermore the difference is impressive: layer III pyramidal cells in the prefrontal cortex are 70% more spinous in the human brain than in the macaque brain (Elston *et al.* 2006).

Is this the result of the size of the human brain? Elston *et al.* (2006) went on to plot the data on a logarithmic scale and to fit the best fit regression line to the data on the size of the prefrontal cortex in non-human primates. The finding was that the human value lies close to this line. In other words, one can predict the microstructure from the overall size of the prefrontal cortex. As size increases, so the power of the basic unit, the pyramidal cell, increases. The more spines, the greater the possibility of integrating information collected by the cells. We return to this in Chapter 7.

Spindle cells

The discussion so far has been limited to pyramidal cells, and these can be found in layers II, III and V in most mammals. But we should also be on the lookout for cell types that are unique to the human brain. Nimchinsky *et al.* (1999) report the existence of large, spindle-shaped cells in layer V in the human brain. They can be found in two areas: the anterior cingulate cortex and the anterior part of the insula. This led Allman *et al.* (2002) to cite these cells as a 'phylogenetic specialization in the human brain'. This title is slightly misleading. It is true that spindle cells cannot be found in gibbons or monkeys, but abundant spindle cells can be counted in the brains of the common chimpanzee (*Pan troglodytes*) and they are also found in clusters in bonobos (*Pan paniscus*), as in the human brain (Nimchinsky *et al.* 1999).

Allman *et al.* (2005) have renamed these neurones 'von Economo neurones' because they were first identified by von Economo (1926). They present counts for the number of these cells in the anterior part of the insula, and the figure that they provide shows that the absolute number is impressively greater in the human brain. But no correction is presented in this paper for the difference in the number of other cells in this area. What is needed is an analysis to see if there are a greater *proportion* of such cells in the human brain. We return to the functional interpretation of spindle cells in Chapter 9 when we consider empathy and theory of mind.

Language areas

There is one final place to look for specializations in microstructure. We know that in right-handers it is the left hemisphere that is specialized for language. So can we find microstructural differences between the left and right hemisphere that can be related to language?

Buxhoeveden *et al.* (2001*a*, *b*) examined stained sections through the temporo-parietal area Tpt, which lies within Wernicke's area. This enabled them to visualize and measure the columnar structure of the cortex.

The cells in neocortex are arranged in a series of vertical mini-columns. The authors measured the width of these columns and the width of the regions between them, which are low in cell bodies, i.e. the neuropil space. They did this in the left and right hemispheres of nine human, eight chimpanzee and seven rhesus macaque brains.

Their first finding was that the columns were larger and there was more space between the cell columns in the human brain than in the brains of chimpanzees and rhesus monkeys (Buxhoeveden *et al.* 2001*a*). This could, of course, reflect differences in brain size, and it would be important to check this by examining the brains of other large mammals. The second finding was that in the human brains there was an asymmetry (Buxhoeveden *et al.* 2001*b*). The column width and neuropil space between the columns were larger on the left than on the right. A similar asymmetry was not found in the brains of the chimpanzees or rhesus monkeys. We will leave further discussion of this finding until Chapter 6, which reviews hemispheric asymmetries in detail.

The other main language area is Broca's area. Amunts *et al.* (1999, 2003) examined stained sections taken through Broca's areas 44 and 45 in the human brain. There was an asymmetry in area 44 but not in area 45: in area 44 there was a higher cell density on the left than the right. This asymmetry was present at birth but tended to increase with age, partly perhaps as the result of language practice (Amunts *et al.* 2003). However, there has been no study of the microstructure of this area in the brains of chimpanzees to see if a similar asymmetry can be found.

Neurochemistry

The study of cyto-architecture is over a century old. We now have more recent methods for studying cells and their receptors. In immunocytochemistry, antibodies are raised against cell-specific proteins, such as enzymes. In receptor autoradiography, radioactively labelled ligands are bound to receptor sites on cells so as to identify the receptors. This method can even be used to compare the distribution of receptor labelling across the different layers of the neocortex (Eickhoff *et al.* 2007).

Cell proteins

Comparative studies using these newer methods are only in their infancy. As an example of what we might find, Preuss and colleagues (1999; Preuss and Coleman 2002*b*) have studied layer IVA of the primary visual cortex in the brains of humans and other primates. This is the sub-layer to which the magnocellular layers of the lateral geniculate nucleus project, bringing information about visual motion. Using immunocytochemistry, the authors showed that in the human brain there are alternating bands that stain for a neurofilament protein or for calbandin. These bands are less marked in the brains of apes and monkeys. Preuss (2001) wonders 'whether this is just the tip of the iceberg' and looks forward to the surprises that might await us when we explore the neurochemistry of higher regions.

As another example, Hackett *et al.* (2001) stained the pyramidal cells in the auditory belt cortex that were positive for the enzyme acetyl-cholinesterase. The staining was less intense in the chimpanzee than in the human brain, and much less intense in the macaque brain.

The problem with observations like this is that it is difficult to assess their functional significance. There are, of course, psychophysical studies that compare the visual or auditory thresholds of human subjects and other primates. Yet the thresholds for motion detection are very similar for macaques and humans (Newsome and Pare 1988) and the audio-grams of chimpanzees and humans are very similar (Stebbins 1978). Of course, these are not really the appropriate measures, since the tests are simply ones of detection. But we do need some way of telling whether small differences, as revealed by immunocytochemistry, are of critical importance for behaviour.

The examples given so far relate to sensory areas, but it is more critical to know if there are similar differences in association cortex. For example, by staining for calbindin, Yanez *et al.* (2005) identified a class of interneurones, the double bouquet cells, in superior temporal area 22 and frontal polar 10. But though they compared the human brain with those of carnivores and rodents, they presented no data for other primates.

Hof *et al.* (2001) do make such a comparison for pyramidal cells in layer V of the anterior cingulate cortex (area 24) (Fig. 9.1) that contain the calcium-binding protein calretinin. These can be found in the brains of humans and great apes. However, these authors also state that they were only able to find such cells in the paracingulate area 32 of the human brain (Fig. 9.1). Chapter 9 reviews the evidence that there is activation in the paracingulate cortex when human subjects mentalize. This might tempt us to relate this to the anatomical finding. The problem is that Hof *et al.* (2001) only report the presence of a few calretinin positive cells in the paracingulate cortex.

Receptors

Immunocytochemistry can also be used to label neurotransmitters such as dopamine. However, a more productive method is to identify the receptors for these neurotransmitters on the post-synaptic cell. This can be done by incubating brain sections with radioactively labelled ligands, using different ligands to bind to the different receptor types. There are a large number of receptor types, e.g. glutamatergic, GABA, 5-HT and their subtypes. Zilles *et al.* (2002; Scheperjans *et al.* 2005*a*; Eickhoff *et al.* 2007) have measured the density of the different receptor types in a wide variety of cortical areas in the human brain. This has enabled them to produce, for each area, what they have called its 'receptor fingerprint'. A fingerprint plots the density of the different receptor types on a radial plot. The term 'fingerprint' was first proposed by Zilles and his colleagues.

These fingerprints can also be measured in the macaque brain. This has now been done for a variety of areas, including visual and motor areas (Kotter *et al.* 2001) and areas within the inferior parietal cortex (Geyer *et al.* 2005). However we do not, as yet, have receptor fingerprints for the chimpanzee brain. The problem is that the method requires fresh brains and these are hard to come by.

The best we can do, therefore, is to compare the receptor fingerprints in the human and macaque brain. Because the brains differ in size, there are likely to be differences in the density of receptors in some of these areas, given the different size of the cells and the different packing density.

What would be more critical would be differences in the *shape* of the fingerprints, i.e. in the relative density of the different receptors. Differences shape should have implications for function. For example, within the human brain the receptor fingerprints clearly differ in visual and motor areas (Zilles *et al.* 2002). Also, the hierarchy of visual and motor areas that one can arrive at on the basis of receptor fingerprints is very similar to the hierarchy based on connectivity patterns (Kotter *et al.* 2001). Work is now in progress to compare receptor fingerprints in the human and macaque monkey brains.

Conclusions

The previous chapter outlined the mental gap between humans and our nearest living relatives. The question for this chapter is to what extent differences in the brain can account for that gap. The most dramatic difference is in relative brain size. The human brain is 3.5 times as large as expected for an ape our size (MacLeod *et al.* 2003). Though cells become larger as brain size increases, there are 6.9 billion cells in the human neocortex compared with 5.5 billion in that of the chimpanzee (Shariff 1953). Total brain size includes, of course, the connections between cells, and cell density goes down with increasing cell size (Shariff 1953). As brain size increases, there is an accompanying increase in the proportion of it that is made up of white matter (Barton and Harvey 2000).

I suggested earlier that one can try to gauge the functional significance of these differences by relating the size of the brain to the size of the brainstem. The dramatic finding is that the gap in relative size between the human and chimpanzee brain is larger than the gap between the chimpanzee and shrew. Reader and colleagues have taken a related measure, that is the neocortex plus basal ganglia, as compared with the brainstem. They find a reasonable relationship between this measure and the degree to which primates innovate and use tools (Reader and Laland 2002; Lefebvre *et al.* 2004).

So, one factor is the number of cells and their connections, after correction for the size of the body. But it matters *where* those cells are. As already mentioned, the neocortex with its underlying white matter forms just 12% of the brain in the shrew (*Sorex minutus*) but as much as 76% in the chimpanzee (Stephan *et al.* 1981). Even within the primates, differences in brain size are accompanied by marked differences in the proportions of the different brain areas. For example, within the neocortex it is cells in the association areas that are critical for learning, memory and decision-making. In the marmoset the association cortex forms just 67% of the neocortex, whereas in the chimpanzee the corresponding value is 83% (Shariff 1953; Passingham 1973).

The human neocortex is over three times as big as predicted for a primate our size (Passingham 1973, 1982). The implication is that the association areas of the human brain must also be at least three times the size predicted. For example, the area of the prefrontal cortex is on average 34 770 mm^2 in the human brain and 6719 mm^2 in the chimpanzee brain (Brodmann 1913). In other words, the prefrontal cortex is five times larger in the human brain, even though a typical person is only 20 kg heavier than a chimpanzee. To give another example, the volume of the superior temporal cortex is 47.2 mm^3 in the human brain and only 12.4 mm^3 in the chimpanzee brain, a difference of 3.8 times (Rilling and Seligman 2002).

But is this difference enough to account for the mental gap? One reaction is to be disappointed with comparisons of the proportions of particular areas, and to look for differences in microstructure as the key (Sherwood and Hof 2007). Others go further. The great neuroanatomist Ramon Cajal wrote that 'the opinion generally accepted at that time that the differences between the brain of non human mammals (cat, dog, monkey, etc.) and that of man are only quantitative seemed to me unlikely and even a little offensive' (Cajal 1917). Cajal was following the common assumption that quantitative changes are unable to produce qualitative differences. I have already questioned this assumption in Chapter 1.

But there is a more important point. Just as differences in overall brain size are associated with differences in the proportions of association cortex, so there are differences in the size of the neocortex that are associated with differences in microstructure. We have already pointed out that as cells get larger, so their density becomes lower (Shariff 1953). This allows an increase in the complexity of the dendritic tree of pyramidal cells, and this gets larger as the surface area of the neocortex increases (Elston 2007). There is an accompanying increase in the complexity of the dendritic tree and in the number of spines, and particularly so in the prefrontal cortex (Elston *et al.* 2006).

But here the argument gets tricky. The density of spines in the prefrontal cortex is directly related to the size of the prefrontal cortex, and the human value can be predicted from data on other primates (Elston *et al.* 2006). But this fact alone will not tell us whether the regression line reflects differences in *scaling* so as to compensate for the increase in size, or whether it reflects the operation of evolutionary selection pressures. In other words does processing power stay constant with increasing size or does it increase? There is one case where we can be certain. This relates to Wernicke's area. It is true that the spacing of mini-columns (Buxhoeveden *et al.* 2001a) might be explained in terms of scaling, but that cannot be true of the *asymmetry* in the width of the mini-columns between the left and right hemisphere (Buxhoeveden *et al.* 2001*b*).

So how far have we come? I have argued that we can go some way towards explaining the mental gap in terms of the number and connections of cells, particularly in the association areas of the neocortex. And these are associated with microstructural changes, e.g. in pyramidal cells. But the most critical factor may be the microstructural specializations for language, for language provides a tool for education and cultural transmission. Chapter 10 will argue that it is this that further ratchets up the mental gap.

Chapter 3

Perception

The previous chapter looked for human specializations by examining the anatomy of the brain. In doing so it made little reference to the functions of the different areas. The rest of the book considers these in detail. It is one thing to say that the human brain differs from other primates in area X, and another to say that this difference in area X explains the difference in behaviour Y. It is to take this further step that this and the succeeding chapters deal with functional anatomy. They do so by comparing what we know of the human brain, from brain imaging, with what we know of the macaque monkey brain.

Two problems are inherent in this comparison. The first is that the common ancestor of macaque monkeys and humans lived as long as 25 million years ago (Kelley 1992; Kumar and Hedges 1998). We cannot draw conclusions about human specializations without knowledge of primates that shared a common ancestor more recently. The lines leading to the chimpanzee and to humans probably diverged around 5–7 million years ago (Kelley 1992; Kumar and Hedges 1998). Yet we are woefully ignorant of the functions of areas in the chimpanzee brain.

Furthermore, it is not clear when there will be an improvement in the situation. Electrophysiological recording requires the insertion of fine electrodes through the skull, and scientists are not prepared to carry out such invasive experiments on chimpanzees. It is true that functional brain-imaging using scanners is not invasive in this way, but current methods do require the subject to lie in the scanner for some time with the head fixed, and this is not practical with chimpanzees. So, for the moment we are left with drawing comparisons with the brains of macaques for which we have a very detailed knowledge of functional anatomy. This has the serious consequence that any conclusions about differences in the functional organization of the brain in humans and other primates must remain tentative, since it is always possible that the chimpanzee brain differs from the macaque brain in the same way as does the human brain. One looks to advances in rthe technology of brain imaging to fill the gap.

The second problem is that most of what we know about macaques comes from electrophysiological recordings in which the activity of cells is measured while the animals perform tasks. Yet most of what we know about human subjects comes from studies using functional brain-imaging. Both positron emission tomography (PET) and functional magnetic brain-imaging (fMRI) make use of the fact that when cells become active in a brain area, there is an increase in the flow of arterial blood to that region. This change in flow is measured directly by PET. It is measured indirectly by fMRI, which monitors the increase in the oxygenation of the blood that occurs with an increase in arterial flow.

Functional brain-imaging differs from electrophysiological experiments in three ways. First, these experiments typically record from cells one at a time, whereas imaging provides an indirect measure of the activity of the whole population of cells in that area. Second, the majority of electrophysiological studies record from one area at a time, whereas imaging gives results for all brain areas at once. Finally, in studies on macaque monkeys, recordings can be taken in discrete cyto-architectonic areas, whereas we have only rough and ready methods for localizing activations in specific cyto-architectonic areas in the human brain (Eickhoff *et al.* 2005*b*).

The result is that comparing results across species is contaminated by these major differences in methods. So the only sound way to make comparisons is to use the same methods in the two species. There are two ways in which one can do this. First, there are circumstances in which one can record from single cells during neurosurgery in patients (Ojemann *et al.* 2002; Williams *et al.* 2004; Quiroga *et al.* 2005). However, such studies will always be rare. The alternative is to carry out comparative experiments using fMRI on macaques as well as human subjects (Orban *et al.* 2004; Nakahara *et al.* 2007). Most of the initial experiments of this sort have been carried out on the visual system. One reason is that it is relatively easy to ensure that both humans and macaques are presented with the identical stimuli and thus that their brains process the same information. This chapter discusses experiments of this sort.

Early visual areas

The primary visual cortex is mapped in a retinotopic fashion. Each area of the retina sends its connections via the lateral geniculate nucleus to a different part of the striate cortex, that is part of the primary visual cortex (V1). We know that in macaques the striate cortex sends connections to a series of prestriate visual areas in turn, and that each of these areas is also mapped in a retinotopic fashion (Zeki 1993). Furthermore, each of these areas is specialized in the sense that the proportions of cells that fire to particular visual features differs between areas. For example, there are cells in area V4 that are sensitive to wavelength, whereas there are few such cells in area MT/V5; correspondingly, the majority of cells in area MT/V5 respond to motion, whereas very few cells do so in V4 (DeYoe and van Essen 1988).

Modern imaging techniques have made it possible to chart these areas in the human brain. If a visual area is retinotopic, this can be demonstrated using fMRI. Stimuli are presented to different parts of the visual field at different times. By presenting a wedge that rotates around the centre, one can plot the upper and lower fields and do so for either the left or right hemi-field; and by presenting expanding rings, one can plot the degree of eccentricity from the centre of the field. In this way it is possible to detect where there is activity in a particular visual area when the visual stimulus is presented to a specific part of the retina (Sereno *et al.* 1995).

The borders between the different visual areas can also be mapped by defining the orientation of the vertical and horizontal meridian. For example, it is known that in macaques the border between the primary visual area V1 and prestriate area V2 lies along the vertical meridian, and that there is a reversal of the retinotopic mapping at this point. This means that this border can also be defined in the human brain by defining the vertical meridian and plotting the retinotopy either side of this border. This method has been validated by using it to map visual areas in the macaque brain, where a comparison can be made between the maps so produced and maps based on anatomical connections and electrophysiological recordings (Brewer *et al.* 2002). Using this technique for the human brain it has proved possible to map primary visual cortex and prestriate areas such as V2, V3a and MT/V5 (Tootell *et al.* 1996).

There is an alternative method for defining these areas in the human brain. This is to make use of the fact that the areas differ in their functional specialization. For example, moving stimuli can be presented to map area MT/V5 (Watson *et al.* 1993; Tootell *et al.* 1995, 1998). There is good agreement between different research groups concerning the location of MT/V5 as mapped in this way (Fig. 3.1). Whereas in the macaque brain it lies in the depth of the superior temporal sulcus, in the human brain it is displaced ventrally near the surface of the middle temporal gyrus (Watson *et al.* 1993; Tootell *et al.* 1996). Orban *et al.* (2003) presented a variety of motion stimuli, and used fMRI to directly

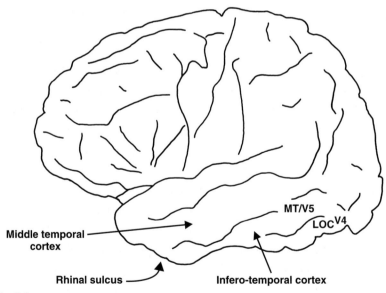

Fig. 3.1

compare motion processing in the macaque and human brain. They report similar activity in the MT/V5 for the two species.

There remains disagreement about the location of area V4 in the human brain. Using coloured stimuli, Zeki and his colleagues located V4 on the ventromedial surface of the human brain on the fusiform gyrus (Bartels and Zeki 2000). By charting the areas on the basis of retinotopic borders, Tootell and his colleagues have identified ventral V4 (V4v) as lying on the lateral surface in the human brain (Hadjikhani *et al.* 1998; Tootell and Hadjikhani 2001) (Fig. 3.1). Van Essen *et al.* (2001) attempted to resolve the issue by warping the macaque maps so as to best fit them to the human maps. They concluded that the best fit suggests that the human homologue of monkey V4 lies in lower part of the lateral cortex.

What, then, is the status of the ventromedial area that has been identified by Bartels and Zeki (2000)? Hadjikhani *et al.* suggest that it be called 'V8' (1998). So, is this area new to the human brain? To find out, Tootell *et al.* (2004) presented coloured stimuli to macaque monkeys in the scanner, and found that most of the activation lay anterior to V4 in the posterior infero-temporal cortex. But it is unlikely that this corresponds to V8 because V8 is retinotopically mapped (Brewer *et al.* 2005). So one possibility is that the area that responds to colour in the human brain is indeed a new area. Brewer *et al.* (2005) propose that it is and therefore call it human V4 or hV4. But the issue is not settled and further study is needed. Hansen *et al.* (2007) have mapped a V4d and a V4v in the human brain, and they suggest that the organization is as in the brain of macaques.

There are other areas of which the status is also unclear. Laarson and Heeger (2006) identify two retinotopic areas in the lateral occipital cortex of the human brain, LO-1 and LO-2. They propose that these are part of the 'lateral occipital complex' or LOC. The LOC was first identified in imaging experiments that compared the presentation of objects with lower level visual features (Malach *et al.* 1995; Grill-Spector *et al.* 2001) (Fig. 3.1). Both LO-1 and LO-2 show a selective response for images of objects in the same way as the rest of LOC (Larsson and Heeger 2006). However, in macaque monkeys, V4 is also sensitive to shape (Hegde and Van Essen 2006), and lesions of V4 cause a major impairment in the ability to discriminate between patterns (Heywood and Cowey 1987). So further work is needed to establish the relation between monkey V4 and human LO-1 and LO-2. Is one of these human areas the homologue of monkey V4 or have one or both of them differentiated out of V4?

These areas lie within the 'ventral visual system', that is the series of visual areas that connect in the macaque monkey from VI through V4 to the infero-temporal cortex (Baizer *et al.* 1991). This is contrasted with the 'dorsal visual system', that is the series of visual areas that connect via V3, MT/V5 and V6 with the parietal cortex (Baizer *et al.* 1991; Shipp *et al.* 1998). Establishing homologies within the dorsal visual system beyond V3a and MT/V5 is as difficult as doing so for the ventral visual system. For example, Press *et al.* (2001) identify a V3b and V7 in the human brain. Only further imaging of the macaque brain will clarify whether these are new areas. For example, Swisher *et al.* (2007) wonder whether V7 is homologous with part of LIP in the intra-parietal cortex in the macaque brain.

We should certainly expect that as the method becomes more sophisticated, studies using retinotopic mapping will reveal yet further areas in the human brain. For example, Hagler *et al.* (2007) have reported a whole series of retinotopic maps in the human parietal cortex. Studies are now needed to see how many of these correspond to areas that can be mapped in monkeys. It may be necessary to use electrophysiological techniques to reveal these maps, given that the macaque brain is so much smaller. The problem is that establishing homologies is difficult, even when one considers some of the early visual areas (Sereno and Tootell 2005).

Whatever the problems, we should keep in mind the possibility that the human brain follows the general rule that the bigger the neocortex, the more the specialized sensory areas (Krubitzer and Huffman 2000; Barton 2007). If there are new specialized areas, we should also look for consequences for human perception. This requires comparative studies. We know, for example, that on average, humans are more sensitive than macaques in visual acuity (DeValois and Jacobs 1971) and in sensitivity to differences in colour (DeValois and Jacobs 1998). But we lack similar psychophysical data for chimpanzees.

Later visual areas and perception

Perception involves more than simple sensory processing of this sort. Mechanisms are needed to recognize forms. Lesions of the infero-temporal cortex (Fig. 3.1) do not cause lower level impairments in visual acuity or contrast sensitivity (Cowey *et al.* 1998; Huxlin and Merigan 1998). Instead they cause impairments in the ability to tell which shape is the odd one out (Huxlin *et al.* 2000) or to identify complex visual stimuli (Mishkin 1972; Gaffan *et al.* 1986). So we need to look beyond the prestriate cortex. This chapter does so for the ventral visual system, and the next chapter for the dorsal visual system.

It has already been mentioned that the presentation of objects leads to activation in area LOC in the human brain (Malach *et al.* 1995) (Fig. 3.1). Drawings of objects have been shown to human subjects and macaque monkeys (Denys *et al.* 2004). When objects were compared to scrambled figures, activations were found in the ventral visual system in both species. In the human brain, as expected, there was activity in LOC extending onto the mid-fusiform gyrus. In monkeys the activity lay within area V4 and the posterior temporal area TEO that lies in front of it. Warping the macaque brain to the human brain suggests that at least the anterior part of the LOC corresponds to TEO in the macaque brain (Denys *et al.* 2004).

A particular class of objects are faces. Tsao *et al.* (2003) presented macaque monkeys with faces and compared the pattern of activation with that evoked by other objects. It has been known for some time that in the human brain this comparison shows activation in an area of the ventral temporal lobe (Kanwisher *et al.* 1997). This area lies in the fusiform gyrus, anterior to the prestriate areas that are retinotopically mapped (Halgren *et al.* 1999), and has come to be known as the 'fusiform face area' (FFA). In the study of Tsao *et al.* (2003) on monkeys, activity for faces was found in V4, TEO and the lower bank of the superior temporal sulcus. The authors suggest that part of this activation may correspond to the fusiform face area in the human brain.

In the above studies, the subjects did not have to perform a task. But to identify an object one needs to be able to recognize it as the same as one that has previously been seen, and to recognize it from different views.

Human subjects have been tested in the scanner for the ability to match an object to one that was presented recently (Ishai *et al*. 1999). The finding was that the activations in the posterior temporal cortex were enhanced compared to passive viewing. There is, as yet, no comparable study with macaque monkeys.

In the study by Ishai *et al*. (1999) photographs for matching were presented from different views; in other words the sample object or face was presented in a different view from the objects or faces between which the choice had to be made. The ability to recognize from different views can be tested by making use of the fact that the activity in the brain when an object is presented for a second time is less than it was when the object was first presented. By presenting the same object twice but in different views it is possible to test whether there is less activity on the second presentation, in other words whether the object representation is 'view invariant'. This pattern of activity has been found in area LOC in the human brain (James *et al*. 2002; Vuilleumier *et al*. 2002).

The same experiment should now be repeated with macaque monkeys. We know that in these animals the ability to recognize objects from different views is impaired by lesions of the infero-temporal cortex (Weiskrantz and Saunders 1984) and of the anterior temporal cortex around the rhinal sulcus (Fig. 3.1) (Buckley and Gaffan 1998). What we do not know is how early in the ventral visual stream there are view invariant representations in macaque monkeys.

Associative knowledge

So far the comparisons made between macaques and humans have not revealed fundamental differences in the organization of the temporal lobe. We should, perhaps, have expected this since the ability to recognize objects or faces, and to do so from any view, is as important for macaques as it is for humans. Where we might expect differences is in the retrieval of information about the objects or faces. The purpose of recognizing objects or individuals is to retrieve knowledge about them. This knowledge is commonly referred to as 'semantic knowledge'. Strictly speaking, this term can only be used for human knowledge, because the word 'semantic' refers to meaning in a language. Much of our semantic knowledge is acquired by association. So we learn that pyramids and palm trees are associated because they are to be found in the same country. It is associations of this sort that form the basis of a test that is widely used to measure semantic knowledge in human subjects, the so-called 'pyramid and palm trees test' (Hodges and Patterson 1995).

A more difficult version of this task was devised for testing human subjects in the PET scanner (Vandenberghe *et al*. 1996). In the experimental condition an object was presented, say a pair of pliers, together with two other objects, such as a spanner and a saw. The subjects had to indicate which of these two objects was associated with the first one, the answer in our example being the spanner because it can grip like a pair of pliers. In the control condition pictures were also presented but the subjects had only to make a perceptual judgement. When these tasks were compared, activation was found throughout the middle and inferior temporal gyrus (Vandenberghe *et al*. 1996); and this result has been replicated with an easier task of the same sort (Price *et al*. 1999).

It is an important finding of these studies that the activation for semantic decisions extends to the most anterior part of the temporal lobe. This includes the tissue of the temporal pole around the rhinal sulcus (Fig. 3.1). Devlin *et al*. (2002) compared the results of seven PET experiments in which the subjects had been required to make semantic decisions about animals, fruit or famous faces. Typical tasks were naming pictures, matching words to pictures, generating names or associating objects by their location. Across the tasks there was activation in common in the ventromedial temporal polar cortex for semantic as opposed to perceptual decisions.

That the activation in the temporal lobe reflects access to semantic knowledge is shown by the fact that atrophy of the anterior temporal lobe can lead to a severe impairment on pictorial tests of associative knowledge (Bozeat *et al*. 2000). The lesions in these cases typically involve the left middle and inferior temporal gyrus, and they can cause a deficit so severe as to merit the term 'semantic dementia' (Galton *et al*. 2001*a*). The most critical area appears to be the anterior temporal cortex including the tissue around the rhinal sulcus (Davies *et al*. 2004).

The mechanism by which associative knowledge is acquired in the human brain may have developed from the mechanism that has been described in the macaque monkey brain. Monkeys can be taught to associate patterns in pairs, and there are cells in the temporal lobe that come to code for these associations (Miyashita and Hayashi 2000). These are called 'pair coding neurones'. If they fire to pattern A, they will also fire to its learned associate, say pattern X. These cells are found in the infero-temporal cortex (Naya *et al.* 2001), and their activity is dependent on inputs from the tissue in the rhinal sulcus (Miyashita *et al.* 1996).

However, there are three major differences between the areas for associative knowledge in humans and macaque monkeys. The first is that human subjects can access their knowledge from words. In the studies already mentioned (Vandenberghe *et al.* 1996; Price *et al.* 1999), semantic knowledge was tested in two ways. The first was to present pictures, but the second was to present the names for the objects, such as 'spanner' and 'pliers'. There was activation throughout the inferior temporal cortex, irrespective of the way in which the subjects retrieved their knowledge.

The second major difference is the presence of a middle temporal gyrus in the human but not macaque brain (Fig. 3.1). One possibility that was mentioned in Chapter 2 is that this is homologous with the depth of the superior temporal sulcus in macaques, as if the tissue within this sulcus has been expanded and flattened out in the human brain. The analogy would be with the middle frontal gyrus in the human brain, which is known to be homologous with the tissue that lies in the principal sulcus of the macaque brain (Petrides and Pandya 1999). However, the chimpanzee does have a middle temporal gyrus. It is frustrating that we cannot, as yet, scan chimpanzees to see whether there is activation in their middle temporal gyrus when they are tested for associative knowledge.

There is a final and over-riding difference. The infero-temporal cortex receives visual information via the ventral visual stream. But the human eye is not very much bigger than the eye of a chimpanzee. Yet the middle and inferior temporal gyrus is 4.1 times as extensive in the human compared with the chimpanzee brain (Rilling and Seligman 2002).

In the somatosensory system there is a principle that the size of the representation in the somatic map relates not to the size of that body part but to the complexity of the analysis of information from that body part. So, for example, if one looks at the representation of the tail in cebus monkeys, there is a very large representation in somatic area 3b (Felleman *et al.* 1983). This is not because the cebus monkey (*Cebus*) has a longer tail than an Old World monkey, such as a macaque, but because the tail of cebus monkeys is prehensile and they use the end of it for active tactile exploration (Kaas 2007).

By analogy, the reason why the middle and inferior temporal cortex is so extensive in the human brain is not because more information arrives from the eye in humans than in chimpanzees. Instead the size of the temporal lobe reflects the complexity of the processing and sorting of that information. The purely visual analysis appears to mainly involve the more posterior parts of the infero-temporal cortex, including LOC. It is the more anterior regions of the middle and inferior temporal gyri that are involved in acquiring and storing knowledge about objects and events in the world, and it is here that humans excel. The expansion of these gyri must reflect, in part, the fact that this knowledge can both be acquired and retrieved through words.

Visual imagery

When we see an object, the information reaches the primary visual cortex V1, and is then passed through a series of relays in the ventral visual system to enable the identification of the object. This is often referred to as 'bottom-up' processing. But human subjects can also be asked to imagine a particular object or shape. If the object is familiar, it has to be recalled from long-term memory. If it is unfamiliar, for example, 'a pink giraffe', the image has to be created anew. The ability to retrieve images involves 'top-down' processing, i.e. the flow of information is from higher to lower areas in the neocortex.

Chapter 1 reviewed the evidence that one can test whether human subjects can successfully imagine items such as the letter F (Kosslyn *et al.* 2001). Kosslyn and others have therefore gone on to use brain imaging to compare activity in the brain when human subjects either see or imagine such stimuli. The general finding is that those visual areas that are active when we actually perceive stimuli are also active when we imagine them (Kosslyn *et al.* 1997, 2001; Ishai *et al.* 2002). For example, when subjects are asked to imagine well-known faces, there is activity in the fusiform face area (FFA), just as there is when the subjects are shown actual photographs of the faces (O'Craven and Kanwisher 2000; Ishai *et al.* 2002).

The visual areas that are activated during imagination include those in which there is a 'retinotopic map'. The images can be said to be 'visual' in that, if subjects visualize a small letter, the activity is restricted to the central part of the retinotopic map, whereas if they visualize a large letter, it extends into the periphery (Tootell *et al.* 1998). The activity can even extend into the primary visual cortex, especially when the subjects have to make fine judgements (Kosslyn *et al.* 2001). This activity is presumably caused by feedback pathways from the prestriate areas.

Not only are the same areas activated during imagination and vision, but also some of the same cells. Kreiman *et al.* (2000) recorded during surgery from areas within the medial temporal lobe, and did so while the patients were conscious. In this way they could establish the selectivity of cells that fired when different objects were presented. In another condition, the patients were asked to imagine each of these objects. Eighty-eight percent of the cells that fired during vision and imagination showed the same selectivity.

Thus, one could argue that any account that we give of the mechanisms that lead to awareness of actual sensory stimuli should apply equally to our awareness of imagined stimuli. But is this true of other animals? Chapter 1 argued that, since other primates are perceptually aware, we should not rule out the possibility that they also experience visual imagery.

The retrieval of images from memory

Given that we cannot ask animals to imagine, we can try to resolve the issue by considering the retrieval of images from memory. The hippocampus and neighbouring hippocampal gyrus lie on the inner or medial surface of the temporal lobe. There is activity in the hippocampus when human subjects retrieve episodic memories as opposed to factual information (Maguire and Mummery 1999). Also, the activity is greater when the subjects report that they 'recollect' the memories in the sense of re-experiencing of the visual context of the episodic memory (Eldridge *et al.* 2000; Yonelinas *et al.* 2005; Steinvorth *et al.* 2006). As expected from these findings, hippocampal pathology can lead to a loss of episodic memory, i.e. of the ability to recollect events (Vargha-Khadem *et al.* 2001). It even affects the ability to imagine scenes that are not in memory but are prompted by brief descriptions (Hassabis *et al.* 2007).

So do hippocampal lesions have an effect on the ability of animals to retrieve memories? Fortin *et al.* (2004) claimed that even in rats, hippocampal lesions impair the 'recollection-like' memory retrieval of odours. It is true that we cannot conclude that healthy rats have the same subjective experience as humans, but it is just as true that we have no proof that they do not. In other research, Gaffan (1992) has shown that damage to the fornix, one of the outputs of the hippocampus, severely impairs the ability of macaque monkeys to remember complex scenes that they have seen just once. The author specifically draws the analogy with human episodic memory.

The second approach would be to see which areas are activated when subjects remember visual items. Wheeler *et al.* (2000) asked subjects to form a vivid image of pictures as they recalled them. There was activity in the prestriate cortex and fusiform gyrus when they recalled the pictures. The activity is greater, the more vivid the subjects report their images to be (Cui *et al.* 2007). It can also be shown that when human subjects recall pictures, the pattern of brain activity that occurred when the pictures were presented is re-instated just before recall (Polyn *et al.* 2005). In principle it would be possible to test whether the same is true when monkeys retrieve visual items from memory.

Of course, the sceptic could argue that, even if this was found, the monkeys do not retrieve a vivid image as humans do. I would try to convince the sceptic by way of an example from perception. If one stimulus is presented to the left eye and a different one to the right eye, the finding is that human subjects report now seeing one stimulus and now the other. So, for example, Tong *et al.* (1998) presented a face to one eye and a house to the other, and the subjects were aware of seeing alternately either the face or the house, with a switch every few seconds. The exciting finding is that there was activity in the fusiform face area when the subject was aware of seeing a face and in a more medial parahippocampal area when the subject was aware of seeing a house. The pattern of activity was the same as when a face or house were actually presented in alternation.

Macaque monkeys also report seeing now one stimulus and now the other during binocular rivalry (Blake and Logothetis 2002). Before testing, the animals are trained to press the lever on the right when they are actually shown one picture and the lever on the left when they are actually shown the other. Sheinberg and Logothetis (1997) then recorded from the temporal lobe while monkeys were presented with stimuli under conditions of rivalry. The authors first tested the responses of cells to a variety of visual stimuli so as to find the effective stimulus for any particular cell. They then presented an effective stimulus, e.g. a face, and an ineffective stimulus, e.g. a starburst pattern. In the infero-temporal cortex, a cell that fired to the face fired when the monkey reported seeing a face, and a cell that fired to the starburst pattern fired when the monkey reported seeing the starburst pattern. Only a small proportion of cells in striate cortex and early prestriate areas showed the same effect. This is not to deny that early visual areas retain 'eye-selective' information (Tong et al. 2006), only to say that the percept involves later areas within the visual stream.

In discussing these findings, Gray (2005) points out that the behavioural findings are the same for human subjects and monkeys, and that the physiological findings also appear to be consistent. To use Gray's delightful terminology, the sceptic can still maintain a 'Ptolemaic' position, arguing that though the phenomena are the same, there is an underlying difference. But the 'Copernican' view would be that until such a difference is demonstrated, it is fair to appeal to parsimony. The point is that the Ptolemaic and Copernican proposals both explain much of the same data on the sun and its planets. It is just that one proposal is the more economical.

I would use the same argument for episodic memory. Chapter 1 presented evidence that there are birds and primates that have 'episodic-like' memory. If it turns out that the activations in fMRI for monkeys are the same as those for human subjects in the experiment by Polyn *et al.* (2005), then I would put the onus on the sceptic to prove that monkeys cannot retrieve visual images.

Imagining at will

I deliberately chose to discuss the retrieval of images from memory because we cannot ask animals to imagine something at will. The ability to do so depends on top-down pathways from the prefrontal cortex to the visual areas in the ventral stream. So, for example, whether subjects are required to imagine faces or houses there is much more activity in the dorsal prefrontal cortex than there is if they are simply shown pictures of faces or houses (Ishai *et al.* 2000). By analysing changes in the covariance between activity in the prefrontal and posterior visual areas, it can be directly shown that, during imagination, the prefrontal cortex influences activity in these visual areas (Mechelli *et al.* 2004).

So can monkeys imagine at will? Chapter 1 argued that monkeys are able to engage in 'willed action', that is to freely select what to do, and Chapter 7 will review the evidence that this ability involves the dorsal prefrontal cortex. Furthermore, top-down signals can be demonstrated in macaque monkeys during memory retrieval. Tomita *et al.* (1999) taught monkeys to associate together pairs of pictures. They then cut the bottom-up pathways that led to one hemisphere, say the left hemisphere. Visual stimuli presented to the right hemisphere could still reach the left infero-temporal cortex via pathways to the prefrontal cortex in the right hemisphere, from there to the left prefrontal cortex, and thence via top-down pathways to the infero-temporal cortex of the left hemisphere. And the authors were able to record activity related to the pairing in the infero-temporal cortex of the left hemisphere. To do this, the information had to pass across the corpus callosum from one hemisphere to another, and the activity was abolished by section of the anterior corpus callosum.

But here the pictures were presented to the monkeys. Humans can imagine objects when nothing has been presented, and no external prompt is given. Furthermore, people can imagine non-existent objects or beings, such as a blue elephant. Here I play the sceptic in arguing that it may well be that only humans can summon up imagery at will.

If this is true, it will be a consequence of the expansion of the prefrontal cortex in the human brain. There is activity in the prefrontal cortex when humans generate items (Petersen *et al.* 1988 Nathaniel-James 2002). Even in monkeys there is self-sustaining activity in the prefrontal cortex, not only during short-term memory tasks (Fuster 1973; Funahashi *et al.* 1989) but also before monkeys freely choose between actions (Procyk and Goldman-Rakic 2006). Yet, there is much more extensive prefrontal activation to visual stimuli in monkeys than in humans (Denys *et al.* 2004). The implication is that the expansion of the prefrontal cortex in humans may be associated with an increase in the amount of self-initiated and self-sustaining mental activity And this will include summoning up visual images at will.

Auditory imagery

Human subjects can also be asked to summon up auditory images. Halpern and Zatorre (1999) required subjects to listen to the beginning of a familiar tune and then complete it in their head. As expected, there was activity in the prefrontal cortex and in the superior temporal cortex, i.e. in the auditory association cortex. However, there was also activity in two motor areas: Broca's area 44 and the supplementary motor cortex (SMA) (Fig. 4.2). It is as if, while they were doing this task, the subjects were humming to themselves.

Human subjects can also be asked to imagine someone talking (McGuire *et al.* 1996*b*; Shergill *et al.* 2002), and again there is activation in the superior temporal cortex. Even more dramatically, the same area becomes activated when patients with schizophrenia 'hear' voices (Dierks *et al.* 1999). Frith (1996) has specifically proposed that these hallucinations result from a breakdown in the process by which we distinguish our own inner speech from the speech of others. This view is supported by the fact that, just before the patients hear the voices, there is activity in the region of Broca's area (Shergill *et al.* 2004).

Internal speech depends on the phonological or articulatory loop. This was first described in relation to experiments on short-term memory for letters or numbers (Baddeley and Hitch 1974; Baddeley 1986). These authors proposed a model in which these items were temporarily held in an articulatory loop. Chapter 1 has already mentioned that, if the letters or numbers are read, they are converted to sound and remembered as such, as shown by the fact that when subjects make errors, they reflect auditory rather than visual confusions, e.g. 'P' for 'D' (Conrad 1972, 1973).

If subjects are given letters to remember, there is activity in the superior temporary cortex, the inferior parietal cortex and a region near Broca's area in the left hemisphere (Paulesu *et al.* 1993). A rhyming task was given for comparison. On this there was no activation in the inferior parietal cortex, only in the region near Broca's area. The study by Paulesu *et al.* (1993) was an early PET experiment, but the basic finding has been replicated using fMRI (Henson *et al.* 2000). Here, memory for letters was compared with a task in which the subjects had to make a judgement about two letters presented simultaneously. One was in capitals and one in lower case, and so the subjects had to silently sound out the letters. There was a peak of activity in the superior temporal sulcus when the subjects matched the letters, and this probably reflects the sounding out. In the memory condition, the activation was in the inferior parietal area 40 and in Broca's area. A meta-analysis of all the relevant studies confirms activations for the phonological loop in inferior parietal cortex, Broca's area 44 and premotor cortex (Vigneau *et al.* 2006).

One can test whether these regions are essential for holding material in the articulatory loop by seeing whether it is possible to disrupt articulatory rehearsal by using transcranial magnetic stimulation (TMS). So, Romero *et al.* (2006) applied TMS to the inferior parietal cortex, area 40, and also to a region near Broca's area. The effect was to increase the time it took the subjects to retrieve the numbers from the list that had been presented. The reason why a more severe impairment was not found is that only short bursts of stimulation were applied, and these only disrupt cortical processing temporarily.

Though the articulatory loop was first described in relation to experiments on verbal short-term memory, the same loop is involved in inner speech when there is nothing to remember. One can study this by asking subjects to silently generate sentences. In a PET experiment,

McGuire *et al.* (1996*b*) report activation in the inferior frontal gyrus. In a follow-up experiment using fMRI, Shergill *et al.* (2002) studied the effect of varying the rate of inner speech. The faster the rate, the more the activity in the left inferior frontal gyrus. Though in these experiments the subjects generated inner speech to command, it is fair to assume that the same areas will be involved in spontaneous inner speech.

Conclusions

The aim of this and the succeeding chapters is to find out whether the anatomical differences described in Chapter 2 can explain the mental gap between humans and our nearest living relatives. To achieve this, we need to find differences that have considerable leverage. There is, for example, no doubt that further studies using immunocytochemistry will turn up more differences of the sort described by Preuss and Coleman (2002*a*) in layer IVA of the primary visual cortex (Chapter 2). But the question is whether differences of this kind have the same leverage as differences of the sort that have been discussed in this chapter. We have pointed to four major differences.

First, there appear to be more visual areas in the human brain than in the macaque brain. Clearly one looks forward to the day when it might be possible to chart retinotopic maps in the chimpanzee visual system, but we should not be surprised if it turns out there are indeed more maps in the human brain. The number of sensory areas is known to increase as neocortical size increases in absolute size (Krubitzer and Huffman 2000; Barton 2007), but the number also increases as the neocortex increases in relation to the size of the body (Krubitzer and Hunt 2007). And the human neocortex is over three times the size expected for a primate of our size (Chapter 2).

If it is true that there are more visual areas in the human brain, that would have some leverage. The reason is that specialized areas of the visual system differ in their sensitivity to different stimulus properties (Zeki 1993). There are parallel streams that operate concurrently (Van Essen and DeYoe 1995), but within each stream there is a hierarchical organization, such that higher areas abstract ever more complex features. For example, the primary visual cortex responds best to small line segments, whereas as one ascends the hierarchy the cells respond best to more and more complex patterns or shapes (Schwartz *et al.* 1983; Desimone *et al.* 1985; Desimone and Schein 1987).

The same effect can be demonstrated with fMRI. If one presents either whole pictures or pictures that are segmented into smaller and smaller pieces, one finds that the higher one goes in the ventral visual stream, the greater the activation the more complete the pictures. This has been shown both for the macaque monkey (Rainer *et al.* 2002) and human visual system (Lerner *et al.* 2001). The effect of having more visual areas that are specialized must be to increase the sophistication of the analysis.

The second factor is the amount of visual association cortex in relation to the visual information coming through the eye. This cortex is involved not only in the identification of objects but also in the retrieval of information that is associated with them. This has been shown by single unit-recording in macaque monkeys (Miyashita *et al.* 1996; Naya *et al.* 1996) as well as by an imaging methodology in which measurements are taken of gene expression during associative learning (Okuno and Miyashita 1996). But there are differences in the acquisition of associative knowledge in monkeys and humans. In humans semantic knowledge can be retrieved from words and not just from visual stimuli. This may be one reason for the expansion in the temporal association cortex. The middle and inferior temporal gyri are 4.1 times larger in humans as in chimpanzees (Rilling and Seligman 2002).

A third difference is that, whereas monkeys and chimpanzees must acquire this knowledge from experience, humans can acquire it via teaching in a language. I know that pyramids go with palm trees because I have had lessons in geography; I don't have to have travelled to Egypt. That humans can acquire their semantic knowledge by teaching in a language is of enormous leverage. It is discussed at more length in the concluding chapter.

The final major difference is also related to language. This is the existence of the articulatory or phonological loop. As one would expect, this is parasitic on the language system. The areas that are activated include the superior temporal cortex within Wernicke's area, the left inferior parietal cortex and the region round Broca's area. Only humans are aware of an internal commentary. We do not know whether monkeys or chimpanzees experience visual imagery, but we can be certain that they do not experience phonological imagery. I speculate in the last chapter that inner speech has a dramatic influence on thinking, thus further racheting up the mental gap.

Chapter 4

Manual skill

The point of perception is to guide action. Humans have specialized not only in semantic knowledge but also in the use to which they put it. Our hominid ancestors adapted to novel and changing environments by inventing a tool kit, and it is our sophisticated technology that has enabled modern humans to colonize the world. This chapter treats our manual skill.

Pyramidal tract

Like Old World monkeys and apes, humans have hands that can grasp objects between the forefinger and thumb. This is called a 'precision grip' to distinguish it from a 'power grip' in which all the fingers close around the object together (Napier 1961). The crucial difference between these grips is that the precision grip involves the ability to move each finger independently. For example, if a monkey picks up a piece of food from a small hole or slot, it needs to use its thumb and forefinger to prize the food out, while tucking the other fingers out of the way (Lawrence and Kuypers 1968). Napier suggested a scale of 1–7 for manual dexterity, and on this scale humans score 7 (Napier 1961). The ability to move each finger independently is at its peak in musicians such as pianists or violinists.

This ability is thought to depend on a subgroup of the pyramidal fibres that run from the motor cortex to the spinal cord (Armand 1984; Porter and Lemon 1993). These are the fibres that terminate directly onto the motor neurones. In the most dextrous primates there are terminations onto the motor neurones that innervate the most distal muscles (Heffner and Masterton 1975; Heffner and Masterton 1983). A re-analysis of the data from those studies, controlling for the relationship between the species, has thrown doubt on the relation of this measure to dexterity, but the analysis included only five data points for primates (Iwaniuk *et al.* 1999).

The terminations in the human brain have been documented by Schoen (1964). However, the data provided by Schoen (1964) for the human brain and Kuypers (1981) for the chimpanzee depend on an old method for charting connections: this involves studying the degeneration of fibres after a lesion. Since the lesions in the chimpanzee and human brain are not comparable, we cannot strictly compare the proportions of the pyramidal fibres that terminate on the motor-neurones in the two species.

However, there are physiological data that are suggestive. The method is to stimulate the pyramidal tract and record the excitatory potentials in the motor neurones or muscles. Using electrical stimulation in macaque monkeys and transcranial magnetic stimulation in human subjects, Nakajima *et al.* (2000) report that in humans the amplitude of the response is roughly double that of the response in the macaque monkeys. This suggests a very strong direct cortical projection to the motor neurones in the human brain.

Motor cortex

The degree of manual skill depends not only on the proportion of pyramidal fibres that terminate on the motor neurones but also on the extent of the cortical area that controls the hand and wrist. This area can be assessed by stimulating the motor cortex at different sites and measuring the resulting movements. This has been done not only in animals (Woolsey 1958) but also in patients during surgery (Penfield and Jaspar 1954). However, there are as yet no data that would allow a proper comparison between the hand area in humans, chimpanzees and macaque monkeys. It could be obtained for macaques by using fMRI to map the areas that are devoted to the fingers, as has been done for human subjects (Indovina and Sanes 2001). Nevertheless, there is indirect evidence that there has been a considerable expansion of the hand area in the human brain. In the human brain this area lies within a large insula deep in the central sulcus. This is referred to as the 'hand knob' (Yousry *et al.* 1997).

Indirect evidence for a difference in the motor cortical representation comes from the observation that lesions that include the motor cortex have a more devastating effect on the control of the arm in patients than in monkeys. In patients they cause a relatively long-lasting spasticity and paresis (Freund 1987). In monkeys they cause an initial weakness but not spasticity, though there are long-term impairments in the kinematics of the wrist and fingers (Hoffman and Strick 1995). However, the comparison may not be fair because, whereas it is possible to make discrete lesions of motor cortex in the macaques (Passingham *et al.* 1983; Hoffman and Strick 1995; Liu and Rouiller 1999), strokes rarely produce infarcts that are restricted to the motor cortex. This matters because the premotor cortex is also involved in the control of actions carried out with the hand and wrist.

Parietal cortex

Information about the body is analysed in primary sensory cortex, Brodmann areas 3, 1 and 2. It is then sent to the parietal association cortex, area 5 (Pearson and Powell 1985). However, the parietal association cortex also receives an input from the dorsal visual system. This comes via the MT/V5 complex (Ungerleider and Desimone 1986) and areas V6 and V6A (Shipp *et al.* 1998). Thus, the parietal cortex is in a position to integrate information about the body and the world immediately around us with which we interact. Whereas the ventral visual stream allows for the identification of objects, the dorsal visual stream is specialized for the control of eye movements and the visual guidance of hand movements, as in reaching for and grasping objects (Milner and Goodale 2007).

The intra-parietal sulcus (Fig. 4.1) divides the superior from the inferior parietal association cortex. This is a deep sulcus in the macaque, chimpanzee and human brains. In macaques it contains a series of specialized areas. These include AIP for the visual guidance of grasping, LIP for the control of saccadic eye movements, VIP for the analysis of optic flow during locomotion and MIP for the control of reaching (Culham and Kanwisher 2001; Grefkes and Fink 2005).

Each of these specialized areas can also be found in the human brain (Culham and Kanwisher 2001; Grefkes and Fink 2005).

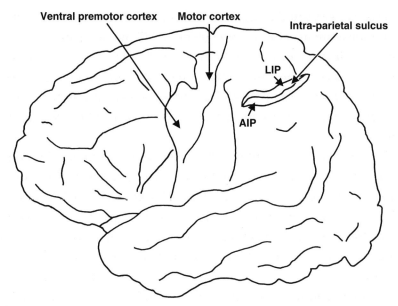

Fig. 4.1

Thus, Culham *et al.* (2003) scanned subjects while they reached for and grasped objects in the scanner. The activity lay anteriorly within the intra-parietal sulcus as in the monkey brain, and the activation was identified as being in area AIP (Fig. 4.1). Area VIP lies further back in the depth of the intra-parietal sulcus. Bremmer *et al.* (2001) used fMRI to identify an area here in the human brain on the grounds that it responded to motion stimuli, whether visual or tactile.

This leaves two areas, LIP and MIP. In the macaque brain, LIP lies on the ventral or lateral bank of the sulcus and MIP on the dorsal or medial bank of the sulcus. Cells fire in LIP when monkeys prepare to make saccades (Colby *et al.* 1996; Snyder *et al.* 1997) and in the region of MIP when they prepare to make reaching movements (Snyder *et al.* 1997). So Hagler *et al.* (2007) scanned human subjects while they either prepared to move their eyes or to point. There were two potential differences from what we know of the macaque brain.

First, in the human brain there are at least four maps both for eye movements and pointing, and these are organized in a retinotopic fashion.

However, we should be cautious. There have been suggestions that there are more than one representation in LIP in macaques (Gattass *et al.* 2005). It would be difficult to compare retinotopic areas in monkeys by using imaging methods because they would be so small. So it will not be an easy task to tell which of the areas identified in the human brain are new and which correspond to areas already known in the macaque brain.

The second potential difference is of more significance. LIP appears to be on the dorsal or medial bank of the intra-parietal sulcus in the human brain (Sereno *et al.* 2001; Hagler *et al.* 2007) (Fig. 4.1). This is a striking difference, and it appears to reflect the expansion of visually receiving parietal cortex in the human brain. There was already an indication of this from Brodmann's (1925) analysis of the cyto-architecture of the human and monkey (*Cercopithecus*) brain. Brodmann commented that in the human inferior parietal cortex, areas 40 and 39 showed a resemblance to area 7, which lies in the inferior parietal cortex in the monkey. But when he came to map the human brain, he located area 7 proper as being in the superior parietal convexity.

There are two other indications that visually receiving parietal cortex has expanded onto the superior surface in the human brain. The first comes from anatomy and the second from fMRI. Rushworth *et al.* (2005) used diffusion tensor imaging to chart the visual connections of the parietal cortex with the superior colliculus in the midbrain. In the macaque monkey, area LIP lies on the lower bank of the intra-parietal sulcus and it is interconnected with the superior colliculus, a nucleus that is involved in the control of eye movements (Clower *et al.* 2001). But in the human brain, the area that is connected to the superior colliculus includes the upper bank of this sulcus and the immediately adjacent superior convexity cortex (Rushworth *et al.* 2005). This is consistent with the results of fMRI studies indicating that LIP lies on the upper bank of the intra-parietal sulcus in the human brain (Sereno *et al.* 2001; Hagler *et al.* 2007; Swisher *et al.* 2007).

The second piece of evidence comes from comparative studies of the macaque monkey and human brain using fMRI (Orban *et al.* 2004).

If human subjects and macaque monkeys are presented with randomly moving dots, there is stronger activity in the intra-parietal sulcus in the human brain (Orban *et al.* 2003). In the human brain, there are four subareas that are sensitive to motion, including two dorsal areas. By comparison, activity has only been found in one ventral intra-parietal area in the macaque brain. The same results have been reported for rotating line segments that give the impression of 3D rotating objects (Vanduffel *et al.* 2002; Orban *et al.* 2003).

Denys *et al.* (2004) also scanned both human subjects and macaque monkeys while they viewed shapes. The location of the resulting activations was then used to constrain the warping of the monkey brain so as to fit the human brain. The degree to which one must warp the monkey brain to do this gives an indication of the degree of the difference between the macaque monkey and human brain. The finding was that there has been a considerable expansion in the visually receiving cortex of the human parietal cortex (Orban *et al.* 2004). In summarizing the data from several of their studies, Orban *et al.* (2006) comment that there has been a large increase in the expanse of the intra-parietal cortex that is devoted to central vision.

It is unfortunate that we do not have any estimates of the size of the parietal association cortex in the macaque and human brains. We only have figures for the total size of the parietal and occipital cortex (Semendeferi and Damasio 2000). This whole region is 4.3 times larger in the human than in the chimpanzee brain. Yet the hand of a person is not so very much bigger than a chimpanzee's, and the visual information that enters the human eye is not so very different from the information that enters the chimpanzee eye. It is clear that the amount of tissue that is available for using vision to guide action is greatly expanded in the human compared with the chimpanzee brain.

Premotor cortex

The parietal cortex sends outputs to the dorsal and ventral premotor cortex (Rizzolatti and Luppino 2001) (Fig. 4.1). The parietal area AIP projects specifically to the ventral premotor cortex (Fig. 4.1). There are cells in AIP that fire when a graspable object is presented and others that fire when the monkey goes on to grasp it (Murata *et al.* 2000). It is not, therefore, surprising that similar cells can be found in the ventral premotor cortex (Raos *et al.* 2006). Correspondingly, when human subjects view objects or go on to perform the appropriate grasp, there is activity both in the intra-parietal cortex and the ventral premotor cortex (Grèzes *et al.* 2003). So the parietal cortex interacts with the premotor cortex so as to allow the sight of the object to guide the pre-shaping of the hand before grasping.

But like the parietal cortex, the motor and premotor cortex are greatly expanded in the human brain. Brodmann (1913) measured the agranular frontal cortex in humans and chimpanzees, that is the cortex in which there is an apparent absence of layer IV that contains granule cells. The agranular cortex comprises the premotor and motor cortex, and it turns out that it is three times larger in the human than the chimpanzee brain, even though the hand of a person is not that much bigger than the hand of a chimpanzee. Unfortunately, we do not have separate measures for the premotor cortex on its own.

The increase in the size of the agranular frontal cortex is of considerable functional consequence. We know, for example, that the dorsal part of the lateral premotor cortex is involved in instructing the motor cortex on the appropriate action given the context (Passingham 1993; Passingham *et al.* 1998). Lesions of this region severely impair the ability of macaque monkeys (Passingham 1985; Petrides 1985) and patients (Halsband and Freund 1990) to use visual cues to retrieve the correct action; and the temporary inactivation of this area using a GABA agonist has the same effect (Kurata and Hoffman 1994). There are also cells in the dorsal premotor cortex that code for the direction of movement, and these cells fire after the visual cue and before the relevant movement (Mitz *et al.* 1991; Cisek and Kalaska 2002). Correspondingly, there is preparatory activity in the dorsal premotor cortex when human subjects are tested on much the same task (Toni *et al.* 1999).

These tasks are 'conditional tasks'. For example, the rule is to turn a joystick to the left if the context is A, but to the right if the context is B, and so on (Passingham 1993; Wise and Murray 2000). In other words, the tasks require flexibility, now doing X and now doing Y. The learning of these tasks in the first place depends on the ventral part of the prefrontal cortex both in macaque monkeys (Wang *et al.* 2000; Bussey *et al.* 2001) and in human subjects (Toni *et al.* 2001). But since there are no direct projections from the prefrontal to the motor cortex, the prefrontal cortex exerts its influence via the premotor cortex (Takada *et al.* 2004).

So, the effect of the expansion of the prefrontal cortex (Chapter 2) and of the agranular frontal cortex (this chapter) must be to enhance the flexibility with which humans can act. In our lifetime we acquire an enormous repertoire of actions that are appropriate in different circumstances. Whether we acquire this repertoire by direct experience or by being told what action is appropriate, we owe our extraordinary behavioural flexibility to the development of the prefrontal and premotor cortex.

Cerebellum

The parietal, premotor and prefrontal cortex are interconnected with the cerebellum, which lies in the brainstem (Schmahmann and Pandya 1997). It is involved in the coordination and timing of movements, and in the process via which movements become automatic with practice (Ramnani 2006). Thus, removal of the cerebellum severely impairs the ability of macaque monkeys to coordinate movements of the hands and legs when climbing (Wirth and O'Leary 1974). The congenital under-development of the cerebellum in children causes a delay in walking with a more lasting impairment due to poor balance and coordination (Yapici and Eraksoy 2005). Similarly, adults with progressive atrophy of the cerebellum have difficulties in balance and walking (Ormerod *et al.* 1994).

The role of the cerebellum in coordination can also be demonstrated by imaging healthy subjects. Ramnani *et al.* (2001) tested the coordination of arm and finger movements, and reported a peak of activity in the cerebellum that was only found when the movements were coordinated. In other words there was no activity at this site for arm movements or finger movements on their own. In another study, Miall *et al.* (2001) tested the coordination of hand and eye movements. They found that the activation in the cerebellum was greater, the more closely these were coordinated.

As motor tasks are practiced, their timing and coordination becomes more stereotyped. Floyer-Lea and Matthews (2004) trained subjects to produce a repeating sequence of forces with their hand. As the subjects learned the task until it became automatic, so there was an increase in activity in the cerebellar dentate nucleus. Inactivation of this nucleus in macaque monkeys causes the animals to make errors on motor sequences that they have previously learned until they were automatic, while having little effect on the acquisition of new sequences (Lu *et al.* 1998). Automaticity requires the coordination of movements in time, and if human subjects learn manual rhythms until they become automatic, there are increases in activity in the cerebellum with learning (Ramnani and Passingham 2001).

Playing the piano requires the pianist to learn both the notes and the rhythms. The cerebellum can be shown to contribute both to performing the series of notes and controlling the rhythm (Bengtsson *et al.* 2004; Bengtsson and Ullen 2006). The degree of activity in the cerebellum is a function of the complexity of the piece. Thus, there is more activity when pianists play pieces from memory than when they simply play scales, even though both are practiced until they have become automatic (Parsons 2001).

This is not to claim that the cerebellum is the only structure that is involved in skilled performance. We know, for example, that the supplementary motor cortex (SMA) (Fig. 4.2) and parietal cortex are also involved in coordination (Stephan *et al.* 1999; Ramnani *et al.* 2001), the learning of timings (Ramnani and Passingham 2001) and the automation of movements (Sakai *et al.* 1998; Toni *et al.* 1998*b*). But the cerebellum is also an essential part of this circuitry, being heavily connected with parietal cortex and the premotor areas, including the SMA (Schmahmann and Pandya 1997).

So we would expect the degree of skill to be related to the development of the cerebellum. It is therefore highly significant that the human cerebellum is 2.8 times as large as predicted for a primate our size (Passingham 1975*b*). This calculation was based on data provided by Stephan *et al.* (1970) from actual brain slices. More recently, further comparative data have been collected from brain slices and also from

MRI scans. When all available data from brain slices are combined with data from MRI, it turns out that the human cerebellum is 2.9 times that expected for an ape our size, and 5.8 times the value for a monkey our size (MacLeod *et al.* 2003).

These comparisons are for the cerebellum as a whole. But we need to distinguish between the vermis, i.e. the medial cerebellum, and the lateral cerebellar hemispheres. In apes and humans it is the lateral cerebellum or 'neo-cerebellum' that is particularly expanded (MacLeod *et al.* 2003). The lateral cerebellum projects to the dentate nucleus of the cerebellum, which sends commentions in turn via the thalamus to the motor and premotor cortex (Middleton and Strick 2000). Relative to body weight, it is the dentate nucleus that is especially expanded in the human brain (Matano and Hirasaki 1997).

But the dentate nucleus does not project only to motor areas. We now know that it also sends connections via the thalamus to the dorsal prefrontal cortex (Middleton and Strick 2001). In fact, the same region of lateral cerebellar cortex that receives an input from the dorsal prefrontal cortex, also returns the connection via the thalamus (Kelly and Strick 2003). Ramnani *et al.* (2006) have confirmed a connection from

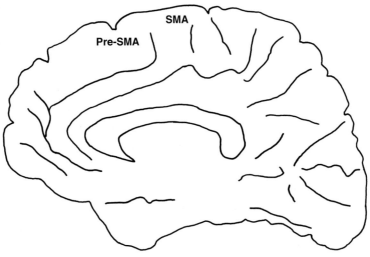

Fig. 4.2

the prefrontal cortex to the pontine nuclei in the human brain, and there is a projection from there to the cerebellum. This projection is relatively more pronounced in the human brain that in the macaque brain (Ramnani *et al.* 2006); this would fit the claim made in Chapter 2 that the human prefrontal cortex is enlarged relative to the rest of the neocortex.

This linkage suggests that the part of the cerebellum that is interconnected with the prefrontal cortex may play some role in cognition, and indeed such a role has been suggested by imaging studies (Kim *et al.* 1994; Desmond and Fiez 1998). However, it is not yet clear what contribution the cerebellum makes to cognitive processing. It is clear that further work needs doing to evaluate all the consequences of the enlargement of the cerebellum in the human brain.

Tools

Humans apply their manual skill to the production and use of tools. Though chimpanzees also use tools, these are crude and the modifications made to the tools are simple. Chimpanzees can strip stems for termite fishing or crush leaves for use as sponges, and they can use stones to crack nuts (Whiten *et al.* 1999); but their survival does not depend on tool use. Modern humans depend critically on the sophisticated technology that they have developed to allow them to adapt to different climates, produce a variety of food and defend themselves.

Tool use

The use of a tool requires that it be regarded as an extension or modification of the limb or body. In other words, it must be incorporated into our 'body schema' (Maravita and Iriki 2004). This can be shown by measuring the interference that is caused when conflicting visual and tactile signals are presented (Maravita *et al.* 2002). If human subjects grasp an object, and are asked to report whether a tactile stimulus is on their thumb (upper) or index finger (lower), they are slower to do so if a visual cue is presented in the location opposite to the tactile signal. This effect is greatly diminished if the visual cues are presented at a distance. Maravita *et al.* (2002) repeated the same experiment with the difference that the subjects now held a golf club in each hand. If the

visual cues are now presented instead on the end of the club, the interference returns if these cues are in a position that is incongruent with
the tactile stimulation. The brain is treating the end of the club as an
extension of the hand.

The mechanism by which this occurs can be studied in macaque
monkeys that have been trained to use rakes to pull in pieces of food.
Iriki et al. (1996) recorded in the parietal cortex. After the monkeys had
been trained, there were cells that fired, not only when visual stimuli
were presented near the hand, but also when these stimuli were presented at the end of the rake. The cells have receptive fields, that is the
area of space within which they are responsive, and it is as if these have
expanded to include the length of the rake.

The parietal cortex is also activated when human subjects use tools.
Inoue et al. (2001) scanned subjects while they picked up a small cylin-
der with a pair of tongs. In the control condition the subjects use their
hand to pick it up. The activity related to the use of the tool was in the
intra-parietal sulcus. This is consistent with the results of a PET study
on monkey in which they used rakes to draw in food. Even after controlling for movement, there was still activation in the intra-parietal
sulcus when they did so (Obayashi et al. 2001).

The activity in the parietal lobe could reflect two processes. The first
relates to the automation of manual skill. When human subjects learn a
motor sequence until it becomes automatic, there is an increase over trials in the activity in the parietal cortex (Sakai et al. 1998; Toni et al.
1998b). The second process relates to the retrieval of action knowledge
from the sight of the tool. If human subjects are scanned while they
demonstrate the use of an object in pantomime, there is activity in the
left intra-parietal sulcus and inferior parietal cortex, even after controlling for movement (Rumiati et al. 2004). These are not the only areas
that are activated (Lewis 2006), but we know that the parietal cortex is
critical because lesions of the left parietal cortex can cause the syndrome
of apraxia (Kertesz and Ferro 1984; Rushworth et al. 1998). Ideomotor
apraxia shows as an impairment in performing movements to command (Geschwind 1965) or in copying movements (De Renzi et al.
1983; Kimura 1993). Ideational apraxia shows as an impairment in

demonstrating the use of an object in pantomime (De Renzi and Lucchelli 1988).

So would parietal lesions cause apraxia in monkeys? Of course, one could study the effects of parietal lesions on the use of tools as rakes, and they would probably be impaired. But patients with apraxia can usually use objects such as a toothbrush if they are given it to handle. Their problem is in accessing the appropriate action just from the *sight* of the object. Unlike human subjects, monkeys cannot be asked to demonstrate in pantomime. However, they could be asked to choose between videos, where one showed the appropriate action and the other an inappropriate action. We know that some patients with ideomotor apraxia have trouble with this task (Rothi *et al.* 1985).

The ability to demonstrate the use of an object requires the ability to access the semantic system (Rothi *et al.* 1997). Kellenbach *et al.* (2003) presented photographs of tools to subjects and asked them to judge either what actions were appropriate or what the tools were used for. Activations that were associated with action knowledge were found in the left intra-parietal cortex, and activations that were associated with semantic knowledge of the function were found in the left posterior temporal lobe. As we have seen in Chapter 3, it is the left hemisphere of the human brain that is specialized for semantics. We return to this in Chapter 6 on cerebral dominance.

Tool making

The difference between simple tool use and tool making is that the latter requires planning as well as manual skill. Chapter 7 documents the role of the prefrontal cortex in planning and we would therefore expect it also to be involved in tool making. Of course, planning can also be involved in complex tool-use. In a PET study, Obayashi *et al.* (2002) taught macaque monkeys to use two tools in sequence. First they had to use the short rake to retrieve the longer one, and then to use that one to draw in the food. As expected, there was activation, not only in the parietal cortex, but also in the prefrontal cortex.

Monkeys do not make tools, and though chimpanzees do so we cannot at the moment scan them. PET can, however, be used with human subjects using[18] fluoro-2-deoxyglucose as a tracer. Because this decays slowly, the subjects can make tools before scanning, and the appropriate activations can be detected. Stout and Chaminade (2007) required subjects to strike a flake off a cobble, as in Oldowan tool-making. The comparison task was simply striking two cobbles together in an uncontrolled. As expected, there was activity in the parietal cortex and premotor cortex.

The subjects in this experiment were novices, and all they were asked to do was knock a flake off the cobble, with no specification as to the type of flake. In other words, little planning was required and there was no sequence of movements. This may account for the lack of activation in the prefrontal cortex. There is independent evidence that the prefrontal cortex is activated when human subjects plan a series of movements to demonstrate the use of a tool (Johnson-Frey et al. 2005). So, in a follow up study, Stout et al. (pers. comm.) scanned three expert stone-knappers while they made a complex tool, an Acheulian hand-axe. Here the core must be edged, thinned and shaped in a complex series of moves. This process was associated with activation in the right prefrontal cortex, with the peak lying just near the inferior frontal sulcus. Chapter 7 will also review imaging data showing that there is activity in the prefrontal cortex when subjects plan a series of moves on a problem solving task (Dagher et al. 1999; Unterrainer et al. 2004).

Imitation

A stone-knapper learns their trade partly by imitation and partly by verbal instruction. It is a requirement that the apprentice closely observes the detailed movements that are made by the demonstrator, and copies them exactly. This is true imitation as opposed to 'emulation' in which the same goal is achieved but not necessarily via the same exact set of actions.

Imitation and emulation can be tested in chimpanzees by setting up alternative ways that a problem may be solved. One can then see whether the observer uses the particular method that has just been demonstrated. Chimpanzees can be shown to use the general method that they observed (Whiten et al. 1996; Myowa-Yamakoshi and Matsuzawa 2000), but they are more likely to achieve the end result in their own way and less likely to copy the details of the demonstrator's actions (Call *et al.* 2005). Tomasello and Carpenter (2005) presented three chimpanzees with boxes and the chimpanzees were given the opportunity to observe actions that turned on coloured lights. The actions were either arbitrary, as in touching the forehead to the box, or non-arbitrary, as in touching one of two attachments. Rather than copying the exact movements, the chimpanzees found their own way of achieving the same goal.

Whiten *et al.* (1996) specifically compared chimpanzees and young children on a problem in which there were alternative ways of achieving the goal. The children were more likely to imitate the elements, whereas the chimpanzees were more likely to achieve the goal with their own behavioural repertoire. However, on one of the components, the chimpanzees did strictly imitate. In a follow-up study, Horner and Whiten (2005) showed that chimpanzees were more likely to emulate if they could see how the mechanism worked, and more likely to imitate if they could not.

But we cannot study the neural basis of imitation in chimpanzees. Electrophysiological experiments can only be carried out on macaque monkeys. Kumashiro *et al.* (2003) have recently claimed that macaques will imitate a human demonstrator so long as they have been taught to attend to what the person is doing; for example, opening a puzzle box. Unfortunately, the report is descriptive and does not present data about the baseline rates for performing the particular actions. It is true that macaques can learn to pick photographs in a particular order by watching a trained monkey doing so (Subiaul *et al.* 2004), but this test does not require the observer to imitate the specific movements. The animals can succeed by emulation, i.e. by achieving the same goal in their own way.

Electrophysiological studies of the macaque brain have suggested a mechanism by which this could occur. Cells were first reported in the ventral premotor cortex, which fired both when the monkey performed an action and when it observed the experimenter performing the same action, for example, picking up a piece of food (di Pellegrino *et al.* 1992; Gallese *et al.* 1996). These cells were called 'mirror neurones'. They are found in particular in area F5 of the ventral premotor cortex as defined on the basis of staining for cytochrome oxidase (Rizzolatti *et al.* 2001). If the monkeys have long experience of watching the experimenter using a tool, cells in this area also fire when the monkeys simply observe the use of the tool (Ferrari *et al.* 2005). There are also cells with mirror properties in the anterior part of the inferior parietal lobe, i.e. in area PF (Rizzolatti *et al.* 2001; Fogassi *et al.* 2005). These cells provide a common coding for actions performed by the subject and the actions that the subject observes. It is as if the subject 'simulates' the action that is observed (Gallese and Goldman 1998; Rizzolatti *et al.* 2001).

Activity has also been found in the human premotor and parietal cortex when subjects observe actions (Buccino *et al.* 2001; Grezes *et al.* 2003). The same premotor and parietal areas are activated both when subjects observe hand actions and when they themselves later perform the actions (Buccino *et al.* 2004). Activity can also be recorded when subjects simply observe tools being used. Jarvelainen *et al.* (2004) scanned subjects using magneto-encephalography and reported changes in activity in motor cortex when subjects watched chopsticks being used. The activity was greater if the actions had a specific goal; that is, if the chopsticks were used to pick up and transfer food rather than being simply moved to an empty plate. The effect was also more pronounced the more the subjects had themselves used chopsticks during the last year.

These results suggest that motor representations are activated when human subjects observe actions. To prove this, Buccino *et al.* (2001) compared the observations of actions performed by the hand, foot or mouth. The argument was that if motor representations were evoked, they should occur in the area that represents that body part. The result was that activity could indeed be found in different parts of the somatic map in parietal cortex and motor map of premotor cortex depending on the body part observed. This is strong evidence for the conclusion that this activity reflects the firing of mirror neurones in the motor system.

Further evidence for motor simulation comes from studies in which human subjects observe actions that they can simulate with activity compared with actions that they cannot. This can be achieved by presenting subjects with movements that are either biologically possible or are not (Stevens *et al.* 2000). The finding is that there is only activation in motor cortex and parietal cortex when the subject observes the movements that are possible, that is movements that they can simulate.

The better one is at skilled movements, the better one can simulate them. So, Calvo-Merino *et al.* (2005) presented dancers with dance forms in which they were or were not expert. The subjects were either professionals in classical ballet or in capoeira, a Brazilian martial dance form. There was enhanced activity in the premotor and parietal cortex when experts saw the dance form that was in their motor repertoire. This enhancement was not due simply to their greater visual familiarity with their style. It was only found when dancers observed ballet moves that were specific to their own gender, even though they were as visually familiar with moves performed by the opposite gender (Calvo-Merino *et al.* 2006).

The suggestion is that it is the ability to simulate actions when observing them that makes it possible to imitate them, because there is a common code for the actions as observed and performed (Rizzolatti *et al.* 2001). Iacoboni *et al.* (1999) therefore scanned subjects while they imitated finger movements. They found more activity in the parietal cortex and in Broca's area 44 when the subjects imitated the movements rather than simply observing them.

One's first thought is that it is puzzling that there should be activity in Broca's area for imitation of actions with the hand. It makes one wonder whether there is mirror neuronal activity in the area that is thought to be homologous to Broca's area in the macaque brain (Petrides *et al.* 2005). Though Rizzolatti *et al.* (2001) have recorded mirror neuronal activity on the convexity of the ventral premotor cortex in area F5, they have not yet recorded from cells deep in the arcuate sulcus in the region identified as area 44 by Petrides *et al.* (2005).

So, Nelissen *et al.* (2005) scanned macaque monkeys using fMRI while they observed actors on a screen. As one would expect, they found activity in the convexity cortex of F5, but they also report activity in the depth of the arcuate sulcus, in a region that appears to correspond to the area identified by Petrides (2005) as the homologue of

Broca's area 44. However, we cannot properly assess this finding without three further experiments. First it has to be shown by direct electrophysiological recording that the same cells are also active when the monkey performs the same actions. Second, we need to know whether any mirror cells that are found fire only when the monkey watches a very specific movement. Gallese *et al.* (1996) classified the cells in the premotor cortex in terms of the degree to which the cells fired for specific movements, and for many cells the match between the action that was performed and the observed action did not have to be exact. Finally, we need to know whether the cells in macaque area 44 fire when a monkey emulates or even imitates. Only when we know this can we draw a proper comparison between the mirror system in macaques and humans.

Conclusions

It is a fundamental fact about modern humans and our hominid ancestors that we have adapted by specializing in technology. It is this that has enabled us to become generalists. So what is it about our brains that has made this possible?

There are several factors with significant leverage. Consider first our manual skill. This results from the expansion of the hand area within the motor cortex and the proportion of motor cells that project directly to the motor neurones. It is enhanced by the enlargement of the premotor and parietal association areas in relation to the size of the hand. The motor cortex, premotor cortex and SMA form the 'agranular' motor cortex, i.e. cortex lacking a layer IV with granule cells. Combined they are nearly two times as large as predicted for a primate our size (Passingham 1975*b*). Finally, skill is further promoted by the development of the lateral cerebellum or 'neo-cerebellum', which is interconnected with these areas. Apart from the neocortex, this is the structure that has most enlarged in the human brain when controlling for body size (Passingham 1975*b*). It is involved not only in coordination and timing but also in the automation of skill.

But making tools requires more than manual skill, it also requires the ability to imagine the finished product and plan the series of moves that will achieve it. In making a hand axe, the knapper has to be able to see potential in a lump of stone. Chapter 3 has already claimed that humans may be unique in being able to imagine at will, and Chapter 7 will document the evidence that it is the development of the prefrontal cortex that is responsible for the human ability to plan. The ability to devise tools also makes demands on the ability to engage in causal reasoning (Johnson-Frey 2003), and Chapter 8 will suggest a critical role for prefrontal cortex in such reasoning.

It is, however, no good having the skill and ability unless there are also the means for acquiring it. Humans can do so in two ways. The first is by strict imitation. One cannot learn how to fashion an Acheulian hand-axe by emulation. While imitation probably depends on a mirror neuronal system, the mirror neurones must fire both when watching skilled movements and when performing the *identical* movements. It is not enough for the match to be a rough one. In the paper on cells in the premotor cortex by Gallese *et al.* (1996) the movements were simple ones, such as touching or picking up peanuts, and there was no requirement that the monkey touch or pick up the peanuts in an identical fashion. The human mirror neuronal system must be tuned much more specifically to allow exact imitation.

But there is another way that skills can be passed on and this is by giving verbal instructions and demonstrating the precise moves. Chapter 10 will argue that teaching is unique to humans, and that teaching in a language is a particularly powerful method. As mentioned in the last chapter, we acquire much of our semantic knowledge in the classroom. The evidence from apraxia demonstrates that our knowledge of the actions that are appropriate for an implement is integrated with the semantic system in the left hemisphere.

Learning by instruction has the advantage that it saves time. A monkey must learn by trial and error over many days or months. Yet, I can simply tell you what to do, and you can do it immediately. Sakai and Passingham (2003, 2006) gave verbal instructions to subjects, and then scanned them during the period after the instruction but before they carried out the task. There was continuous activity during the delay in the frontal polar cortex, area 10, and this reflected preparation to perform the particular type of task. The data suggested that this area sets up the appropriate task by interacting with posterior areas that are involved in the performance of that task. It is true that one can also give non-verbal instructions to monkeys; for example, a specific tone telling the animal that on this trial it should choose the picture that matches the sample (Wallis *et al.* 2001). But it takes very many trials to teach the meaning of the tone. The difference is that language enables humans to give an infinite variety of instructions which can be immediately obeyed.

Chapter 5

Speech and language

The essential human skill is that of speaking. Apart from parrots, only humans can speak, and we can speak in sentences. While apes that have been reared in the laboratory can understand some spoken words of English, and can learn some of the gestures of sign language, we still do not know whether they are able to master rules of grammar. The procedures for teaching apes are also arduous; yet human infants pick up language at an astonishing rate, and without any directed programme for teaching them. Though it is possible to teach chimpanzees gestures, deaf children spontaneously invent their own (Goldin-Meadow and Mylander 1983, 1998). This chapter is central to our search for specializations of the human brain.

Hearing words

Speech uses arbitrary symbols to refer to objects and events. Though pictograms may have originally depicted the items to which they refer, most spoken words have no such history of being iconic; so their referents must therefore be learned. Chapter 1 indicated that this is within the capability of chimpanzees. Kanzi can pick out from a picture book the object that is appropriate for a word that he hears over headphones (Savage-Rumbaugh and Lewin 1994). There is also convincing evidence that the dog Rico can understand many words of English (Kaminski *et al.* 2004). No-one has yet shown that macaques can do this, but this may simply be because monkeys have not been reared in such close proximity with humans.

Lesions of Wernicke's area in the human brain impair the ability to understand spoken words (Naesser 1994), and this area lies posteriorly in the superior temporal cortex. Electrical stimulation of this area causes errors in the identification of phonemes (Ojemann 1983).

The connections of the superior temporal cortex are well described in monkeys (Galaburda and Pandya 1983). The primary auditory cortex sends connections to the immediately neighbouring region, which projects in turn to the convexity cortex of the superior temporal lobe. There are then projections from there to the upper bank of the superior temporal sulcus (Seltzer and Pandya 1994).

In macaques, the superior temporal cortex also projects to the posterior region Tpt (Fig. 2.4). This lies in the posterior part of the superior temporal cortex. As mentioned in Chapter 2, in the human brain this area has expanded onto the inferior parietal convexity cortex (Galaburda and Sanides 1980). We do not know whether it is restricted to the temporal lobe in chimpanzees.

Just as infero-temporal cortex is visual association cortex, so the superior temporal cortex is auditory association cortex. In macaque monkeys there are cells in the superior temporary association cortex that fire to complex auditory stimuli, and some of these fire to specific monkey calls (Rauschecker et al. 1995). As one would expect from this finding, lesions of the left superior temporal cortex in macaques impair their ability to discriminate between monkey calls (Heffner and Heffner 1986).

Though monkeys do not speak, they can discriminate between phonemes that are voiced, such as /ba/, /da/ and /ga/, and those that are unvoiced, such as /pa/, /ta/ and /ka/, although they are less sensitive to variation in voice onset time than human subjects (Steinschneider et al. 1995). In macaque monkeys there are cells in the primary auditory cortex that fire to the onset of voicing (Steinschneider et al. 1995). Again, lesions of the superior temporal cortex have the expected effect, impairing the ability of monkeys to discriminate between phonemes (Dewson et al. 1969).

The abilities of other primates are not confined to the perception of individual phonemes. Like human infants, cotton-top tamarins can learn to pick out words from a stream of sounds, i.e. they can segment the stream of speech. This ability was tested by presenting syllable sequences in two artificial languages (Hauser et al. 2001). The tamarins came to orient more to a speaker when it played syllable sequences that were not in the language, evidence that they detected the fact that these sequences were anomalous. In macaque monkeys removal of the superior temporal cortex also impairs the ability to discriminate between sequences of sounds (Dewson *et al.* 1970).

It should not then be surprising that the chimpanzee Kanzi can discriminate between many words of spoken English (Savage-Rumbaugh and Lewin 1994). The auditory mechanisms that allow such discrimination are not necessarily specific to speech. To see whether there are additional mechanisms that are specific to speech, one can compare listening to speech sounds with listening to tones or noise. Noise bursts activate the primary auditory cortex, whereas speech sounds activate the secondary auditory areas in the superior temporal gyrus (Zatorre *et al.* 1992; Jancke *et al.* 2002). Compared with frequency modulated tones, the activity in the upper bank of the superior temporal sulcus is greater for speech sounds, even if they are pseudo words or reversed words (Binder *et al.* 2000). The same result has been found when comparing speech syllables with acoustically matched non-phonemic-like sounds (Liebenthal *et al.* 2005). However, Price *et al.* (2005) argue that there is no area that is specific to speech processing, since the superior temporal sulcus can also be activated by melody. This suggests that the apparently speech-specific activations reflect the recognition of meaningful sounds.

Two PET studies have been carried out on macaques. The first such study reported activity in the superior temporal cortex when monkeys heard calls (Gil-da-Costa *et al.* 2004). The second study compared activity in response to species-specific calls, i.e. coos and screams, with activity in response to non-biological sounds (Gil-da-Costa *et al.* 2006). There was activation in the superior temporal cortex whatever the sounds, but the activation in area Tpt was specific for the species-specific calls.

Meaning

It is clear that the auditory mechanisms for discriminating between single speech sounds are not unique to humans. But words carry meaning. So functional imaging can be used to compare activity for words that do or do not have meaning. Scott and colleagues (Scott *et al.* 2000; Narain *et al.* 2003) matched speech and speech-like stimuli for acoustic complexity. When speech is intelligible, the activity spreads into the anterior part of the left superior temporal sulcus, and also onto the left middle temporal gyrus.

This activity reflects both the retrieval of the referents of the words and the retrieval of semantic information. When subjects are asked specifically to make judgements about meaning, activity is found in the left middle temporal gyrus, extending into the inferior temporal cortex. This is true whether the subjects make semantic judgements about words that they hear (Demonet *et al.* 1992) or about words that they read (Price *et al.* 1997; McDermott *et al.* 2003). Booth *et al.* (2002) specifically compared semantic judgements for spoken and read words, and report activity in common in the left middle temporal gyrus.

Chapter 3 has already argued that the mechanism by which semantic retrieval occurs could be based on an associative mechanism already found in macaque monkeys. This involves cells in the temporal cortex that code for learned associations between pairs of pictures after the animals have been taught a delayed associative task. One type of cell fires to both members of a pair once the association between them has been learned; the other type fires prospectively when one member has been presented and the associate is going to be presented (Sakai and Miyashita 1991; Naya *et al.* 1996). Cells have also been recorded in the human temporal lobe that are particularly active during the early stages of verbal paired-associate learning (Ojemann and Schoenfield-McNeill 1998).

There is the difference that in the case of spoken words, it is an auditory cue that allows the retrieval of a visual stimulus; in other words the coding is cross-modal. But cells have also been reported in the monkey brain that fire on a cross-modal associative task. Zhou and Fuster (2000) trained macaques on a delayed visual–tactile task. There were cells in the somatosensory cortex that fired during the delay after the visual stimulus had been presented and before the tactile stimulus was presented.

Such a mechanism could be involved in the retrieval of the referent of a spoken word. But there are three crucial differences in relation to human language. The first is that what makes language special is not this associative mechanism, but the *purpose* for which words are used. In a language, words or symbols are used to communicate, that is to say 'A' and in so doing to allow another person to mentally retrieve A'. There must be an intention to communicate and an understanding of the effect of the communication on the mental state of the partner. It is here that humans probably differ from chimpanzees, and we therefore devote a whole chapter (Chapter 9), to the understanding of mental states.

The second major difference is the size of the temporal lobe in humans. The left superior temporal cortex is 3.8 times as big in the human brain as in the common chimpanzee (*Pan troglodytes*) (Rilling and Seligman 2002). The left middle and inferior temporal cortex are 4.1 times larger in the human brain. It is true that the complexity of the information that is conveyed to the ear through speech is much greater than the complexity of the information that a chimpanzee hears in the wild. But, in spite of this difference in the inputs, it is clear that the sophistication and depth of the analysis of that input is immeasurably greater in the human brain.

The final difference has already been noted in Chapter 3. This is that it is the left temporal lobe that is activated when subjects retrieve the meanings of words or make judgements about those meanings. The next chapter discusses cerebral dominance in detail and, in particular, the specialization of the human left hemisphere for phonology and semantics.

It might be thought that there must also be brain specializations for reading. However, writing is a relatively recent invention in human history, and there has not been time for evolution to modify the circuitry of the brain. It is true that there is activity in the 'word form' area of the left fusiform gyrus when subjects read words or pseudowords (Dehaene *et al.* 2002). But we should not be surprised to learn that there is also activity in the same area when objects are presented (Price and Devlin 2003). An area that is used to analyse the form of objects has been exploited to analyse the form of written words.

Of course, written words have to be linked to their referents. But the association of written words with meaning uses the same mechanisms as for spoken words. Callan *et al.* (2005) taught Japanese subjects the association between unfamiliar Korean or Thai ideograms and the appropriate phonemes. There was an increase in activity in the superior temporal sulcus (Callan *et al.* 2005), just as for intelligible speech (Narain *et al.* 2003).

Articulation

While chimpanzees may be able to access the meanings of spoken words or visual symbols, they are unable themselves to speak. Lieberman (2006) has argued that this is partly a matter of vocal anatomy. In adult modern humans the skull has an angled base, with the larynx positioned low in the throat. Post-mortem studies suggested to Lieberman (1975, 2006) that this contrasted with a high position for the larynx in the chimpanzee. However, MRI scans of living chimpanzees indicate that in fact both the larynx and the hyoid, which supports the tongue, descend rapidly during development (Nishimura *et al.* 2006). X-rays of tamarins (*Saguinus oedipus*) and dogs (*Canis familiaris*) also indicate that during the production of loud calls, the larynx is lowered (Fitch 2000).

It is not the position of the larynx but the central control of breathing and of movements of the larynx and articulators that is critical. The intercostal muscles function to coordinate inspiration and expiration, and in modern humans there is an enlargement of the spinal cord at the thoracic level due to the complexity of the spinal regulation of these muscles (MacLarnon and Hewitt 1999). This reflects the need to precisely coordinate breathing and speaking.

There are important differences between humans and chimpanzees in the coordination of breathing and the production of sound. Chimpanzees produce a breathy panting sound that is reminiscent of laughter, but each pant is produced once during each brief expiration or inspiration (Provine 1996). Thus, their laughter is closely coupled to their breathing. By contrast, when humans laugh they produce vowel-like sounds that result from the chopping of a single expiration. When humans speak, they are able to produce a series of phonemes for each expiration.

The central control of breathing can be studied using imaging. When humans voluntarily inspire or expire, there is activity in the motor cortex and premotor cortex, including the supplementary motor area (SMA) (Ramsay *et al.* 1993) (Fig. 4.2). The coordination of breathing with speech has been examined by comparing two conditions. In one the subjects vocalized 'buy Bobby a poppy', but without moving the mouth or tongue, and in the control condition they mouthed it silently (Murphy *et al.* 1997). Here the experimental condition involves the coordination of breathing with speech, but does not involve movement of the articulators. Activity reflecting this coordination was reported in the motor and premotor and SMA.

Normally, of course, one does move the articulators when speaking, and imaging can again be used to study this. Voluntary retraction of the tongue is associated with activity in the motor and premotor cortex and the neighbouring frontal operculum (Corfield *et al.* 1999). The control of the articulators has also been examined in the study by Murphy *et al.* (1997) that was mentioned in the previous paragraph. In an additional comparison, the authors constrasted articulating 'buy Bobby a poppy' aloud with vocalizing it without moving the mouth or tongue. Articulation involved the motor cortex, premotor cortex and neighbouring operculum, and these activations were bilateral. As expected from these results, strokes that involve the operculum can cause oral dyspraxia, a disruption in the articulation of speech (Dronkers 1996).

Unfortunately, there have been no studies that have compared the size of the oral motor representation in humans and chimpanzees or monkeys. This representation can be mapped by electrical stimulation, as in the studies by Penfield and Jaspar (1954) during surgery on patients. The cortical motor area controlling the larynx can also be mapped by electrical stimulation, and in monkeys it lies in the ventral premotor cortex, and particularly in the frontal operculum (Hast *et al.* 1974; Simonyan and Jurgens 2002). However, there have been no studies that directly compare these areas in humans and other primates.

The cortical motor areas for the mouth and larynx send connections to nuclei in the brainstem. We have comparative measurements for the hypoglossal nucleus. It is here that the motor-neurones for the tongue originate. The value for the human brain is 24% greater than predicted for a monkey or ape but the difference is not statistically significant (Sherwood *et al.* 2005*a*). But the crucial factor is not the size of these brainstem nuclei, but the directness with which the motor areas connect to them. Chapter 4 reviewed the evidence that the ability to move the fingers independently depended on direct projections onto the motor-neurones in the spinal cord. Simonyan and Jurgens (2003) have traced the descending projections from the cortical larynx area in squirrel monkeys (*Saimiri sciureus*). The finding is that there are no direct projections to either the hypoglossal nucleus or to the nucleus ambiguus where the motor-neurones for the larynx originate. Yet, there are direct motor connections from the cortex to these nuclei in the human brain (Kuypers 1958; Iwatsubo *et al.* 1990). I confess to being overjoyed when I learned that this was so. Here is an anatomical specialization that relates to our most distinctive characteristic, i.e. our vocal skill.

Broca's area 44

Broca's area 44 lies anterior to the cortical area that is specialized for articulation (Fig. 5.1). It is a crucial observation that stimulation of Broca's area can impair the ability to name correctly, even when the patients retain the ability to speak (Penfield and Roberts 1959). In other words, it can produce aphasic errors. It has long been assumed that permanent damage to Broca's area causes a severe non-fluent aphasia. But as already mentioned in Chapter 2, small lesions that are confined to pars opercularis (area 44) do not produce a long-lasting impairment in producing speech (Mohr *et al.* 1978; Damasio and Damasio 1989). To produce such an effect, the lesion needs to be more extensive (Alexander *et al.* 1990). It is not clear whether the critical factor is that it should also include pars triangularis (area 45), which lies anterior to area 44, or that it should undercut the white-matter fibres that pass beneath these areas. A lesion that invades this white matter will disconnect the temporal lobe from the whole inferior frontal gyrus.

Imaging has the advantage that the activation peaks lie in the cortex, and can be confined to specific areas. So, the specific contribution that is made by area 44 can best be studied by scanning healthy subjects.

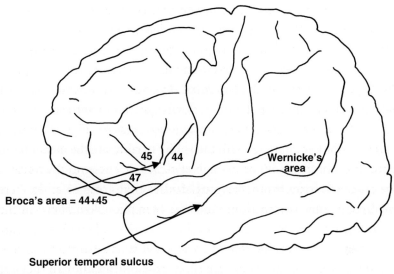

Fig. 5.1

Because of the classical doctrine that Broca's area is specialized for speech, studies have concentrated on its role in phonological processing. Several tasks have been used to study this.

One is word repetition. In two PET studies, the subjects heard single words and repeated them; in the control condition they also heard words but always said the word 'crime'(Price *et al.* 1996). Thus, the subtraction of the control from the experimental condition removes activity due simply to hearing and speaking. Activity due to repetition was found in Broca's area 44. A peak lying just inferior to this area has also been reported when subjects read pseudowords as opposed to real words (Hagoort *et al.* 1999). Pseudowords must be sounded out, whereas the name of a word can be accessed via a link between the shape of the whole word and its semantics. Another task involves the generation of words. The subject is required to produce words beginning with a particular letter, such as 't'. Several PET studies have reported activity for letter fluency in and around Broca's area, pars opercularis (Mummery *et al.* 1996; Warburton *et al.* 1996; Paulesu *et al.* 1997).

Two meta-analyses of the activation peaks on phonological tasks shows a clear clustering around this region (Poldrack *et al.* 1999;

Vigneau *et al.* 2006). To find out whether the activity is essential for phonological tasks, one can use transcranial magnetic brain stimulation (TMS). Two studies have required subjects to decide whether two words that are visually presented sound the same, as in 'vein' and 'pane' (Nixon *et al.* 2004; Gough *et al.* 2005). In both cases stimulation over pars opercularis interfered with performance. This contrasts with the effects of stimulation over the more anterior areas 45 (Fig. 5.1) and 47. Here stimulation interferes with the ability to compare the meanings of words but not their sounds (Gough *et al.* 2005). These results confirm the evidence from brain-imaging studies that areas 45 and 47 are involved in semantic processing and area 44 in phonological processing (Poldrack *et al.* 1999).

But what is the specific role of area 44 if it is not the production of the individual sounds? There are three possibilities, though they are not exclusive. The first depends on our understanding of premotor cortex in general. We know that it is involved in the learned selection of movements, i.e. the retrieval of the movements that are appropriate for the context (Passingham 1993). By analogy, the role of Broca's area could be to retrieve the appropriate words.

The second possibility is that it is specialized for the retrieval and manipulation of sequences (Hoen *et al.* 2006). Gelfrand and Bookheimer (2003) presented either three syllables or three hums, and required their subjects to mentally manipulate the sequence, either changing the order or deleting one item. In a control condition the subjects also engaged in articulation but did not have to manipulate the sequences. In the contrast between the conditions, there was a peak of activity at the top of Broca's area, and this was true for the hums as well as for the syllables.

There is a third and related possibility. This is that Broca's area contributes particularly to the production of grammatical sequences. We will return to this suggestion in a later section.

Area 44 in monkeys

As mentioned in Chapter 2, Broca's area 44 can also be found in the brains of monkeys and chimpanzees. So has it changed its functions in the human brain? The first question is whether it is involved in vocalization in monkeys and apes. In the squirrel monkey (*Saimiri sciureus*), electrical stimulation of the anterior cingulate cortex (Fig. 7.2) evokes calls (Jurgens 1970; Muller-Preuss and Jurgens 1976), and lesions that include this area decrease the rate of spontaneous vocalizations (Kirzinger and Jurgens 1982). In turn, there are projections from the cingulate vocalization area to area 44 (Muller-Preuss and Jurgens 1976). Area 44 also receives an input from the cortical larynx area (Simonyan and Jurgens 2005).

Yet lesions of area 44 do not affect the rate of spontaneous vocalizations in squirrel monkeys (Kirzinger and Jurgens 1982). This could be taken to imply that the calls of other primates are simply evoked by emotion and are not under voluntary control. On this view the difference is that in hominid evolution, mechanisms evolved for the voluntary control of sound production.

But one can challenge this claim. Macaque monkeys have been trained to produce a call only while a white light was on. Calls at other times led to a delay before the light was turned on again (Sutton *et al.* 1974). The finding was that after training the monkeys did indeed learn to call when the light came on. And there is an even more impressive demonstration. In this the monkeys were trained to produce a 'coo' when a red light came on and a 'bark' when a green light came on (Sutton *et al.* 1978). And they were able to do so. In other words, they were able to select the appropriate call even though the stimuli were neutral and not associated with emotion. Hihara *et al.* (2003) even claim that their macaques learned to produce different coos depending on whether they wanted food or a tool for raking in food.

So if monkeys have control over their calls, would lesions abolish it? The effect of lesions was tested using the first paradigm where the animals were trained to call when a light came on (Sutton *et al.* 1974). As expected, lesions of the anterior cingulate cortex had a severe effect. One monkey could no longer be induced to produce voluntary calls, and the second monkey produced calls that were sporadic and of shorter duration. But, surprisingly, lesions that included part of area 44 had no effect.

But this does not settle the matter, and for two reasons. The first is that the lesions did not remove all of the tissue in the depth of the arcuate sulcus that we now know corresponds to area 44 (Petrides *et al.* 2005). Stimulation of this area in macaque monkeys evokes movements of the jaw and lips (Petrides *et al.* 2005). And there is a second reason for thinking that the issue remains open. This is that the more critical test would be to see whether lesions in this region impaired the ability to produce *discriminatory* calls. In other words, would they prevent the animal from producing a coo or bark depending on which cue was presented?. After all, we know that lesions of the neighbouring premotor cortex impair the ability of monkeys to produce hand movement A given cue X and hand movement B given cue Y (Halsband and Passingham 1985; Petrides 1987).

For these reasons, I think that it is still possible that area 44 is involved in the voluntary control of calls in other primates. But this is not to say that there has been no significant change in Broca's area during human evolution. This point is best made by referring to the evidence that in the human brain this area is involved in grammatical processing. This is the topic of the next section.

Grammar

Aphasic patients with large frontal lesions that include Broca's area can suffer from 'agrammatism' (Alexander *et al.* 1989). This is evidenced by 'telegraphic speech', i.e. a failure to use function words such as 'the' or to generate morphological markers, as in plurals or past tenses. However, as noted previously, the lesions in these cases tend to result from extensive strokes. The specific contribution of area 44 can be isolated by scanning healthy subjects.

Take morphological markers, for example. Heim *et al.* (2003) required subjects to decide whether a word was a preposition or a noun. In another condition the subjects had to decide the gender of a noun. In both conditions there was activity in area 44 extending into area 45. In a study by Suzuki and Sakai (2003) the subjects judged whether there are anomalies in noun–verb agreement, and again there was activity in area 44.

An alternative is to study word order. Dapretto and Bookheimer (1999) required subjects to judge whether sentence pairs had the same meaning. For example, the pairs might be 'the pool is behind the gate' and 'behind the gate is the pool'; these pairs differ in syntax. In the comparison condition, the pairs might be 'the car is in the garage' and 'the auto is in the garage'; these pairs share the same syntax. There was a peak of activity in Broca's area when the pairs differed in syntax. Activity has also been reported in this general region when subjects judge word order errors compared with spelling errors (Embick *et al.* 2000*b*), The greater the complexity of the sentence, the greater the activation in Broca's area (Friederici *et al.* 2006).

There are two possible objections to the conclusion that the activity reflects grammatical processing. The first is that sentences that differ in their syntax may also differ in their semantics. One way of avoiding this is to use pseudowords. This has been done in two studies. Moro *et al.* (2001) presented sentences using quasi-Italian pseudowords. The subjects had to detect anomalies in order or agreement. Again there was activity in Broca's area 44. Indefrey *et al.* (2001*b*) also used pseudowords, requiring the subjects to detect errors of case or number marking. The peak of activation lay just above Broca's area.

A second objection is that the subjects may subvocally rehearse sentences when making judgements about syntax, and thus the activity in Broca's area may reflect this rehearsal. To rule out this possibility, subjects have been asked to make judgements about sentences while saying the word 'double' repeatedly so as to prevent internal rehearsal (Caplan *et al.* 2000). Even though rehearsal was suppressed, the more complex the syntax the greater was the activity in Broca's area.

This is not to claim that working memory plays no role in processing sentences. The further displaced a verb is in a sentence from its canonical position, the greater the working memory load, and the greater the activation in Broca's area (Fiebach *et al.* 2005). However, Sakai *et al.* (2003) included a verbal memory task as a control task. Compared with this control, there was still activity in Broca's area when the subjects made decisions about syntax.

The findings described so far relate to the ability to make judgements about syntax. However, one can also scan subjects while they produce sentences. In one such study, the subjects were shown scenes that consisted of an arrangement of coloured shapes (Indefrey *et al.* 2001a). In the critical condition, the subjects described the scene in full sentences, as in 'the red square launches the blue ellipse', and in a control condition they preserved only the local syntactic structure, as in 'red square, blue ellipse, launch'. The activity for this comparisonlay partly in Broca's area 44 and partly in the premotor cortex posterior to it.

One can also scan subjects while they learn new grammatical rules. Musso *et al.* (2003) scanned German speakers while they learned some basic rules of Italian or Japanese grammar. For comparison they taught them rules that do not exist in any language: they call these 'unreal' rules. The authors report learning-related increases in activity in the left Broca's area, but claim that this was only true for the 'real' rules. On this basis, the authors argue that this area is specialized for the learning of the rules that are found in natural languages. But to be sure of this conclusion, one would have to show that there were no other differences between the real and unreal rules; for example, in the demands made on working memory.

In summary, there is general agreement between imaging studies that the general region of Broca's area is involved in judgements about grammatical sentences and in the production of grammatical speech. This conclusion is supported by the results of a meta-analysis of studies on sentence processing (Vigneau *et al.* 2006). But the fact that there is activity in this region does not prove that that activity is essential for these processes. There is also, for example, activity in other regions, such as the superior temporal cortex, when subjects make judgements about the grammaticality of sentences (Embick *et al.* 2000a).

To find out whether Broca's area is indeed necessary for grammatical processing, one can try to interfere with that processing by applying transcranial magnetic brain stimulation to the general region of Broca's area. Shapiro *et al.* (2001) applied stimulation to an area just anterior and superior to Broca's area, and found that it interfered with the generation of plurals for verbs but not for nouns. Studies are now

needed in which the coil is aimed directly at Broca's area, pars opercularis, and subjects are required to make judgements about grammar.

Broca's area and vocal learning

Children have to learn the words and grammatical rules of their native
language. In the early years they do this without formal training. Simple
exposure to language is enough. In this way they differ radically from
other primates. The closest analogy is with song birds (Wilbrecht and
Nottebohm 2003). For example, if exposed to specific sequences of syllables, canaries and zebra finches learn to produce them Tchernichovski
et al. 2001; Liu *et al.* 2004; Gardner *et al.* 2005). Chapter 4 suggested that
imitation depended on mirror neurones. In the case of song learning,
these would be neurones that fire both when the bird produces a syllable and when it hears that syllable. We know that song learning depends
on two structures (Wilbrecht and Nottebohm 2003): these are 'area X' in
the paleostriatum, part of the basal ganglia, and the hyperstriatum ventrale caudale (HVC), now reclassified as a cortical structure (Jarvis *et al.*
2005). The relative size of the HVC correlates with the number of song
types in the repertoire (Devoogd *et al.* 1993). It is an exciting finding
that in swamp sparrows (*Melospiza georgiana*) there are mirror neurones that fire both when the bird sings a particular note sequence and
when it hears it (Prather *et al.* 2008).

So are there mirror neurones in Broca's area? Most of the data relates
to mirror neurones for imitating hand actions. Chapter 4 has already
described an fMRI study that showed that there is activity in this area
when macaque monkeys observe humans performing arm movements
(Nelissen *et al.* 2005). There is also activity in human Broca's area 44,
both when the subjects observe hand actions (Buccino *et al.* 2001) and
when they imitate them (Iacoboni *et al.* 1999).

This activity can be found in the same area that is activated when
subjects speak (Hamzei *et al.* 2003). So one might wonder if it actually reflects subvocal naming of the actions. To control for this,
Iacoboni *et al.* (1999) included control conditions in which the subjects
moved the finger that was marked. If they named the finger in the imitation condition, they would have done so in the control conditions,

and thus activity due to naming would have been subtracted out in the comparison.

Why, then, is there activity in Broca's area for the imitation of hand actions? It has been suggested that the answer may be that human spoken language developed from a gestural system, and that gestures were learned by imitating the gestures made by others (Rizzolatti and Arbib 1998; Arbib 2005; Gentilucci and Corballis 2006). Consistent with this proposal, there is activity in the general region of Broca's area when deaf subjects view manual signs, imitate signs or sign the names of things (Petitto *et al.* 2000; MacSweeney *et al.* 2002; Emmorey *et al.* 2003). Furthermore, electrical stimulation of pars opercularis induces errors in naming in deaf signers (Corina *et al.* 1999).

But even if this suggestion were correct, we would still need to understand how a gestural system was converted to a vocal system. The answer may lie in the fact that electrical stimulation of Broca's area (44) in macaque monkeys elicits both the mouth and hand movements (Petrides *et al.* 2005). In the neighbouring ventral premotor cortex there are also mirror neurones that fire both when a monkey makes mouth or ingestive movements and when it observes them (Ferrari *et al.* 2003). The association with feeding is confirmed by the finding that in macaques electrical stimulation of the ventral premotor cortex causes the hand to move to the mouth, with accompanying mouth movements (Graziano *et al.* 2002).

MacNeilage (1998) has therefore proposed that the mechanisms for speech evolved from the control of ingestive processes. The hypothesis is that there are cycles of mandibular oscillation associated with chewing, sucking and licking that took on communicative significance. For example, monkeys and apes engage in lip-smacking and teeth-chattering displays when submitting to more dominant animals. MacNeilage (1998) suggests that it is here that one should look for the origin of the alternating cycles of opening and closing of the mouth during the production of vowels and consonants. These cycles can be detected in the babbling of babies before they learn to speak (MacNeilage and Davis 2000).

But speech has to be learned by listening to others. So is there any direct evidence that there are mirror neurones in Broca's area that fire both when subjects hear sounds and when they themselves produce them? There is activation in ventral premotor area F5 when macaque monkeys listen to species-specific calls (Gil-da-Costa *et al.* 2006), but the paper does not comment on whether this activation extended into the sulcal area identified by Petrides *et al.* (2005) as area 44. Nor do we know whether the same area would be active when monkeys themselves produce calls.

Fortunately, we have convincing evidence for humans. This comes from a study in which Italian subjects listen to words of Italian (Fadiga *et al.* 2002). When they heard a word such as 'birra', which involves tongue movements, there was an increase in the excitability of the tongue muscles. The effect was specific since it was not found when the subjects heard a word such as 'biffa' which involves lip, but not tongue movements. The change in excitability has been shown to be correlated with activity in Broca's area (Watkins and Paus 2004). In other words, when we hear a word, it is as if we subvocally repeat it.

Genes

There is another link between the learning of speech and song learning in birds. This relates to the 'FoxP2' gene. This gene was recently discovered when a genetic analysis was performed on the 'KE' family. This is a three-generational family in which half the members have a very severe non-fluent developmental aphasia and half are unaffected (Vargha-Khadem *et al.* 1995). We now know that the disorder in the affected members is the result of a point mutation in the FOXP2 gene on the q arm of chromosome 7 (Lai *et al.* 2001). The normal gene codes for a putative transcription factor, but we do not know the function of this transcription factor nor how a mutation in the gene disturbs chemical processes that are involved in brain development.

We do know, however, that FoxP2 is expressed in area X in the zebra finch at the time after hatching when vocal learning occurs, and in the same area in adult canaries when they are learning a new song (Haesler *et al.* 2004). It is also expressed in the analogous regions in parrots and hummingbirds. It is true that its expression is not limited to these areas and that it is also found in birds that do not learn song.

But nonetheless, it is found predominantly in sensori-motor circuits (Haesler *et al.* 2004).

The critical experiment is to reduce the levels of FoxP2 in area X, and this has been done by Haesler *et al.* (2007). The effect was that the zebra finches still learned song but it was a less precise match to the song to which they had been exposed during development. For example, syllables were omitted or repeated in error. FoxP2 is also known to be expressed in cortical structures in birds, and similar studies are therefore needed that interfere with this expression in the HVC. In the human brain, FoxP2 is expressed both in the striatum and the cortical plate (Lai *et al.* 2003; Teramitsu *et al.* 2004).

The next step is to investigate the evolution of the FoxP2 gene. Disappointingly, there are no amino-acid substitutions that are shared between song-learning birds and humans (Webb and Zhang 2005). However, Zhang *et al.* (2002) have reported that, along with one other gene, the FoxP2 gene is the most accelerated of the 120 genes that they studied, with two amino acid changes compared with chimpanzees.

It is tempting to conclude that this is the key to the development of speech. But this involves a leap of faith that cannot currently be justified. It assumes that there was only one genetic change that was associated with the development of speech. Yet, linkage studies suggest a variety of chromosomes are involved in disorders of language (Newbury *et al.* 2005). Of course, genes that are involved in individual differences between modern humans may not be the same as the genes that differentiate humans from chimpanzees. The genes that we need to look for are ones that are conserved across the human population, and this is true of the FoxP2 gene (Marcus and Fisher 2003). But it is certain that there must be many more genes that are involved in the human ability to learn speech.

There are other reasons for caution. The primary impairment caused by a mutation in the FoxP2 gene in humans is poor articulation (Vargha-Khadem *et al.* 1995; Watkins *et al.* 2002*a*). The affected members of the KE family speak; they just speak in a way that it is difficult to understand. Variants in the FoxP2 gene have also been reported in three members of another family that were diagnosed with a verbal dyspraxia (Macdermot *et al.* 2005). It is possible that the basic problem in the KE family and these probands is one of the sequencing (Lieberman 2002). Articulating words clearly makes high level demands on sequencing and coordination.

It is true that the affected members of the KE family also tend to be impaired in generating morphological markers. Gopnik (1990; Gopnik and Crago 1991) initially claimed that they were poor at generating regular plurals and past tenses, which are rule based, but not at producing irregular formations, which are learned as lexical items. But it turns out that in fact they are poor with irregular as well as regular forms (Watkins *et al.* 2002*a*). It remains to be demonstrated whether the grammatical impairments are independent from the articulatory impairment. One possibility is that a fundamental problem in sequencing affects not only articulation but also grammatical processing.

There is another reason for caution. This is that the KE family are not simply impaired in their speech. They also have oral dyspraxia, i.e. they are poor at copying sequences of mouth movements (Alcock *et al.* 2000). Furthermore, the mean non-verbal IQ of the affected members is just 83, that is one standard deviation below average (Watkins *et al.* 2002*a*). Nonetheless, the pathology in the affected members of the KE family is relatively restricted to motor structures, the caudate nucleus, inferior frontal gyrus, premotor cortex and cerebellum (Watkins *et al.* 2002*b*; Belton *et al.* 2003). The areas that are under-activated when they speak are also motor areas, i.e. Broca's area and the basal ganglia (Liegeois *et al.* 2003).

For the moment we should resist regarding FoxP2 as the key to the evolution of human speech. As Marcus and Fisher (2003) suggest, it provides an 'entry-point' into the problem. It will certainly not provide the whole solution.

Conclusions

Though work on the FoxP2 gene is exciting, we are a very long way from knowing how genes such as this influence structure. Nor is it clear what microstructural changes have been required to allow the learning of grammatical rules. It is true that connectionist networks have to be devised to learn the rules for generating the past tense (Plunkett and Marchman 1993) or to learn long-distance grammatical dependencies (Elman 1993). An analysis of corpora of spoken language has revealed many statistical regularities, and connectionist networks can make use of these (Bates and Elman 1996; Elman 2005).

But, although such networks can be powerful (McLeod *et al.* 1998), it is the *structure* of the network that determines whether a rule can be learned (Elman 2005). It is implausible that there were no modifications in the microstructure of the circuits in the evolution of the human brain. The next chapter therefore reviews what we know of the microstructural specializations of the language areas in the human brain.

Chapter 6

Cerebral dominance

The last chapter dealt with language as studied by brain imaging. Though not always stated, the activations were predominantly in the left hemisphere. This is, of course, what would be expected from what we know of cerebral dominance for language. In right-handed subjects it is strokes in the left hemisphere that cause aphasia, i.e. impairments in speech and language.

Cerebral dominance for language is best established by administering the Wada test (Milner 1975; Rasmussen and Milner 1977). In this, sodium amytal is infused into the blood supply that distributes to the left or right hemisphere. If language is represented in that hemisphere, the infusion of sodium amytal causes a temporary aphasia. For safety reasons these studies are only carried out in patients who are to undergo surgery, where it is necessary to establish which hemisphere is specialized for language so as to avoid causing a severe aphasia as the result of the surgery. In a sample of 262 patients with no signs of early brain damage, language was represented in the left hemisphere of 96% of right-handers, and in the right hemisphere of only 4% of right-handers (Milner 1975). For left-handers the picture was mixed: in 70% language was represented in the left hemisphere, in 15% in the right and in 15% in both hemispheres.

Attempts have also been made to establish language dominance using brain imaging. There have been many studies that have specifically compared the results from imaging and the Wada test. The tasks used have ranged from semantic decision concerning single words (Binder *et al.* 1996), the generation of words (Adcock *et al.* 2003) and the generation of semantic associations between words (Baciu *et al.* 2005). The degree of concordance with the Wada test depends both on the task used and the method for quantifying dominance, but in the optimal case it can be 100% (Baciu *et al.* 2005).

The subjects used in these studies have been patients with epilepsy, and so the numbers of subjects have been limited. But in an imaging study of 100 right-handed healthy subjects, Springer *et al.* (1999) report that 94% showed left dominance and just 6% a bilateral representation of language. These figures are very similar to those presented by Milner (1975) based on the Wada test.

Given the association between language dominance and handedness in humans, it is natural to assume that both handedness and dominance are unique to the human brain. Indeed this position has been strongly argued by Crow (1998a, 2002, 2007). He specifically suggests that cerebral asymmetry and handedness are the key to the speciation of *Homo sapiens*. The following two sections therefore investigate whether there is any evidence for handedness and anatomical cerebral asymmetry in apes. The final section reviews evidence for functional specialization in the left and right hemispheres in humans, and considers whether there are indications of any such specializations in other primates.

Handedness

Handedness is assessed in humans across a wide range of skills. These include writing, throwing, using scissors, striking a match and so on (Oldfield 1971). People differ in how strongly handed they are. In a very large sample assessed over six tasks, 78% of subjects were consistent in their use of the right hand and 5% in their use of the left hand (Annett 2004). The remaining 17% either used different hands for different tasks, or used either hand. Annett (2004) relates these proportions to her theory that there is a 'right-shift gene' in the human population.

So, when studying handedness in other primates, the question is not whether an individual animal has a habitual hand preference, but whether there is a shift towards right-handedness in the population. McGrew and Marchant (1997) carried out a meta-analysis of 10 studies of handedness in chimpanzee populations. Of 387 animals that showed a statistically significant handedness, 59% were right-handed. However, Palmer (2002) re-analysed the data, and showed that there was no significant tendency towards right-handedness if one excluded the animals from the studies by Hopkins (1994, 1995, 1996). These studies were on captive chimpanzees at the Yerkes Primate Centre.

Palmer (2002) also pointed out that the number of observations for each animal was not the same. He therefore re-analysed the data from the paper by Hopkins (1994) and showed that the tendency towards right-handedness became non-significant if animals were excluded for which there were less than 26 observations. Hopkins and Cantalupo (2003) responded by repeating the tube test from their earlier study in 132 chimpanzees, making sure to obtain 80 observations for each animal. On this test the animal uses the index finger of one hand to extract peanut butter from a tube, while the other hand holds the tube (Hopkins 1995). The results were that on this test 71 animals were right-handed, 29 left-handed and 32 ambidextrous. These results were consistent with those from an earlier paper in which 98 of the same animals had also been tested, and in which care had been taken to present the tube randomly to either hand (Hopkins *et al.* 2001).

This control was necessary because it is possible that handedness in captive chimpanzees results from interactions with people. For example, if they are hand-reared, captive animals may imitate the handedness of their handlers; and roughly half of the chimpanzees in the sample reported for the Yerkes laboratory were hand-reared (Hopkins *et al.* 2004). However, the proportions of hand-reared animals differ across three different colonies of chimpanzees and yet the right-hand bias remains constant (Hopkins *et al.* 2004).

Hand-rearing is not an issue in wild populations. Yet Lonsdorf and Hopkins (2005) report a small population tendency towards right-handedness in chimpanzees that use stones to crack nuts in the wild. Here the movements are ballistic, as in throwing, and captive chimpanzees also show a population tendency towards right-handedness when throwing (Hopkins *et al.* 2005). But if they were like people, one would expect them to also use their right hand when performing other skilled actions. Yet, when wild chimpanzees fish for termites, the population tendency is towards holding the stem in their left hand (Lonsdorf and Hopkins 2005).

These last comparisons are based on small numbers, but they make the point that handedness in chimpanzees is not comparable to handedness in people. First, the population tendency on any one test is much less marked than in the human population. In the report by

Hopkins and Cantalupo (2003), just 54% of their animals used their right hand for the tube test, and 24% their left hand, the rest being ambidextrous. Second, the degree of bias reduces, the more tests of handedness are taken into account (Hopkins and Pearson 2000). These results compare with 78% of people who were found to be consistently right-handed across six tasks and only 5% who were consistently left-handed (Annett 2004). When assessed just on writing and throwing, 85% of the same sample used the right hand for both tasks and only 7% the left.

Why, then, the much stronger bias in humans? There were two developments in hominid evolution that could have promoted such a strong hand preference. The first is the manufacture of tools and the second the throwing of weapons. The manufacture of a stone tool, such as a flake, requires one hand to support the core and another to perform a rapid striking movement. There is an advantage in always using the same hand to strike, and the other to support. Even in chimpanzees, handedness is most obvious on tasks that require the use of both hands, as on the tube test. The second development was the manufacture of hafted spears for hunting and defence. Throwing such weapons requires a rapid snapping movement of the arm. Again there is an advantage to always using the same arm to make rapid movements. Thus, the two hemispheres have become specialized for different roles, the left hand for support and the right for rapid movements.

Asymmetry

Handedness is related to cerebral dominance for language (Milner 1975). So is there an anatomical basis for cerebral dominance? An anatomical asymmetry between the two hemispheres of the human brain was first reported by Geschwind and Levitsky (1968). They cut along the superior plane of the temporal lobe to reveal 'the planum temporale' in post-mortem brains. They then measured the area of the planum, excluding the primary auditory regions in Heschl's gyrus. The finding was that the planum was larger on the left in 65% of the brains and on the right in 11% of brains.

Given that these brains were from adults, the obvious question is whether the asymmetry was present at birth or developed with experience. We know, for example, that the left pyramidal tract is larger than the right (Rademacher *et al.* 2001) and that its development is influenced by practice at the piano (Bengtsson *et al.* 2005). Witelson and Pallie (1973) therefore studied the size of the planum temporale in 14 neonate and 16 adult brains. The area was larger on the left 79% of the neonates, a figure comparable to the 69% for the adult brains.

Larger samples can be collected by analysing the MRI scans of healthy subjects. In one study of 67 right-handed subjects, the left planum temporale was larger than the right in 72% of subjects (Foundas *et al.* 2002). However, Westbury *et al.* (1999) point out that the results depend on the way in which the area or volume of the planum temporale is measured. They confirm a bias towards to the left if the 'knife-cut method' is used, taking a slice along the top surface of the temporal plane. However, they argue that, due to the complexity of the gyral anatomy in this region, this method may give a misleading impression. Nonetheless, a later study, using a different method to measure grey matter, confirmed a greater amount of grey in the left than right planum temporale in 142 healthy adults (Watkins *et al.* 2001).

The situation for Broca's area is less clear. An initial study of 10 post-mortem brains by Galaburda (1980) reported that Broca's area was larger on the left in six brains, and on the right in just one brain. Foundas *et al.* (1998) went on to analyse the scans of 16 right-handers. They measured the mean surface area of pars opercularis, which very roughly corresponds to area 44, and of pars triangularis, which very roughly corresponds to area 45. For pars opercularis they report that nine brains showed an asymmetry favouring the left, three the right and four no asymmetry. The asymmetry was more marked in pars triangularis, where the corresponding figures were eleven left, one right and four symmetrical. However, the data are not consistent. Tomaiulo *et al.* (1999) measured pars opercularis in the scans of a larger sample of 54 brains, and did not find an asymmetry favouring the left.

The advantage of taking measurements from MRI scans is that one can also assess the handedness of the subjects. Habib *et al.* (1995) reported a greater asymmetry towards the left planum temporale for 24 consistent right-handers compared with 16 non-right-handers. However, in a later study with a larger sample of 67 subjects, there was no relation between the size of the planum temporale and handedness (Foundas *et al.* 2002). It was larger on the left in 71% of the 48 subjects who wrote with their right hand and 74% of the 19 subjects who wrote with their left hand.

But there is a problem with trying to relate handedness to asymmetry, and this is that the majority of the left-handers will actually be left dominant for language (Milner 1975). Thus, the more critical measure is not handedness but cerebral dominance for language. Two groups have measured asymmetries from MRI scans and compared the results with cerebral dominance for speech as assessed directly the Wada method. Foundas *et al.* (1994) studied the planum temporale and report that of the 11 patients with speech dominance in the left hemisphere, all had an asymmetry favouring the left. One patient had language dominance in the right hemisphere, and in this subject it was the right planum that was larger. But Dorsaint-Pierre *et al.* (2006) studied 20 patients with left-hemisphere dominance for speech and 11 with right-hemisphere dominance, and report that there was an asymmetry favouring the left irrespective of speech dominance. It is clear that larger samples are needed to settle the issue.

Attempts have also been made to relate asymmetries in Broca's area to cerebral dominance for language. Foundas *et al.* (1996) measured pars triangularis and report that nine out of the ten patients with left-sided cerebral dominance had an asymmetry favouring the left; the one patient with right-sided dominance had the reversed asymmetry. This time the results were confirmed by the study by Dorsaint-Pierre *et al.* (2006) with a larger sample. Here there was more grey matter in the left pars opercularis in the group with left speech dominance, and more in the right for the group with right speech dominance. This is the most convincing demonstration that asymmetries can be related to dominance for speech.

Ape brains

If it is true that anatomical asymmetries are related to language in the human brain, one might not expect such asymmetries in ape brains. It came as a surprise, then, when there was a report that the left planum temporale was larger than the right in 14 of the 15 chimpanzee brains in which the planum temporale could be quantified (Gannon *et al.* 1998). This corresponds to a figure of 93% favouring the left. This is higher than the 70% that is typically found for the human brain, but the sample size of chimpanzee brains is small and may not be representative of the population. But Crow (1998*b*, 2004) points out that the method was the crude one of inserting pieces of flexible plastic into the exposed lateral fissure, and this may give an inaccurate estimate given the variation in gyral morphology.

So Cantalupo *et al.* (2003) studied the MRI scans of 22 chimpanzees, and took the measurements in the standard way. The left planum was larger in 14 and the right in 2. Here the leftward bias was 63.6%, much closer to the typical value for human samples. The asymmetry was statistically significant and thus confirms the results of a previous study using a smaller sample (Gillisen 2001). In that study, the left planum was reported to be larger in seven chimpanzees, and the right in one, though due to the small sample size the asymmetry just failed to reach statistical significance.

One can also check for asymmetry in pars opercularis, the homologue of Broca's area in the chimpanzee brain (Sherwood *et al.* 2003). Cantalupo and Hopkins (2001) measured this area in 25 chimpanzees, and report a significant asymmetry that favoured the left. Their table suggests that in 14 animals the asymmetry was towards the left and in 6 towards the right, though it is difficult to tell where to put the criterion for equality between the hemispheres. These figures are similar to those of Foundas *et al.* (1998) for 16 human brains, but in both cases the sample was small.

There is, however, a problem in basing measurements of asymmetry on sulcal landmarks, as in pars opercularis and pars triangularis. Sherwood *et al.* (2003) have carried out a cyto-architectural study of pars opercularis in the chimpanzee, and found a poor correspondence between area 44 and the sulcal landmarks. They therefore comment that the delineation of this area on the basis of gross morphology may give misleading results. It is clear that a new study is needed in which comparisons between left and right are based on the areas as defined by cyto-architecture.

Of course, the point made by Sherwood *et al.* (2003) also applies to studies of pars opercularis in the human brain. There is also only a very approximate correspondence between area 44 and pars opercularis, and area 45 and pars triangularis in the human brain (Amunts *et al.* 1999). There is considerable variability in the borders of these areas in the human brain. Thus, we need to define Wernicke's area and Broca's area in term of cyto-architecture to see if the asymmetries hold for areas as defined in terms of microstructure. We do this in the next section.

Asymmetry in microstructure

Wernicke's area

The cyto-architectural area Tpt lies within Wernicke's area, and includes tissue in the planum temporale (Galaburda *et al.* 1978). These authors therefore carried out a cyto-architectural study of Tpt in four post-mortem brains. In these brains, the left planum as defined by sulci was larger in three of the brains, and larger on the right in the fourth. Tpt as defined by cyto-architecture was larger on the left in the first three brains, but did not differ between the sides in the fourth.

It is, of course, an easy comment that a larger sample is needed. Given the fact that visual inspection of histological sections for cyto-architectural borders is so labour-intensive, a larger sample could be achieved by using automatic methods to scan the cortex and determine the boundaries (Schleicher *et al.* 1999). Suppose that this had been done, and the results for Tpt confirmed those of Galaburda *et al.* (1978). We would still need to repeat the measurements of Tpt in the chimpanzee brain to see if the asymmetry is unique to the human brain. Only then could we relate it with some degree of certainty to the lateralization of language.

So Buxhoeveden *et al.* (2001*b*) compared the microstructure of Tpt, not only in the human brain but also in chimpanzees and macaque monkeys. They measured the width of cell columns (mini-columns) within this area and the distance between columns. In the human brain, the column width and neuropil space between the columns were larger on the left than on the right. Across a series of studies, the difference is of the order of 14–17% (Buxhoeveden and Casanova 2002). The crucial finding is that a similar asymmetry was not found in the brains of chimpanzees or monkeys. The spacing between columns will have implications for connectivity. Seldon (1985) measured the extent of the branching of the dendrites of the cells in the secondary auditory areas of the human superior temporal cortex, and found that it was larger in the left than the right hemisphere.

Two further studies have looked at features that relate to connectivity in the human brian. In the first, Hutsler (2003) measured the sizes of the large pyramidal cells in layer III in the auditory cortex and in Wernicke's area. The 'magnopyramidal cells' have very large cell bodies and axons, and are thus fast-conducting. The finding was that there were more such cells in the left than right superior temporal cortex. This is consistent with the independent observation that the axonal bundles that underlie the superior temporal cortex are larger on the left than the right (Anderson *et al.* 1999*a*) These findings suggest that speed may be at a premium in a system that is processing a rapid stream of sounds.

In the other study, Galuske *et al.* (2000) specifically measured the interconnectivity between cells within the left and right superior temporal cortex. They injected fluorescent tracers, and identified patches of interconnected cells. They report that the spacing between these patches was 20% larger on the left than the right. It is unfortunate that the method used in this study is invasive, and will not therefore be repeated on the chimpanzee brain.

Broca's area

There are also microstructural differences between the left and right Broca's area in the human brain. Amunts *et al.* (1999) identified areas 44 and 45 by cyto-architecture in 10 human brains. They report that area 44 was larger on the left than the right in all 10 brains. Furthermore, in area 44, the density of cells was higher on the left than the right in 8 brains. Thus there is more space between the cell bodies on the right than the left. A study is now needed to find out whether a similar asymmetry is or is not present in area 44 in the chimpanzee brain.

The study by Amunts et al. (1999) analysed data from MRI scans. Hayes and Lewis (1993, 1995) measured the size of the pyramidal cells in layer III in histological sections of Broca's area 45. The mean cell size was the same on the left as on the right, but there were more very large pyramidal cells on the left. Also, the length of the dendrites correlated with cell size on the left but not on the right (Hayes and Lewis 1996).

Two issues arise from these studies of microstructure. The first is whether the asymmetries are specific to language areas. Hutsler (2003) compared the superior temporal cortex with the neighbouring angular gyrus, and report that there is no asymmetry in the latter. Hayes and Lewis (1995) compared Broca's area 45 with prefrontal area 46 and the motor cortex. There was no asymmetry in the size of the pyramidal cells in the motor cortex, and indeed in prefrontal cortex the asymmetry favoured the right.

The second issue is whether differences in microstructure between the left and right precede the development of language or result from experience with language. Amunts et al. (2003) have tackled this issue in relation to Broca's area. They studied the brains of 16 children, ranging in age from 3.5 months to 12 years, together with 16 adults. As in their previous study, cell density was measured by an automated method (Schleicher et al. 1999). The adult-like pattern of asymmetry in area 44 was not reached until the age of 11 years. There are two possible explanations, though they are not mutually exclusive. The first is that the developmental process is itself delayed, the second that language practice has an influence over that development. The second explanation suggests a study of the brains of chimpanzees that have been exposed to language or undergone training in using symbols. The cyto-architecture of area Tpt and Broca's area could be established by using automated methods (Schleicher et al. 1999) to make measurements from MRI scans.

Functional specialization

When anatomical asymmetries were discovered in the human brain, it was naturally assumed that they reflected the human specialization for language. But, as we have seen, anatomical asymmetries are not unique to the human brain. So it is important to establish whether there are also differences between the functions of the two hemispheres in animals.

Calls

Though chimpanzees do not learn their calls, it has already been mentioned that many song birds, such as canaries or zebra finches, produce complex sequences of sounds, and learn new variants each season (Nottebohm 1991, Tchernichovski *et al.* 2001). One area that is centrally involved is the hyperstriatum ventrale, pars caudale (HVC) (Nottebohm *et al.* 1976). The crucial finding is that there is strong evidence for functional dominance. For example, in the canary (*Serenius canarius*), left-sided lesions in this area severely disrupt the ability to produce songs, whereas right-sided lesions do not (Nottebohm 1977).

Macaque monkeys do not produce complex calls. However, they do discriminate between the calls of their own species. Japanese macaques (*Macaca fuscata*) are better at discriminating 'coos' on the basis of the timing of the peak fundamental frequency, when the coos are presented to the right ear rather than to the left (Petersen *et al.* 1978). This suggests a left-hemispheric advantage. The same advantage was not shown when Japanese monkeys discriminated on the basis of pitch, a feature that is not relevant for communication (Beecher *et al.* 1979). Nor was it shown when other species of macaque discriminated between the coos of Japanese monkeys (Beecher *et al.* 1979; Petersen *et al.* 1984).

There is also a strong tendency for rhesus monkeys (*Macaca mulatta*) to turn their right ear towards a loudspeaker when their own species-specific calls are played (Hauser and Andersson 1994). This effect was not found when they were played the calls of a bird, even though they were familiar with the calls (Hauser and Andersson 1994); nor was the effect found when 'grunts' and 'barks' were manipulated so as to change the temporal characteristics of the calls with the aim of making them unfamiliar (Hauser *et al.* 1998). However, the preferred side is not constant across species. For examples, vervet monkeys (*Cercopithecus aethiops*) tend to turn their left ear to the speaker (Gil-da-Costa and Hauser 2006).

Though the experiments on macaques suggest a left-hemisphere advantage, this is more directly tested by comparing the effects of left-sided and right-sided lesions. Heffner and Heffner (1986) therefore played the same coos to Japanese monkeys as had been used in the experiments described above by Petersen *et al.* (1978). In five animals, the left superior temporal cortex was removed and in five the right. The results were clearcut: the left-sided lesions led to a severe impairment in discrimination on the basis of the temporal characteristics of the calls, whereas the right-sided lesions had little if any effect.

It is open to someone to argue that the lesions may not have been symmetrical and of the same size, though they do appear to be when one inspects the lesion diagrams provided. However, this objection does not apply to imaging studies in which the degree of activation is compared between the hemispheres. Poremba *et al.* (2004) scanned rhesus monkeys with PET. They presented species-specific calls such as grunts, coos and barks, and for comparison they presented scrambled calls. There was more activity in the anterior-most sector of the superior temporal lobe on the left than in the right, and this effect was only found for the species-specific calls. However, this effect was not replicated in a later PET study (Gil-da-Costa *et al.* 2006). It is not clear what accounts for the difference between the results of the two studies. It could be due to the fact that the earlier study included more monkeys and presented a wider variety of calls.

Visuo-spatial processing

In the human brain, the specialization of the left hemisphere for language is complemented by a specialization of the right hemisphere for visuo-spatial processing. For example, it is more common for right- than left-sided lesions to cause spatial neglect of stimuli presented in the contralateral visual field (Ringman *et al.* 2004). Neglect can be tested by presenting two stimuli simultaneously, one to the left and one to the right. Patients with right parietal lesions tend to fail to report the stimulus presented on the left, an effect that is called 'extinction' (Vuilleumier and Rafal 2000).

That the right hemisphere is indeed specialized for the analysis of visuo-spatial stimuli has been confirmed in an fMRI study by Stephan *et al.* (2003). They presented subjects with words, and required them either to engage in verbal processing, detecting the letter A, or in visuo-spatial processing, detecting whether the red letter was to the left or right of centre of the word. Though the identical stimuli were presented for both tasks, the activations that were specific for verbal processing were in the left hemisphere, and the activations that were specific for visuo-spatial processing were in the right hemisphere.

Macaques can be tested on visual extinction by teaching them to report whether a stimulus is on the left or right, and then seeing which stimulus they report on trials in which two stimuli are presented simultaneously, one on each side. After unilateral parietal lesions, the monkeys fail to report the stimulus that is presented in the contralateral visual field, i.e. the field opposite to the lesion (Lynch and McLaren 1989). Temporary inactivation of tissue within the intra-parietal sulcus also causes monkeys to miss targets in the contralateral visual field on a visual search task (Wardak *et al.* 2002). The monkeys are less likely to make saccades towards the contra-lesional target.

However, the crucial issue is whether there is a difference between the effects of right- and left-sided lesions. Gaffan and Hornak (1997) provide data for six macaques with parietal lesions of which four were on the right and two on the left. There was no difference in the severity of the neglect according to the side of the lesion. The tentative conclusion, based on very small numbers, must be that there is no evidence for specialization of one hemisphere in macaque monkeys for visuo-spatial processing.

This leaves open the possibility that there is specialization in the chimpanzee brain. To find out, Hopkins and Morris (1989) tested two chimpanzees, Sherman and Austin, animals that had been trained to make requests by pressing symbols on a keyboard. A figure was presented with two horizontal lines, one short and one long, and the task was to move the cursor up if the shorter line was above the longer line, and down if it was below. The figures were presented either to the left, and thus to the right hemisphere or to the right and thus to the left hemisphere. Sherman was faster to make the judgement if the figure appeared on the left, irrespective of whether he used the left or right hand to move the joystick that controlled the cursor. Austin showed the same effect, but only when he used the left hand, i.e. the hand controlled by the right hemisphere. The effect needs to be confirmed on more animals.

Face processing

In the human brain the right hemisphere is not just specialized for spatial processing. It is also dominant for the perception of faces. As already mentioned, if pictures of faces are shown to subjects in an fMRI scanner and a comparison made with objects, there is activity in the 'fusiform face area' or FFA (Kanwisher *et al.* 1997). For five of the ten right-handed subjects, the activity in the FFA was only found in the right hemisphere, and in the other subjects it was greater in the right than the left hemisphere.

Right hemispheric dominance for face processing can be demonstrated in another way. This can be done by presenting 'chimeric' faces: these are constructed by making up a whole face by adding a left-half face and a different right-half face. Levy and colleagues (1983) took photographs of the same people either with a smiling or neutral face, and made up chimeric faces in which the smile was either in the left-half face or in the right. The task was to identify which of the two faces was 'happier'. The consistent finding was that subjects chose the face in which the smile was on the left half of the face, i.e. presented in the left visual field and thus to the right hemisphere (Levy *et al.* 1983; Levine and Levy 1986).

This experiment has been repeated with chimpanzees. Morris and Hopkins (1993) taught three chimpanzees, Sherman, Austin and Lana. The task was to choose a human face with a happy expression, rather than a human face with a neutral expression. The animals were taught this discrimination for a series of photographs. They were then presented with a pair of chimeric faces, and again required to pick the one with the happy expression. Two of the three chimpanzees were significantly more likely to pick the face with the happy expression on the left. There was a tendency in the same direction for the third chimpanzee but it was not significant. The authors compared these results with their own data for human subjects. The chimpanzees favoured the face with the happy expression on the left in 62% of trials, and the humans on 63% of trials. However, since only two of the three chimpanzees showed a significant effect, it is clear that the experiment needs to be repeated on a larger sample of chimpanzees, so as to see if there is a genuine population bias.

This has not yet been done, but an analysis has been performed on the symmetry of facial expressions in a large sample of chimpanzees. Fernandez-Carriba *et al.* (2002) have done such an analysis for 36 chimpanzees. Videos were taken, and still photographs selected for five categories of facial expression, such as the play face or bared-teeth display. Objective measures were taken of the length and area of the left half and right half of the mouth, and these measurements were performed 'blind', i.e. by someone who did not know the hypothesis being tested. The results showed a significant tendency towards facial asymmetry, favouring a greater length and area in the left-half mouth. Given this asymmetry in the production of facial expressions, it is important to see if one could confirm an asymmetry in the perception of these expressions.

That there may indeed be such an asymmetry is suggested by the findings of an fMRI study on macaque monkeys (Pinsk *et al.* 2005). The animals were presented with faces so as to identify areas in which the activation was greater for faces than objects. Two regions were identified in superior temporal sulcus and the posterior one has been suggested to be the homologue of the fusiform face area in the human brain (Tsao *et al.* 2003). The activations were bilateral, but the size of the activated area was larger on the right than the left, as in the human brain.

The selection of action

There is one final crucial respect in which there is specialization between the two hemispheres in the human brain. This concerns the selection of action. To understand it, one can draw a comparison with the specialization of the right hemisphere for visuo-spatial processing. Here there is activity in the right parietal cortex, irrespective of whether the subjects attend to stimuli in the left (contralateral) or right (ipsilateral) visual field (Corbetta *et al.* 1993; Nobre *et al.* 1997). By contrast, there is activity in the left parietal cortex mainly for stimuli in the right (contralateral) visual field, with little representation for stimuli in the left (ipsilateral) visual field). Thus, the right parietal cortex represents both visual fields and the left parietal cortex mainly the contralateral visual field.

There is a corresponding dominance for the selection of movement in the left parietal cortex. Rushworth *et al.* (2001) used transcranial magnetic brain stimulation to temporarily interfere with activity in either the left or right parietal cortex. The task for the subjects was to select between finger movements on the basis first of a warning cue and then an instruction cue. Interference over the left inferior parietal cortex delayed movements with either the right (contralateral) or left (ipsilateral) hand. Thus, the left parietal cortex is involved in the control of both hands. Interference over the right parietal cortex only affected movements of the left (contralateral) hand.

This pattern is replicated in the premotor cortex. Schluter *et al.* (1998) used transcranial magnetic brain stimulation during a task in which the subjects had to move one finger given cue A or B, and another finger given cue C or D. Stimulation over the left premotor cortex delayed movements with either hand, whereas stimulation over the right premotor cortex only delayed movements with the left hand. When the same task was given in a PET study, activity was found in the left parietal and premotor cortex irrespective of the hand that was used (Schluter *et al.* 2001).

These results have a parallel in the syndrome of apraxia. This has already been described in Chapter 4. The critical finding is that it is lesions of the left parietal cortex that produce apraxia (Kimura 1993; Rushworth *et al.* 1998); and this is true even though it is usually the left hand that is tested. The reason is that in many apraxics, the lesion extends into the left motor cortex, thus affecting the right arm.

It could, of course, always be argued that the reason why apraxia results from left-hemisphere lesions is that the patients tend to be aphasic.

This is because the lesions are usually large and thus they also involve the language areas. So perhaps the patients are impaired at pantomiming actions because they fail to understand the instructions or to name the objects. But it is unlikely that this is the correct explanation. As mentioned in Chapter 4, Rumiati *et al.* (2004) carried out a PET study in which the subjects were required to copy a gesture or pantomime the use of an object. Because the subjects might subvocally name the gestures or objects, control conditions were included in which the subjects were required to name them aloud. The activity in the left parietal cortex remained after the activity for naming was subtracted.

So why is the left hemisphere dominant both for language and for the selection of action? One possibility is that the reason is that they involve similar operations. Both speech and non-verbal actions must be generated (Corballis 1991) and their production involves processes of selection. This makes it intriguing to know whether there is any specialization of the left hemisphere of chimpanzees for the generation and selection of actions. Since we can neither use transcranial magnetic stimulation nor brain imaging, interest gives way to frustration.

Conclusions

It will be clear that there is radical specialization between the hemispheres in the human brain. The left hemisphere is specialized for phonological, semantic and grammatical processing, and the right hemisphere for visuo-spatial processing. The result is that unilateral lesions can cause severe impairments, aphasia or spatial neglect. Furthermore, posterior lesions of the right hemisphere lead to an 'apperceptive agnosia', i.e. a perceptual disorder in which the patients are poor at recognizing objects and at matching them under laboratory conditions (Warrington 1982; Warrington and James 1988; Bottini *et al.* 1991). By contrast, posterior lesions of the left hemisphere can lead to an associative agnosia, i.e. a disorder in which the patients can visually match objects but cannot retrieve facts about them (Warrington 1982). This results from lesions of the left middle and inferior temporal gyrus, and, if the lesions are extensive, gives rise to an impairment so severe as to be called a 'semantic dementia' (Garrard and Hodges 2000; Galton *et al.* 2001*b*).

Yet, with the exception of the superior temporal cortex, it is not common for unilateral lesions to cause behavioural impairments in monkeys. The reason is that each hemisphere processes information from the contralateral space. So if stimuli are presented in free vision, they can still be processed by the intact hemisphere, which processes information from the visual field ipsilateral to the lesion. Monkeys with unilateral infero-temporal lesions are only impaired if the stimuli are presented to the contralateral field (Merigan and Saunders 2004).

Contrast the situation in the human brain where the specialization for higher order processing is not by visual field. The right hemisphere is specialized for analysing the visual characteristics of objects, whereas the left hemisphere is specialized for analysing the semantic characteristics of objects. This re-organization goes with the specialization of the left hemisphere for language. Whether knowledge about objects is tested by presenting pictures or words, the activation is in the left infero-temporal cortex (Vandenberghe *et al.* 1996; Price *et al.* 1999).

Why has this re-organization occurred? One possibility was put forward by Ringo *et al.* (1994). They argued that the key is that it takes time for information to pass between the hemispheres across the corpus callosum. This becomes a problem the larger the brain. Ringo *et al.* (1994) calculate that the time could be 25 ms in the human brain. They suggest that where a continuous flow of information between the hemispheres is required, the time lags may become prohibitive for efficient information processing. So, the larger the brain, the greater the pressure for one hemisphere to handle a particular operation. In this way, operations can rely on connections within one hemisphere rather than connections between the hemispheres. This would be particularly important where the operation required fine discriminations of temporal information, as in the perception and production of speech. It is intriguing that the most clearcut cases of dominance that we know of in other animals involve the production of song in song birds (Nottebohm 1977) and the discrimination of the temporal features of calls in macaques (Heffner and Heffner 1986).

There is another possible reason for hemispheric specialization. Levy (1977) pointed out that in the absence of functional specialization, there is duplication of function between the hemispheres. For example, each infero-temporal cortex in a monkey does the same thing. This duplication could be regarded as inefficient, and it can be avoided by functional specialization between the hemispheres.

But if specialization is an advantage, why is the human brain specialized in a way that the monkey brain is not? The obvious suggestion is that the development of language placed a premium on the efficient use of cerebral space. Imaging studies show that, outside the classical language areas, much of the left temporal lobe and prefrontal cortex is devoted to semantic processing (Vandenberghe *et al.* 1996; Price *et al.* 1999). If this processing were duplicated in the right hemisphere, the brain would have to be considerably enlarged. Cerebral dominance pays in efficiency.

Chapter 7

Decision-making and planning

The previous two chapters have dealt with language, and the last chapter will argue that language greatly amplifies the mental gap between humans and chimpanzees. Take planning as an example. Humans can make long-term plans concerning actions weeks or months ahead, and in doing this they can articulate their plans. This chapter discusses the brain mechanisms that underlie our ability to make decisions and plan.

Voluntary decisions

Much of our life is spent making voluntary decisions. Should I buy a cell phone or CDs? Should I have lunch now, or continue working? These decisions are all voluntary in the sense that it is up to us. No-one else is telling us what to do.

Human subjects can be scanned while they make decisions of this sort. Rather than requiring subjects to make real-life choices, the first imaging experiments presented simple decisions, such as in which of four directions to move a joystick (Deiber *et al.* 1991) or which of two fingers to move (Frith *et al.* 1991). The critical comparison was between decisions that the subjects made of their own accord, and decisions where there was no choice because the subjects were told which movement to make. Decisions of the first type may be said to be 'free' in the sense that they are not prompted by the experimenter.

The classic finding is that there is activity in the dorsal prefrontal cortex (Fig. 7.1) when a comparison is made between actions that the subjects freely choose and actions that are specified by the experimenter (Deiber *et al.* 1991; Frith *et al.* 1991). However, these studies leave it unclear whether there is simply more activity when the decisions are free, or whether prefrontal activity only occurs in the free-selection condition. In a later fMRI study, Rowe *et al.* (2005) scanned subjects

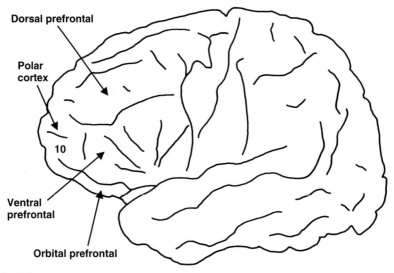

Dorsal prefrontal

Polar cortex

10

Ventral prefrontal

Orbital prefrontal

Fig. 7.1

during both types of response, and measured prefrontal activity versus baseline. It turned out that there was no activity in the prefrontal cortex unless the choice was free.

The decisions that have been discussed so far concerned simple movements. But can the results be generalized to other decisions? Frith *et al.* (1991) sought to find out by including a condition in which the subjects had to decide what word to produce. They could generate any word that they liked so long as it began with a particular letter, such as 'S'. To control for speaking, in the comparison condition the subjects simply said the word 'next' on each occasion. Again there was activity in the prefrontal cortex when the two conditions were compared. These results have been confirmed in many subsequent studies. The dorsal prefrontal cortex is activated whether the decisions concern movements, words or numbers (Spence *et al.* 1998; Jahanshahi and Dirnberger 1999; Spence 1999; Frith 2000; Jahanshahi *et al.* 2000).

And the decisions do not have to be arbitrary. The same result is found when taxi drivers spontaneously decide in the scanner which route to take during a computer game that involves navigation through a city (Spiers and Maguire 2006*b*). Here the decision is up to the taxi driver, but it is not arbitrary because some routes will actually be better than others. To give another example, the dorsal prefrontal cortex is also activated when pianists improvise on a series of notes that are presented on the screen (Bengtsson *et al.* 2007).

Frith *et al.* (1991) suggested that the prefrontal activity reflected 'willed action'. They took this term from William James (1890) who used it to refer to actions that are preceded by the idea, or as we would say now the 'representation', of the action. He distinguished them from automatic actions for which this is not the case. In all the experiments described so far, the comparison conditions have involved actions that were routine and automatic; for example, moving the finger that was touched or always saying the same word (Frith *et al.* 1991).

Actions can become routine or automatic by repeated practice. If subjects are given a finger sequence to learn by trial and error, there is activity in the prefrontal cortex as they generate the moves (Jenkins *et al.* 1994; Toni *et al.* 1998*a*). However, if they learn the sequence and then practice it for 45 minutes, the prefrontal activity gradually declines until it reaches baseline levels when the task has become automatic (Toni *et al.* 1998*a*). Similarly, if subjects are asked to generate verbs that are appropriate to particular nouns, there is extensive activity in the prefrontal cortex, but this disappears as the task is repeated again and again with the same nouns, so that the responses become stereotyped through repetition (Raichle *et al.* 1994).

It is a critical finding that once a task has become automatic, it is possible to re-activate the prefrontal cortex simply by instructing the subjects to attend again to what they are doing (Rowe *et al.* 2002). This is true even though the same movements are being performed. Thus, the activity in the prefrontal cortex reflects attention to the selection of action (Passingham *et al.* 2005). Shallice and colleagues (Shallice 1982; Shallice and Burgess 1998) have suggested that the prefrontal cortex forms a 'supervisory attentional system', i.e. it is involved when there are demands on attention because the decisions are not routine.

Working memory

This conception appears, at first sight, to be at odds with what we know about the functions of prefrontal cortex in animals. Goldman-Rakic (1987, 1998) reviewed the literature on prefrontal cortex in macaque monkeys, and concluded that the prefrontal cortex is essential for 'working memory'. By this term she referred to the ability to hold recent items 'on line' so as to guide the appropriate behaviour.

There are two strands of evidence for this claim. First, it has long been known that macaque monkeys with lesions in the dorsal prefrontal cortex make many errors when tested on spatial memory tasks (Mishkin 1957; Goldman *et al.* 1971). For example, on the spatial delayed response task, the animal must remember for a few seconds where it saw a peanut and must respond to that location after the delay. Second, if one records the activity of cells in the prefrontal cortex during that delay, one finds many cells that continue to fire throughout, i.e. after the cue has been presented and before the response is made (Fuster and Alexander 1971; Funahashi *et al.* 1989). In her classic paper, Goldman-Rakic (1987) proposed that the reason why prefrontal lesions impair performance on delayed response tasks is that, in the absence of this delay-related activity, the animals fail to remember the location.

It is important to notice that Goldman-Rakic (1990) used the term 'working memory' rather than 'short-term memory'. Working memory does not simply refer to the ability to hold information in mind for a few seconds. Baddeley and Hitch (1974) introduced the term into the literature to account for our ability to perform mental operations, such as arithmetic. Suppose that someone is asked to subtract 7 from 100, and then to go on repeating the subtraction. Short-term memory is involved because they have to remember the intermediate numbers, 86 or 79, and so on. But executive functions are also involved because the subject has to generate the next number by performing the operation of subtraction. Baddeley (1986, 2003) put forward a working-memory model in which there are several components. These are a 'central executive' that is involved in decision-making and slave short-term memory systems for holding information on line. Goldman-Rakic (1998) took this model over and suggested a role for the prefrontal cortex, not only in on line maintenance but also in executive operations such as decision-making.

So on delayed-response tasks, does the prefrontal activity that can be recorded during the delay simply reflect maintenance in memory or does it also reflect decisions as to which response to make? In the population of cells, it is possible to detect an increase of activity at the time of presentation of the cue, continuous activity during the delay and a further increase of activity at the time of response (Goldman-Rakic 1992; Goldman-Rakic and Leung 2002). It has been demonstrated that the activity during the early part of the delay mainly reflects maintenance of the cue information, whereas the later activity mainly reflects the selection of and preparation for the response (Takeda and Funahashi 2002). Thus, during the delay there is a transformation from cue to response (Takeda and Funahashi 2004).

So, even in monkeys, the prefrontal cortex is involved in executive operations such as the selection of the appropriate response. This can be directly tested by setting macaque monkeys the task of making arbitrary decisions; in other words, the same task that has been given to human subjects when tested in the scanner. Barraclough *et al.* (2004) gave macaque monkeys the choice between a target on the left and another on the right. It was up to the monkey which response to make, and at the time of choice there was no way of the animal knowing whether the response would be rewarded. This was decided by a computer program, which presented rewards in such a way as to encourage the monkey to respond randomly. There was cell activity in the dorsal prefrontal cortex that related to the choice to be made by the animal.

So monkeys can freely generate responses, but they are no match for humans in the creativity with which they do so. Take, for example, the sentence-completion task. Nathaniel-James and Frith (2002) gave this to subjects in the scanner. Incomplete sentences are presented such as 'The police had never seen the man so. . .'. The subjects have to complete sentences of this sort, and there are an infinite number of endings that they could generate. As one would expect, there is activity in the dorsal prefrontal cortex when they generate their ending.

Or consider the verb-generation task. Here nouns are presented on the screen such as 'cake'. The task of the subjects is to supply a verb that is semantically associated. So they might supply 'cut', 'eat', 'ice' and so on, through many possibilities. Again there is activation in the dorsal prefrontal cortex.

Of course, in the ordinary course of our life we are constantly producing novel sentences. Furthermore, we are aware of engaging in trains of thought that are not immediately prompted by events in the outside world. These have been called 'stimulus-independent thoughts' (McGuire *et al.* 1996*a*). These can occur, for example, during rest periods in the scanning session. During such a resting condition, the subjects are free to think about whatever they want, and there is heightened activity in the frontal polar cortex and anterior cingulate cortex (Gusnard *et al.* 2001; Raichle *et al.* 2001; Gilbert *et al.* 2006) (Fig. 7.2). McGuire *et al.* (1996*a*) asked subjects to rate how frequently they thought about other things during scanning, and found that the more they did so, the greater the activity in the medial prefrontal cortex.

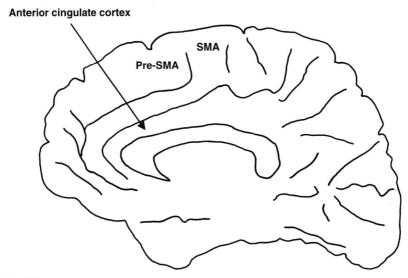

Fig. 7.2

We cannot ask monkeys to rate their thoughts, but we can measure activity in the medial prefrontal cortex and anterior cingulate cortex during rest. Unfortunately, the only study that has been carried out was done while the monkeys were anaesthetized (Vincent *et al.* 2007). The authors measured spontaneous fluctuations in activity so as establish which areas are interconnected, and they found such fluctuations in medial frontal areas. What we now need is a comparative study of activity at rest in awake monkeys and humans. If the activity genuinely relates to self-generated thoughts, we would predict that it would be more extensive in humans.

Awareness of intention

Chapter 1 argued that humans may be unique in being able to reflect on their own thoughts. We are, for example, aware of our intentions and can reflect on them. We know because we can ask the person if they are aware, and they can give a report on the basis of introspection. This was done in the classic experiment by Libet *et al.* (1983*a*). The subjects were instructed to raise their forefinger whenever they wanted. This is like the free-selection task, except that the subjects decide when to move a finger, as opposed to which finger to move. Libet (1983*a*) also required the subjects to time the earliest moment at which they were aware of their intention to act. This was called the 'W' judgement (for 'Will'). It was contrasted with another condition in which the subjects timed the earliest moment at which they were aware that they were making the movement. This was called the 'M' judgement (for 'Movement'). So as to enable the subjects to make these judgements, the subjects viewed a clock face with the second hand moving rapidly. All that the subjects were asked to do was to remember the time of this hand when they were first aware of W or M, and then to report it later.

As already mentioned in Chapter 1, the finding is startling. Subjects report W roughly 150 to 200 ms before the time of the movement. But the BP or readiness potential, as recorded by EEG, starts at least 500 ms before movement. In other words, we can detect the brain's preparing the movement significantly earlier than the time at which the subject is aware of preparing the movement. And the finding is replicable (Haggard and Eimer 1999).

The first question is where the BP has its origin. At least the earlier part of the BP appears to arise from the supplementary motor cortex (SMA) and the pre-supplementary cortex in front of it (pre-SMA) (Erdler *et al.* 2001) (Fig. 7.2). This claim is plausible given that one can record early activity in this area in macaque monkeys between 640 and 1280 ms before a self-initiated movement (Okano and Tanji 1987).

But, the fact that it is possible to record such activity does not prove that that activity has a causal effect on the movement. One way to find out is to prevent the activity. Thaler *et al.* (1995) did so by removing the SMA and pre-SMA bilaterally in macaque monkeys, so as to see whether this abolished self-initiated actions. The animals had been taught to raise their arm into empty space whenever they wanted a peanut: it was up to the monkeys when they raised their arm. So as to exclude any prompting by external stimuli, the task was carried out in total darkness. The effect of the lesion was clearcut. After surgery the monkeys rarely raised their arms. This was not because they were unable to move their arm or were no longer motivated, since they would still raise their arm in response to an external cue such as a tone.

Given that preparatory activity in the SMA and pre-SMA is essential for self-initiated movements, one wonders if it is this activity of which one is aware before such movements. Lau *et al.* (2004) tried to find out by using fMRI to scan subjects while they performed the Libet task. When subjects judged the time of W compared with M, there was enhanced activity on the borders between the pre-SMA and SMA. This suggests that at some point human subjects become aware of the increase in preparatory activity, but this activity has to build up to a critical point for the subject to be aware of it.

So in this case it is not the awareness of intention that causes the movement (Wegner 2002, 2003) as a philosopher who believes in dualism would claim. But one need neither be a dualist nor fight the battle on this ground. The movements chosen in these experiments are simple and semi-automatic, and thus the Libet task requires subjects to pay attention to something of which we do not normally need to be aware.

So Lau *et al.* (2006) compared the scans for different subjects because the subjects differed in the degree of attention that they paid to the task, and thus in the enhanced activity in the pre-SMA. The finding was that the more attention subjects paid to the task, the earlier they reported that their intention occurred. In fact, those that paid the least attention did not report their intention as occurring before the movement at all.

The implication is that the task of paying attention to intention affects the phenomenon that is being measured. The subjects are asked when they are first aware of the 'urge' to move. Yet, in everyday life we are not usually aware of these urges, since there is no reason to direct our attention to them. We usually initiate simple finger movements without thinking about them. The task is pretty automatic. It is our plans that we attend to and of which we are aware. We return to these plans in a later section.

There are two potential differences between intentional actions as performed by human and animals. The first has been the subject of this section. Humans are aware of their intentions, whereas we do not know whether this is true of animals. We know in the case of humans because we can direct them to pay attention to their intentions. Chapter 9 will extend this finding by showing that humans can reflect, not only on their own intentions but also on those of others.

The second potential difference is that humans can veto their intentions at will (Libet *et al.* 1983*b*). We know that they can do so because we can set up an experiment in which we ask the subjects to move a finger whenever they want, but to sometimes veto their intention. We have objective evidence that they can do so, because if the subjects are scanned there is activity in the medial frontal cortex when they do so (Brass and Haggard 2007). It is intriguing that the activity lies in the paracingulate sulcus. Chapter 9 will review the evidence that there is activity in the same area when humans reflect on themselves. This is compatible with the suggestion that the ability to veto actions at will depends on the ability to reflect on one's own intentions.

Setting goals

Intentional actions are goal-directed. Like other animals, we perform those actions that favour survival. In other words, we too have basic needs and must find ways of satisfying them. So it is not surprising that we share mechanisms for representing the value of such things as foods and drink.

In macaque monkeys there are many cells in the orbital frontal cortex (Fig. 7.1) that fire selectively when macaque monkeys are expecting rewards (Tremblay and Schultz 1999). Some of these cells code for reward preference (Schultz *et al.* 2000), and others for specific amounts of reward (Wallis and Miller 2003). But the crucial finding is that many of them code for the value to the animal of the rewards rather than for their sensory aspects (Padoa-Schioppa and Assad 2006).

The current value can be manipulated by taking a particular food, for example, and feeding it to the animal until it is satiated. This food then becomes less preferred, and cell activity in the orbital frontal cortex reflects this change (Rolls *et al.* 1989). The same phenomenon can be demonstrated in the human brain. Experiments with human subjects have taken a smell (Gottfried *et al.* 2003) or a taste (Kringelbach *et al.* 2003) of a food, and have then exposed the subjects to it until the subjects found it subjectively less pleasant. In both cases, activity in the orbital frontal cortex decreased as the food became less attractive. This is what would be expected if that activity reflected the current value of the food.

There are also cells in the anterior cingulate cortex (Fig. 7.2) of macaques that monitor the level of reward so as to guide the next response (Shima and Tanji 1998). These cells fire when the monkeys find that there is no reward. As one would expect from this, the temporary inactivation of this area impairs the ability to change behaviour subsequently (Shima and Tanji 1998). Similar activity can be found in the anterior cingulate of humans. Williams *et al.* (2004) taught patients to use a decrease in reward as a cue to choose an alternative action on the next trial. During surgery they found many cells in the anterior cingulate cortex that fired specifically to the sign for reduced reward. Furthermore when, for clinical reasons, this area was then surgically removed, the patients were poorer at choosing the alternative action.

So humans share with macaque monkeys the circuitry for representing basic rewards and using them to guide behaviour; but there are three crucial differences. First, psychologists distinguish primary rewards, such as food, shelter and sex, from secondary rewards that are associated with them. In the wild, monkeys work for primary rewards, though in the laboratory macaques can be taught to work for tones that have been recently associated with food (Gaffan and Eacott 1995). It is a feature of human working life that many activities are rewarded with money, i.e. with a token that can be exchanged for necessities such as food or housing. In the human brain there is activity in the orbital frontal cortex when subjects win or lose money (O'Doherty *et al*. 2001).

The second major difference is that humans can set up their own goals. For example, scientists pose problems to themselves for the satisfaction of answering them and novelists write novels because they enjoy telling stories. In the laboratory, subjects can be asked to decide themselves which task to perform; for example, whether to add or subtract numbers that are presented later. When subjects make these sorts of decisions, there is activity in the medial frontal cortex and anterior cingulate cortex, as well as in the dorsal prefrontal cortex on the lateral surface (Forstmann *et al*. 2006; Haynes *et al*. 2007)

Having set themselves goals, humans can also monitor their progress towards them. In a recent experiment, we gave a difficult memory task to subjects (Bengtsson *et al*. submitted). Half of the subjects were told that performance on the task was related to intelligence, and the other half were told that the experimenters were simply piloting the task. During scanning, the first group of subjects were also asked at intervals how they were doing, whereas member of the second group were asked about details of the task presentation. The group who took the task to be a measure of intelligence closely monitored their own performance and showed more activity in the paracingulate cortex (Fig. 9.1). The same area was activated when they reflected on their own performance in answer to the questions on how they were doing.

So humans can set themselves tasks, even if these do not actively promote survival. For example, they can pursue hobbies that earn them no money. But there is a third and crucial difference between humans and animals. This is that humans can set themselves goals that actually militate against their survival by putting themselves in danger. Consider the lifeboat man. Here, the rewards, if there are any, relate to ideas of duty and moral character. We will discuss altruism in chapter nine.

Planning

Many of our goals are long term. Unlike other animals, humans can plan for distant future. The ability to plan can be assessed in human subjects by giving them the puzzle that has come to be known as the 'Tower of Hanoi'. On this there are several pegs: the subjects have to move different-sized rings so as to achieve a target set-up, and they have to do so in the minimum number of moves. So the subjects have a goal and need to plan the sequence of actions so as to achieve that goal. A simpler versions of the task has been devised with three coloured balls, and this has been nicknamed 'The Tower of London' (Shallice 1982). From this a computerized version was developed in which the subjects move balls by touching them on a screen (Morris *et al.* 1988).

There are two ways of testing the abilities of subjects. The first is to require them to actually make the moves; the second is to ask them to consider how many moves are needed without actually making any of them. It does not matter which way the subjects are tested, imaging studies show activity in the dorsal prefrontal cortex, with the activity extending into the frontal polar region, area 10 (Fig. 7.1) (Owen *et al.* 1996; Baker *et al.* 1996; Dagher *et al.* 1999; Rowe *et al.* 2001; Unterrainer *et al.* 2005). As might therefore be expected, patients with large prefrontal excisions are poor at the task (Owen *et al.* 1990). They are also poor at a financial-planning task, which was devised so as to better capture the sorts of plans that humans make in their everyday life (Goel *et al.* 1997). Unlike the Libet task, these tasks are demanding in terms of attention, and subjects are well aware of their mental activity.

So how do we plan? There must be a way of representing possible moves and then of selecting between them. One possible strategy is to imagine performing the moves. This can be done with motor imagery, and Jeannerod (1994, 2006) has suggested that motor imagery is closely related to motor preparation. When humans prepare to perform an action, there is activity in premotor and parietal cortex in advance of the movement (Toni *et al.* 2002). Similar activity can be recorded when macaque monkeys prepare hand movements (Wise and Mauritz 1985; Snyder *et al.* 1997).

When humans plan, they prepare alternative courses of action. So can monkeys do this? Cisek and Kalaska (2002) showed macaque monkeys two potential targets for action, and demonstrated that subpopulations of cells in the premotor cortex coded for each of the potential targets. When the monkeys were instructed as to which of the two targets to select, the activity was reduced to the subpopulation of cells that that coded for that particular action.

In this experiment, there were two alternative possible moves but the monkey was only required to perform one of them. However, when humans solve problems on the Tower of London, they plan a series of moves. Monkeys can also prepare a sequence of moves. Mushiake *et al.* (2006) trained macaque monkeys to move a cursor through a maze. During the period while the monkeys were considering their moves, it was possible to find different cells in the prefrontal cortex that coded for each of the three moves that the monkey was going to make.

So monkeys can prepare a series of movements, but can they imagine them? When humans plan they can mentally rehearse possible moves. Cisek and Kalaska (2004) attempted to demonstrate that monkeys can also do this. The task was the same one as was used in their previous experiment (Cisek and Kalaska 2002). As described above, the monkey saw two potential targets, and after a delay it used a joystick to move a cursor to the target that had been specified. However, an additional condition was added in which the monkey was prevented from moving the cursor, and the experimenter moved the cursor instead. The authors again recorded in the premotor cortex, and found that there were cells that changed their activity just before the experimenter moved the cursor, as if the monkey was mentally representing the correct movement, even though it could not carry it out itself. Of course, the monkey might simply have been predicting the visual direction in which the cursor would move, but the fact that the activity was in a motor area argues against that interpretation.

Is this evidence strong enough for us to conclude that the monkey was 'imagining'? If human subjects are scanned while they imagine finger movements, there is activity in the premotor cortex, as there is in preparation, and this is true even when recordings from the hand muscles show that the hand is still (Gerardin *et al.* 2000). But there is also activity in the prefrontal cortex during imagination, just as there is during visual imagination. Unfortunately, Cisek and Kalaska (2004) only recorded in the premotor cortex. Thus, a critic could argue that the monkeys were simply preparing to move the cursor, even though recordings showed that the hand muscles were silent. The difference is that by definition, imagination involves awareness, whereas preparation need not. After all, the BP starts some time before we are aware of our intention to move.

We know that humans can imagine because we can ask them, and the experiment by Gerardin (2000) and others like it show that humans can imagine movements at will. The fact that they can do so means that they can, to use the words of Tulving (2005), engage in 'mental time-travel'. When subjects are asked to imagine future events, there is activity in the frontopolar cortex, area 10, as well as in the hippocampus (Addis *et al.* 2007). The activity in the hippocampus supports Tulving's (2005) suggestion that there is a link between the capacity for episodic memory and the ability to imagine the future. In the study by Addis *et al.* (2007), the hippocampus was active both when retrieving episodic memories and when imaging future episodes. As a consequence, amnesic patients with hippocampal lesions are poor at imagining future events (Hassabis *et al.* 2007).

The essence of mental time-travel into the future is planning for events when the behaviour serves future needs rather than current ones. So can chimpanzees represent future needs? Chapter 1 described an experiment by Mulcahy and Call (2006) in which they showed that apes could save tools for future use. The authors argue that this demonstrated that the apes could engage in future planning, even when the tools were to be used many hours later. However, while the experiment does indeed show that the animals save the tools so as to use them in the future, it does not prove that they can represent what their need will be in 14 hours time. At the time that the chimpanzees left the room with the tools, they did not know when they would be let back in. And the apparatus in the neighbouring room remained in sight.

How, then, can we account for the fact that humans can plan for future needs? Evidence was reviewed earlier in this chapter that, when human subjects generate alternatives at will, there is activity in the dorsal prefrontal cortex. We also know that when they summon up images there is activity in the same area, whether those images are perceptual (Kosslyn *et al.* 1997) or motor (Gerardin *et al.* 2000). There is now convincing evidence that the most anterior part of the prefrontal cortex, i.e. the frontal polar cortex, area 10, is involved in what has been called 'prospective memory' (Burgess *et al.* 2003). This term refers to the on-line representation of future-task goals, and we know that when subjects represent these there is continuous activity in the frontal polar cortex (Sakai and Passingham 2003, 2006). And, as mentioned in Chapter 2, the relative size of the human frontal polar cortex is two times that of the bonobo (Semendeferi *et al.* 2001).

Mental trial and error

The advantage of thinking ahead is that one can engage in mental trial and error. Psychologists often teach animals tasks by trial and error: one response is rewarded, another not. The only way that the animal can find the answer is to try particular responses and discover the outcome. But outside the laboratory trial and error is risky; the wrong response may lead to danger or even death. The advantage of mental trial and error is that one can eliminate this alternative before actually putting it into action. We know that humans can do this, because, for example, they can solve the Tower of London by evaluating the various moves in their head, seeing whether they would be successful, and dismissing ones that would not lead to the goal (Baker *et al.* 1996).

So, are humans unique in being able to engage in mental trial and error? We know that monkeys can consider various options in a visual maze before deciding how to reach the goal (Mushiake *et al.* 2001) and, as mentioned above, we know that there are cells coding for the future moves on the maze (Mushiake *et al.* 2006). But here the options are visible: the monkeys can follow the paths with their eyes and see whether they are or are not blocked. Humans differ in that, in the absence of visual cues, they can imagine particular actions. For example, they can imagine they are playing tennis or walking through their house and, while they do this, there is activation in the appropriate areas: motor areas when they imagine playing tennis, and spatial areas when they imagine themselves walking (Owen *et al.* 2002). The consequence is that humans can represent many alternatives, evaluate the outcomes and take into account a wide variety of considerations in making their choice.

This requires the integration of information about all the possibilities. It has been suggested that such integration takes place in a 'global workspace'(Dehaene *et al.* 1998; Dehaene and Naccache 2001; Dehaene and Changeux 2004). This concept bears some relation to the 'central executive' of Baddeley (2003). The crucial difference is that both Dehaene and colleagues (Dehaene *et al.* 1998; Dehaene and Naccache 2001) and Baars and Franklin (2003) have produced computational models that allow of testable predictions. The critical notion is that there is a stage at which information-processing becomes integrated (Baars 2002; Baars and Franklin 2003). The suggestion is that at earlier stages, the processing is carried out by distributed specialized processors that can operate in parallel. But where the response is not automatic, information must be integrated so as to determine the appropriate response.

Prefrontal cortex is ideally suited for such integration. It is the only cortical area that receives information from all five sense modalities, and the information that it receives is already highly processed. The prefrontal cortex receives inputs from all the other regions of association cortex (Barbas 2000; Miller and Cohen 2001). Thus, it can be regarded as sitting at the top of the hierarchy of information processing (Fuster 1997; Passingham *et al.* 2005). In this sense it can be regarded as part of a global workspace.

Central to the notion of a global workspace is that the contents are accessible to awareness. But does mental trial and error demand awareness? We know that choosing between alternatives need not do so. In an experiment by Dijksterhuis *et al.* (2006), subjects were asked to choose between cars. The cars were to be compared on a wide range of criteria. There was an objectively correct choice, and the surprising finding was that the subjects were more likely to choose this car if, before they made their choice, they were prevented from consciously thinking about it by being given a distracting task which consisted of solving anagrams.

This shows that we can compare alternatives without being aware of doing so. But the choice that was presented in the experiment was one that simply required an impression of the overall worth of different cars. There are other situations that do not just present a choice between several items. A general might have to compare the likelihood of success of several different possible strategies in battle. It is in such cases that it is helpful to be aware of what is going on in one's head.

Conclusions

The success of humans in colonizing such a variety of environments depends on several highly developed abilities. These include mental trial and error, being creative in proposing solutions to problems and planning for the future.

When humans engage in mental trial and error, they compare several alternatives, estimate the relative costs and values, and weigh up any moral issues. This is a major step in evolution. It is much safer to deliberate first than to simply try out the alternatives and learn by error. Many factors can influence our decisions, as can be seen from Darwin's list of reasons why he should or should not marry (Desmond and Moore 1991). Darwin's list included concern for the distant future, i.e. his care in old age. The ability to deliberate and think about events far into the future has revolutionized human mental life.

The behaviour of monkeys and apes tends to be determined by fewer factors, and by ones that are relatively immediate. Much of their behaviour can be accounted for in terms of responses to the current external context. By contrast, much of human mental life is inner-directed and influenced by factors in the long term. In line with this, the prefrontal activation to visual stimuli is much more extensive in macaque monkeys than in humans (Denys *et al.* 2004). Unfortunately, there are no complementary data comparing the self-sustaining activation of the prefrontal cortex during spontaneous thoughts. However, there are frequent claims that patients with very large prefrontal lesions are more 'stimulus bound' (Knight *et al.* 1995; Mesulam 2002).

There are two interpretations of the difference between humans and animals in deliberation and planning, though they are not mutually exclusive. The first is that these differences arise from specializations of the prefrontal cortex in humans. The second is that they are the consequence of the fact that humans have language and can thus articulate reasons for action.

Chapter 2 discussed the size of the human prefrontal cortex. It relied mainly on the data of Brodmann (1912) on the whole prefrontal cortex and the data of Semendeferi *et al.* (2001) on the frontal polar cortex, area 10. Both studies agree that the prefrontal cortex is proportionately much more extensive in the human brain. For example, Brodmann (1912) found that the prefrontal cortex formed 28.4% of the area of neocortex in humans compared with only 16.9% for the chimpanzee. The data for the frontal polar cortex are particularly intriguing since this area is particularly involved in preparing for future tasks (Burgess *et al.* 2003).

Along with differences in size, and thus in cell numbers, there are also differences in the peak branching complexity and number of spikes for prefrontal pyramidal cells (Elston *et al.* 2001). For example, the number of spines is roughly 1.9 times as great in the human brain compared with the macaque brain. Since other cells make contact on these spines, the implication is that more information can be integrated onto each cell in the human prefrontal cortex. The result is a brain with an unparalleled ability to integrate information.

But what of the fact that humans can represent the distant future? Here we can appeal to the ability of humans to imagine at will and to articulate goals and plans. Imagination can cope with some cases: for example, in considering breakfast tomorrow I can imagine the cereal packet, milk and coffee. But one cannot plan the strategy for a battle this way. Here the general must deliberate not only with others but also with himself, and it is in such situations that one 'hears' oneself thinking. Hearing one's thoughts has the same effect as writing them down, as Darwin did when debating whether to get married. It draws attention to the relevant issues. The production of an explicit representation of the alternatives allows one to note, rehearse, review and reflect on them.

Philosophers mark the difference between decision-making in humans and animals by saying that only humans base their decisions on 'reasons'. The notion is that only humans can formulate reasons for what they do, and this is because they alone have language. The next chapter therefore considers reasoning.

Chapter 8

Reasoning

Since the time of Descartes, the ability to reason has been taken as a mark of humanity. If one takes the line that reasoning requires language, then it necessarily follows that only humans can reason. But, as mentioned in Chapter 1, Levine *et al.* (1982) have described a patient with brain damage that eliminated inner speech, and yet the patient could still reason successfully on a non-verbal test of reasoning.

The implication is that an animal without language might be able to solve similar problems, even if they were simpler ones. Gillan *et al.* (1981) tested the chimpanzee, Sarah, on a very basic task of analogical reasoning. She was presented with shapes or objects and required to complete an analogy of the form 'A is to B as C is to ?', and here she had to choose between D or E. Having been taught a series of tasks of this type, she could then solve new problems in one trial. For example, she succeeded on the problem 'key is to lock as tin is to ?' by choosing a tin opener rather than a paint brush. And this was not because of a simple association between the tin opener and the tin, because she also solved the problem 'letter is to pencil as tin is to ?' by choosing the paint brush rather than the tin opener.

So language is not necessary for all types of reasoning. But, given language, humans can also evaluate propositions. For example, philosophers consider syllogisms and solve problems in formal logic. So this chapter tackles the thorny question of the relation between language and thought. The reader should be warned that there has long been controversy over whether humans 'think in language' and the most common view amongst cognitive psychologists is that we do not. The mental representations in which we think are not the words of our native language (Allport 1983). Nor do the words of this language constrain what we can think (Pinker 2007). This chapter argues for a more nuanced position. This is that there are two advantages of language in relation to thought. The first is that language provides a very efficient way of teaching concepts and cognitive operations. The second is that inner speech allows us to attend to particular contents of our thought, such as the relations between items.

Concepts and categories

Language provides labels for concepts and categories, such as 'primates' or 'similarity'. But words are not needed to form categories: animals can do so. Pigeons, for example, can pick out pictures in which there are people, even though the people differ in identity, size and other respects (Hernstein *et al.* 1976). Similarly, macaque monkeys can be trained to pick out exemplars of a category (Schrier *et al.* 1984; Bhatt *et al.* 1988; D'Amato and Sant 1988). Critically, they can do so when each exemplar is presented for one trial alone, in other words before feedback is given as to whether the choice is right or wrong. This ability depends on cells in the prefrontal cortex that fire similarly to exemplars within the same category (Freedman *et al.* 2001, 2002).

Though categories can be learned without language, verbal labels provide a highly efficient means for teaching them. Plunkett *et al.* (2007) describe a series of experiments in which 10-month-old infants were presented with cartoons of fictitious animals. They were familiarized with the division of animals into two categories. After this, the infants were shown pairs of animals, and their eye movements were monitored. It was assumed that, if the infants had learned the categories, they would look longer at the animal that belonged to neither category. If, during the familiarization phase, the labels were presented randomly, irrespective of the category membership, this interfered with learning. If a single label was presented for the two categories, the infants came to categorize them as one.

The effect of providing labels can also be studied in chimpanzees. Premack and Premack (2003) tested the the ability of the chimpanzees Sarah, Elizabeth and Peony to see that two identical objects AA were the same as two other identical objects BB but not as two non-identical objects CD. This task tests for the *abstract* notion of similarity, since the relation of similarity between the two objects A is the same as the relation between the two object B. The chimpanzees failed. They were then taught to use plastic symbols for 'same' and 'different'. Only after this did the chimpanzees succeed in mastering the abstract notion of similarity. Here the claim is not that the chimpanzees thought in the symbols, but that teaching them the symbols was a good way of teaching them the abstract concepts.

Non-verbal reasoning

It has already been admitted that language is not necessary for analogical reasoning with shapes or objects, as in the experiments with the chimpanzee Sarah (Gillan *et al.* 1981). The Raven's Matrices is a much more complex version for human subjects. It involves presenting three lines of patterned shapes. The subject has to complete the last item in the third row, using the progression in the first two rows to derive the general rule. The answer is therefore provided by analogy. The test has been given to human subjects in the MRI scanner (Christoff *et al.* 2001). The authors found activity in the middle frontal gyrus (area 46). However, the more complex the reasoning, the more the activity extended into the frontal polar cortex (area 10). Bunge *et al.* (2005) also report activation of the polar cortex when subjects evaluate whether one word pair, such as 'bouquet-flower' is or is not analogous to another word pair such as 'chain-link'.

A simplified test of analogical reasoning was given to subjects by Duncan *et al.* (2000). A line of four figures was presented, and the subject had to pick the odd one out, and this could be done by deriving the rule that was followed by the other items. Again, there was activity in prefrontal area 46, but there was also activity in the intra-parietal cortex. Parietal activation was not reported in the study by Christoff *et al.*(2001), but this is probably because the control condition also required the derivation of a rule, however simple. The Raven's Matrices test is used as a non-verbal test of general intelligence or 'g'. That is why Duncan *et al.* (2000) called their paper 'A neural basis for general intelligence'. People differ in intelligence, and their scores on the Raven's Matrices correlate positively with the activity in the prefrontal and parietal cortex when they perform a cognitive task (Gray *et al.* 2003).

The score on spatial measures of *g* have also been shown to be strongly related to the amount of frontal grey matter (Thompson *et al.* 2001). Chapter 2 has already pointed out that the prefrontal cortex is greatly expanded in the human brain (Brodmann 1912). This is true in particular of the frontal polar area 10 (Semendeferi *et al.* 2001), which is activated during complex problems (Christoff *et al.* 2001). There is no scale that would allow us to make a formal comparison of *g* in humans and chimpanzees, but it is clear that if one were to be constructed that was suitable for chimpanzees, humans would be at one extreme of that scale.

Verbal reasoning

By definition, problems in verbal reasoning are problems that are posed in words or symbols. Though chimpanzees have been taught to press symbols on a keyboard (Savage-Rumbaugh 1986), there are no reports that they can produce a proposition, and this is a precondition for reasoning with symbols. Yet, humans can evaluate syllogisms and even entertain hypotheticals and counterfactuals.

The fact that the problems are posed in verbal form, does not mean that they have to be solved by 'thinking in langage'. Of course, the first stage is that the meaning of the proposition must be interpreted. But there is disagreement over what happens next. Some, such as Braine (1998), argue that deduction is a *syntactic* process in which the reasoner extracts the logical form of the premises and then follows formal rules to as to reach their conclusions. Others, such as Johnson-Laird (Johnson-Laird 1999, 2001), argue that deduction is a *semantic* process in which the reasoner uses mental models to work out the relations. Goodwin and Johnson-Laird (2005) specifically suggest that wherever possible, these are iconic, as, for example, with spatial imagery.

We might hope that imaging would give us clues as to the actual processes that are involved. After all, subjects can be scanned while they evaluate syllogisms that are presented in verbal form. Of course, one must include a control condition in which similar sentences are read and understand, so as to subtract the effect of understanding the meaning of the words. Even after this, there is, however, a problem in interpreting the results of such an experiment. This is that if one finds activity in language areas, it may not be clear whether this reflects syntactic or semantic processes. There could, however, be one clear result. If the activity was confined to the intra-parietal cortex, this would indicate the use of spatial imagery, since there is extensive evidence for activations in this region during spatial tasks (Culham and Kanwisher 2001).

The first finding is that when subjects evaluate verbal syllogisms, there is activity in the left Broca's area. The activations included both area 44, in the case of deductive reasoning, and area 45, in the case of both deductive and inductive reasoning (Goel and Dolan 2004). Though there is an association between activity in area 44 and phonological processing and activity in area 45 and semantic processing (Poldrack *et al.* 1999), the data merely point to linguistic processing without favouring the syntactic or semantic hypothesis. There was additional activity in the intra-parietal cortex, just as when subjects reason with visuo-spatial material.

In this experiment the syllogisms were presented in sentence form. But humans can also engage in deductive reasoning with symbols. For example, they can evaluate whether the following is true: 'all p are b, all b are c, therefore all p are c'. So Goel *et al.* (2000) specifically compared syllogisms that were presented in symbols with syllogisms that were presented in sentences. As one would expect from the previous experiment, in both cases there was activity in the left Broca's areas 45 and 44. However, the results also suggested an association between symbolic logic and visuo-spatial reasoning, since there was more activity in the intra-parietal sulcus in the case of the symbolic logic. In the case of the sentences, there was more activity in the middle temporal gyrus and this may reflect the operation of semantic processes.

Humans are capable of more complex propositional logic. For example, they can evaluate whether the following inference is valid: 'if p then q; if not q, then not p'. In propositional logic this is called 'Modus Tollens'. Noveck *et al.* (2004) presented inferences of this sort to subjects in the scanner. For Modus Tollens there was activation in the inferior frontal cortex just below Broca's area 45. However, there were also activations in frontal and parietal areas outside the classical language areas. But the most striking finding was that all the activations were in the left hemisphere, i.e. the dominant hemisphere for language. Chapter 6 reviewed the evidence that the left hemisphere is specialized for linguistic processing. But the fact that there are left-hemisphere activations for symbolic reasoning does not tell us whether they are associated with phonological, syntactic or semantic processing. Nonetheless, it does suggest that language plays some role in reasoning. Again this is not to claim that the mental representations are words. It could be, for example, that the activations reflect the process by which we become aware of our thoughts via inner speech.

Arithmetic

The brain areas that are active during reasoning are also active when human subjects carry out arithmetic operations (Houde and Tzourio-Mazoyer 2003). There is activity in both parietal and prefrontal cortex when subjects engage in calculations (Zago *et al.* 2001). In the last chapter, the task of serially subtracting 7s from 100 was used as a protypical task that makes demands on the working memory system, and thus on the prefrontal and parietal cortex.

Clearly macaque monkeys cannot calculate in this way. The limit of their ability is that, like birds (Koehler 1950), they can estimate the numerosity of items up to 7 or so (Nieder 2005), and can respond to changes in numerosity. Thus, they can choose reliably between small quantities of fruit, taking into account pieces of fruit that they watched being taken away, that is 'subtracted' (Sulkowski and Hauser 2001). And they are surprised if they see the addition of a piece of fruit leading to an incorrect or 'impossible' number rather than to the correct number (Flombaum *et al.* 2005). These abilities depend on cells that can be found in the parietal (Nieder and Miller 2004) and prefrontal cortex (Nieder *et al.* 2002), which code for different numbers.

There is, however, a distinction between estimating and enumerating or counting out. The parrot, Alex, was taught to say the appropriate number for arrays of up to six items (Pepperberg 1987), and when presented with two arrays under separate cups could say the total, so long as it was not larger than four (Pepperberg 2006). Similarly, the chimpanzees, Ai (Matsuzawa 1985) and Sheba (Boysen *et al.* 1995), can indicate the numeral that applies to small sets of items, and Sheba can give the total for two arrays (Boysen and Berntson 1989). It is not clear, however, whether these animals are estimating total numerosity by remembering the sets or genuinely enumerating and then adding.

True calculation requires the ability to enumerate. Though humans can estimate numerosity (Dehaene *et al.* 2004), they can also enumerate, and this works for big numbers. They can be taught the rules of addition, subtraction and so on, because they can be taught in a language. When calculating, we can also become aware of the mental operations via the contents of the phonological loop. To investigate the role of language, Dehaene *et al.* (1999) imaged subjects while they were either estimating the result of a numerical operation or engaging in exact arithmetic. Estimation was associated with activity in the intra-parietal sulcus. This suggests a relationship between estimating and spatial processing (Hubbard *et al.* 2005). It is as if numbers are spatially arranged along a line, the 'mental number line' (Dehaene *et al.* 2004).

By contrast, exact calculations involving two two-digit numbers were associated with an activation in the left angular gyrus. Activations here have also been reported by others for calculation (Zago and Tzourio-Mazoyer 2002; Simon *et al.* 2004). The crucial finding is that there is overlap with the area of the left angular gyrus that is activated for a simple language task, detecting target phonemes within simple words (Simon *et al.* 2004). This strongly suggests that subtraction also involves left-hemisphere phonological mechanisms. Confirmation that the left angular gyrus is crucially involved in calculation comes from the observation that electrical stimulation here causes a disturbance in calculation (Roux *et al.* 2003).

The obvious question is whether the parietal activations genuinely represent the executive process of calculating or simply the requirement to hold numbers in memory while performing calculations. Gruber *et al.* (2001) therefore presented serial calculations and control tasks on which numbers or letters had to be substituted, and intermediate values kept in temporary memory. There was a region in the left angular gyrus that was more active for calculation than for the memory of numbers alone.

In the same paper, there was extensive activation in the left inferior frontal gyrus when subjects engaged in complex calculations, and the same has been reported in other studies (Dehaene *et al.* 1999; Hubbard *et al.* 2005). Gruber *et al.* (2001) therefore devised a control task called 'pseudo-calculation' in which letters rather than numbers were manipulated by substitution. When calculation was compared with this control task, there was activity in Broca's area 44 and 45. This relates to the extra load on numerical processing in calculation.

Causal reasoning

The previous sections have considered reasoning with patterns, words, logic symbols and numerals. This leaves a type of reasoning that has proved crucial in the development of technology and science. Humans can reason about causal relations. They can consider, not just whether A is associated with X, but whether A causes X. This is not to say that animals have no understanding of causal relations. If you teach a rat that A is followed by outcome X, and then that A+B is followed by the same outcome, the animal will attribute X to A alone. If presented with B on its own, the rat will not expect X, even though on every trial that it was presented, B was associated with X (Dickinson 1980). In other words, it is not sufficient for a stimulus to be associated with a particular outcome for the rat to relate them.

Motivated by the work on rats, Fletcher *et al.* (2001) taught human subjects that particular fictitious drugs represented by pictures had particular outcomes. For example, 'Dugetil' leads to 'Huxley syndrome'. The authors report activation of the dorsal prefrontal cortex and intra-parietal cortex at the beginning of learning, but this activity fell off as the relationship was learned. However, if then 'Dugetil' was not followed by 'Huxley syndrome', these areas were re-activated. Furthermore, the authors found even more activity in the prefrontal cortex if the subjects had been taught that drug A did not lead to syndrome X, and in a subsequent trial A was followed by syndrome X. The authors conclude that the dorsal prefrontal cortex forms part of a system for the learning of causal relations. Others have shown that it is also activated when subjects evaluate causal relations that they already know; for example, that erosion is caused by tides (Satpute *et al.* 2005).

Following up their work on fictitious drugs, Turner *et al.*(2004) drew on a further paradigm that had been developed for rats. If A predicts X, and A+B predicts not X, B is interpreted as preventing X. If now B+C are presented followed by X, the rat predicts X very strongly indeed when presented with C on its own. The interpretation is that C must be very powerful to overcome the effects of B. This is called 'superlearning' (Aitken *et al.* 2000).

So Turner *et al.* (2004) taught human subjects that food A, e.g. banana, was followed by an allergy, and then that bananas and mushrooms did not lead to this allergy. The final stage was to present mushrooms and pears followed by the allergy. The subjects rated pears as particularly allergenic. In line with the predictions of the subjects, when C was presented on its own, there was activation in both the dorsal and ventral prefrontal cortex during the superlearning condition.

There is, however, a crucial difference between humans and animals. Human can intervene so as to establish causal relations. If A causes B, then B will not occur if you intervene and prevent A. Blaisdell *et al.* (2006) have tried to demonstrate that rats understand interventions. The animals were taught that a light A led to X and Y, where X was a tone and Y was food. They were then taught to press a lever to bring on the tone. Even though both the tone and food had previously been paired with A, the animals did not look for food on hearing the tone. The authors argue that the rats realized that generating the tone by an alternative cause, i.e. lever pressing, had no effect on the cause of the food, i.e. the light. However, the experiment is not convincing. Though the light was paired with both the tone and food, it was not paired with both of them simultaneously in the same trials. Furthermore, there is the fundamental difference that the rats were taught this 'intervention'. Humans intervene of their own accord.

It is the human capacity to intervene that has led to the development of our technology. This is not to deny that chimpanzees can learn to use simple tools (Whiten *et al.* 2005). The chimpanzee Sarah can also choose the tool that would have a particular effect; for example, a knife when presented with a cut apple or water when presented with a wet apple (Premack and Premack 1994, 2003). But a chimpanzee's understanding is very limited compared with that of humans. To take an example suggested by the Premacks, humans have long understood the relation between seeds and growth, but it was their ability to reason causally that has led them to intervene by deliberately planting the seeds.

In other words, humans have an *explicit* understanding of causality. It is a general rule that the prefrontal cortex is activated during the explicit processing of rules. It is not, for example, activated when subjects learn motor sequences implicitly, but it becomes activated when with further practice they come to have an explicit knowledge of the sequence (Grafton *et al.* 1993). The prefrontal cortex is not activated if subjects perform a sequence automatically and without attention, but it is re-activated when subjects are required to pay attention to the sequence (Rowe *et al.* 2002). The activation of the prefrontal cortex when subjects work out causal relations (Fletcher *et al.* 2001) reflects the explicit processing of causal relations.

Conclusions

The last chapter related the human ability to engage in mental trial and error, and to plan for the distant future, to the expansion of the prefrontal cortex. In this chapter, the prefrontal cortex has been shown to be also involved in the formation of concepts, calculation and causal reasoning. At the same time, the parietal cortex has also been shown to be involved in reasoning and calculation. The pre-eminence of humans in these abilities results from the expansion of the prefrontal and parietal cortex (Chapters 2 and 4).

The other crucial difference is the development of language. This is not to take the strong line that no reasoning can occur without language. Indeed, we know that much of our thought occurs automatically and without awareness (Velmans 1991; Jackendoff 1997). But, at the same time, we are often aware of 'talking to ourselves' and, in particular, when faced with a difficult problem. In other words, one way in which we are aware of the content of our thoughts is by virtue of experiencing the phonological images that are associated with them

(Jackendoff 2007). Of course, we are also aware of visual imagery, but phonological imagery gives us access to our thoughts in a way that is not available to chimpanzees.

One might have hoped to be able to use imaging to show whether the phonological loop is used during thought and there are data that are consistent with this proposal. The inferior frontal gyrus, including Broca's area 44, is activated during deductive reasoning (Goel *et al.* 2000), calculation (Gruber *et al.* 2001) and the evaluation of causal relations (Satpute *et al.* 2005). These data are suggestive, though they do not distinguish between activations that reflect semantic and phonological processing.

It should not, however, be controversial that the phonological loop is often engaged during thought. After all it is our common experience that we have a mental life in which we hear an inner conversation, however patchy and fleeting it may be. What is controversial is the advantage of using the phonological loop during thought. Jackendoff (2007) suggests that inner speech provides 'something new to pay attention to'. But why should inner speech be more potent than visual imagery? The difference is that visual imagery is graphical, whereas verbal imagery is analytic. Only verbal imagery allows predication, as in 'Freddie is a dog', or logical connections between situations, as in 'Joe takes an umbrella because it is raining' (Jackendoff 2007). In other words, the power of imaged language comes through the combinatorial structure of language.

This is speculation. What we need is an experimental test, and the truth is that there has not been one. Jackendoff (2007) can only offer an anecdote. He refers to the work of Kegl *et al.* (1999) on the introduction of education in Nicagura for deaf individuals who had no previous exposure to language. Because they were now in a community, the members quickly developed a novel sign language. Jackendoff (2007) cites an interview with one individual who was exposed to this language relatively late in life. This person signed that 'I didn't even know what it meant to think. Thinking meant nothing to me'. It is not that this person did not think beforehand: it is that he was now aware of thinking in a new way. The implication is that now he had access to a better way of thinking.

Chapter 9

Social cognition

Humans are unrivalled in intelligence, and so the previous two chapters have been devoted to cognition. But humans are also specialized in the way in which they have adapted socially. All human societies depend critically on cooperation and exchange. In a complex society, different groups of people make their own contribution by adopting specialized roles and developing particular skills. This entails the sharing of resources, whether directly in the form of food or equipment or indirectly in form of tokens such as money. Such societies cannot operate unless individuals can understand the intentions of others.

The term 'social cognition' is used here to cover the wide range of abilities that are required. These include empathy, joint attention, the understanding of beliefs and other mental states, and the capacity for altruism. Herrmann *et al.* (2007) summarize the results of experiments in which they compared chimpanzees and orang-utans with children of two and a half years on six aspects of social cognition. The children outclassed the chimpanzees and oranges on five of the six tests. Clearly humans have specialized to be skilled in social cognition.

Empathy

Social cohesion is underpinned by the ability of one individual to empathize with another. We know what it feels like to be happy, sad, alarmed or in pain. In the laboratory, pain provides a good example. Singer *et al.* (2004*b*) investigated couples. The female partner was scanned while she watched painful electrical stimulation being applied to the hand of her male partner. The ratings of unpleasantness showed that the female partner showed empathy for her partner. Whether the subjects watched stimulation of their partner or were stimulated themselves there was activity in two areas. The first was the anterior cingulate cortex, which lies on the medial frontal surface (Fig. 9.1).

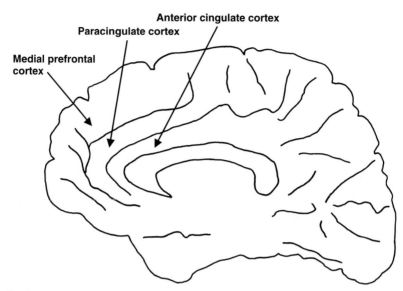

Fig. 9.1

The second was the anterior insula, which lies at the bottom of the lateral fissure that divides the temporal lobe from the parietal lobe (Fig. 9.2). These activations reflect the emotional response. There was only activation in somatic areas and in a caudal part of the anterior cingulate cortex when the subject themselves suffered pain.

The same effect works with videos. The anterior cingulate and insula are also activated when subjects view videos showing faces in moderate pain (Botvinick *et al.* 2005). Again these same areas were involved when subjects experienced thermal pain themselves. The effect even works with still photographs: the same results are found when subjects view photos of hands and feet in very uncomfortable positions (Jackson *et al.* 2005). The degree of activation in the anterior cingulate cortex and anterior insula correlates with the degree of pain shown in faces, as well as with the degree of empathy shown by the observer (Saarela *et al.* 2007)

Empathy is not restricted to pain, anxiety and discomfort. We are also sensitive to the feelings of disgust in others. Wicker *et al.* (2003) presented subjects with noxious smells and reported activity in the anterior cingulate cortex and insula. The same areas were activated

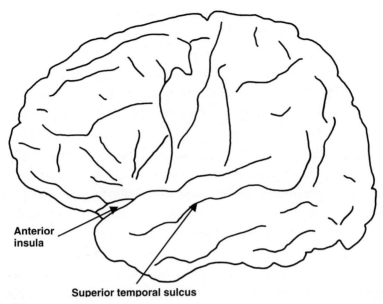

Anterior
insula

Superior temporal sulcus

Fig. 9.2

when the subjects viewed videos of a person leaning forwards over a glass and expressing disgust at the smell. The case is strengthened by the observation of a patient with a lesion in the insula. As expected, he was impaired at recognizing the emotion in faces that expressed disgust (Calder *et al.* 2000).

Wicker *et al.* (2003) suggest that empathy depends on mirror neurones. These have been described in earlier chapters. For example, cells in the ventral premotor cortex fire both when a monkey lip smacks and when it sees a person protruding the lips (Ferrari *et al.* 2003). Mirror neurones were first described in the motor system, i.e. in the premotor and parietal cortex (Rizzolatti *et al.* 2001). But structures such as the anterior cingulate cortex and insula are not part of the skeletal motor system.

However, they do have connections to the viscero-motor system. In macaques, electrical stimulation of both the anterior cingulate cortex and insula produce autonomic and viscero-motor changes (Kaada 1960). Mirror neurones have not been looked for in these areas in monkeys, but they have been described in a patient undergoing surgery on the anterior cingulate cortex. The cells fired both when the patient received noxious stimulation and when he watched someone else receiving similar stimulation (Hutchison *et al.* 1999).

It is unfortunate that it is not feasible to record specifically from the large spindle-shaped cells that can be found in layer V of the anterior cingulate cortex in the human but not the macaque brain (Nimchinsky *et al.* 1999). These are abundant in the human brain and are found in clusters. As already mentioned in Chapter 2, they were first identified by von Economo (1926), and so Allman *et al.* (2005) refer to them as 'von Economo neurones'. Because these cells are also found in the anterior insula, Watson and Allman (2007) suggest that they may be involved in the representation of internal somatic states. It was in the anterior insula and anterior cingulated cortex that Singer *et al.* (2004*b*) reported activation when subjects feel empathy. But the suggested link between empathy and spindle cells is weakened by the observation that subjects with autism spectrum disorders score low on a scale of empathy (Wakabayashi *et al.* 2007), and yet a preliminary study found no reduction of spindle cell numbers in the anterior insula in four subjects with autism (Kennedy *et al.* 2007).

Chimpanzees also feel empathy, comforting others that are in distress (Preston and de Waal 2002). It may or may not be coincidence that there are spindle cells in the anterior cingulate cortex of chimpanzees, including clusters of them in bonobos (Nimchinsky *et al.* 1999). There are numerically many more in the human brain (Allman *et al.* 2005), but unfortunately in this paper the absolute numbers of spindle cells are presented rather than the proportion of these cells out of the total number of cells.

The fact that chimpanzees will comfort others shows that they show more than empathy in the restricted sense of emotional contagion. It indicates that, like humans, they can feel sympathy for others. However, in humans this extends to altruistic acts. The ability to feel the emotions of others is a necessary condition for altruistic acts, but it is not a sufficient one. We return to altruism in a later section.

Joint attention

When one animal sees another in an emotional state, it looks round to see what is causing that state. For example, there may be a predator nearby. There are various clues as to where the predator might be: one is stance and another is eye gaze.

So does joint attention depend on mirror neuronal mechanisms? The way to find out is to see if there is activity in the same areas both when the subjects move their eyes and when they observe eye movements. Pelphrey *et al.* (2005*b*) found activity in the superior temporal sulcus (Fig. 9.2) and frontal eye fields when subjects watched an animated face in which the gaze shifted to one side. But there are two reasons for doubting that this experiment demonstrates the operation of mirror neurones. The first is that studies in monkeys have failed to find mirror neurones in the superior temporal sulcus. Though the cells fire when the monkeys watch people carrying out actions (Jellema and Perrett 2003), they do not fire when the monkeys act themselves (Rizzolatti pers.com.). The second problem is that the subjects were not required to fixate, and thus the activation in the frontal eye fields could have been due to the subjects' own eye movements. The experiment needs to be repeated while the subject fixates a central point.

However, there is more to joint attention than simply following gaze. It involves understanding the significance of the gaze, such as the intentions of the other person. For example, children with autism can discriminate the direction of gaze, but they do not understand its significance. Baron-Cohen (1995) describes an experiment in which children were shown a cartoon face looking at one of four sweets or candies. The children with autism were poor at saying which candy Charlie preferred.

So Pelphrey *et al.* (2005*a*) compared healthy subjects with subjects with autism, and showed them videos in which the eyes either shifted gaze to a target or into empty space. If the observer understands the intentions behind eye movements, they should be surprised by the shift into empty space. In the healthy subjects there was an increase in activity in the superior temporal sulcus when the eyes looked into empty space, i.e. when the eyes did not move as expected. There was no such activity in the subjects with autism. But while it could be argued that the results suggest that a specific mechanism is impaired in the brains of autistic subjects, it does not follow that that mechanism is necessarily unique to the human brain. To find out whether this is the case, the behavioural experiment needs to be carried out with chimpanzees to see whether they too are surprised when they see someone's eyes move into empty space.

Intentions

The point of viewing the actions of others is that they provide an indication of what the actor intends to do. To isolate the judgement of intentions, one needs conditions that are matched for movement but which differ in that intentions are inferred in one condition but not in the other. For example, Castelli *et al.* (2000) constructed videos in which geometric shapes moved around. In one set of videos, the shapes could be interpreted as interacting with others, as if to influence them; in the other set, the movements of the shapes were random. Healthy human observers ascribed intentions to the first but not the second set (Castelli *et al.* 2000). In the scanner, two areas in which there was more activity for the first set of videos were the superior temporal sulcus (Fig. 9.2) and the medial prefrontal cortex (Fig. 9.1). Activity in these areas was also correlated with the degree to which the observers judged the items to involve intentions.

In our everyday life we do not normally view shapes interacting. However, one gets the same results if one uses a real-life task. Spiers and Maguire (2006a) studied taxi drivers and adapted a video game for use in the scanner. The taxi drivers were required to drive a taxi through a representation of the streets of London. When they were thinking about the intentions of pedestrians or the drivers of other cars, there was activity in the superior temporal sulcus. There was also activity in an area within the medial frontal cortex, the paracingulate cortex (Fig. 9.1).

The obvious next step is to scan subjects who are known to be poor at judging intentions. So Castelli *et al.* (2002) tested subjects with Asperger's syndrome. The advantage of studying these subjects is that, though they have some autistic features, they are of normal intelligence. However, they are usually impaired at 'second-order' theory of mind, judging, for example, what John thinks that Mary thinks (Abell *et al.* 1999). As expected, in the experiment by Castelli *et al.* (2002), these subjects were less likely to ascribe intentions to the shapes. And, correspondingly, there was less activity in their superior temporal sulcus and medial prefrontal cortex.

So does the ability to judge intentions depend on mirror neurones? As already mentioned, these have been recorded in the premotor (Gallese *et al.* 1996) and parietal cortex (Fogassi *et al.* 2005) in macaque monkeys. And there is activity in these same areas when human subjects observe either simple (Buccino *et al.* 2001) or complex actions (Calvo-Merino *et al.* 2005). By simulating a movement when observing it, the subject can understand the actions of others (Gallese and Goldman 1998; Rizzolatti *et al.* 2001).

But do mirror neurones enable one to read the *intentions* behind the action? Fogassi *et al.* (2005) have argued that they do. They recorded from mirror neurones in the inferior parietal cortex. There were cells that fired differently when the animal picked up a piece of food, depending on whether the animal was going to eat it or place it in a cup. And some of these were mirror neurones, i.e. they fired in the same way when the animals watched the experimenter picking up an object with a particular goal in mind. But here the intention was provided by the context; for example, by whether the object was edible or not, or by what had happened previously in the block of trials. In other words, it was the animal's knowledge that told it the intention.

There is an alternative to the notion that we understand actions by simulating them. We learn to predict physical events by observation and by developing causal theories. So presumably we could also learn to predict social events in the same way. The term 'theory–theory' has been coined to refer to causal theories concerning mental states (Gopnik and Meltzoff 1997).

So how could we distinguish between simulation theory and theory–theory? Calvo-Merino *et al.* (2006) carried out a study on ballet dancers. The idea was that there are some moves that only men perform and others that only women perform. Yet, both men and women are visually familiar with all the moves, since they practice and dance together. So they know the names of all the moves and can make predictions about how they would go. Yet, in the study, there was more activity in the parietal and premotor cortex when the dancers watched the moves they could do themselves than when they watched the moves that they do not do. This supports the idea that they simulated the moves that they could do.

But these activations are in the motor system. So why, when subjects judge the intentions of others, is the activity in the medial frontal (Castelli *et al.* 2000) and paracingulate cortex (Spiers and Maguire 2006*a*) rather than in the motor system? The answer is provided by a beautiful study carried out by Wheatley *et al.* (2007). The subjects watched a moving stimulus, such as a spinning top, but in one condition the background was a picture of an ice-rink, whereas in the other it was a picture of dry land. The background biased the interpretation of the viewers, such that when they saw the top spinning on ice it brought a skater to mind, whereas when it was spinning on dry land it was interpreted as inanimate.

The results are startling. In both conditions there was activity in the parietal and premotor cortex. This presumably reflects the operation of the mirror system in predicting future movements. But there was only activity in the superior temporal sulcus and paracingulate cortex when the subjects viewed the objects against a background that suggested that they were animate, e.g. the top on ice. This presumably reflects the operation of a system for social interpretation. In other words, we need to distinguish mechanisms for predicting movements from mechanisms for interpreting minds.

Beliefs and other mental states

Chapter 1 argued that only humans can reflect on their own mental states, such as beliefs. It is the ability to do this that allows us to infer the mental states of others (Frith 2007). Evidence that this is so comes from the finding is that there is activity in the paracingulate cortex, both when subjects reflect on their own characteristics or mental states and when they reflect on those of others (Ochsner *et al.* 2005; Amodio and Frith 2006; Northoff *et al.* 2006). This is consistent with the hypothesis that we interpret the mental states of others by 'putting ourselves in the same situation'.

Many studies have reported activation of the paracingulate cortex when subjects reflect on the beliefs and other mental states of others. One of the earliest, used stories (Fletcher *et al.* 1995): the subject read them and then had to answer a question. The questions were of two types: the first asked about mental states, as in 'why did the burglar do this?'; the second asked about physical events, as in 'why did the alarm go off?'. When a comparison was made between stories requiring the attribution of mental states and physical stories, there was differential activity in the paracingulate cortex.

This area turns up in a wide range of studies that have been conducted since. Gallagher and Frith (2003) have reviewed imaging studies in which subjects infer mental states, i.e. in which they 'mentalize' (Frith and Frith 2006). The review points to common activation in the paracingulate cortex. This is true not only when subjects read stories about others (Gallagher *et al.* 2000; Vogeley *et al.* 2001) but also when they look at cartoons (Brunet *et al.* 2000; Gallagher *et al.* 2000). In the latter study, the cartoons were taken to make demands on mentalizing if one needed to attribute false belief or ignorance so as to understand them.

So as to directly test false belief, Grèzes *et al.* (2004*b*) required actors to pick up a box and sometimes gave them false information about the weight of the box. Videos were taken and were shown to subjects in an fMRI scanner. The observers were specifically required to judge when the actor had a false belief. They were able to do this by watching the adjustments made by the actors as they picked up the box. When the observers judged that the actor had a false expectation, there was activity in the superior temporal sulcus and medial frontal cortex.

Amodio and Frith (2006) suggest that there is a posterior to anterior gradient on the medial frontal surface. They point out that the peaks for reflecting on mental states tend to lie anterior on the medial frontal surface to the peaks for monitoring one's own actions. Lau *et al.* (2006) also report that the peak for attending to intention is anterior to the peak for attending to the movement itself. The proposal is that the more anterior one goes, the more abstract the representations. It is the most anterior segment that allows the meta-cognitive process of reflecting on thoughts.

This gradient reflects a hierarchy of abilities. Chimpanzees are aware of their bodies, and can compare their reflection with their own body (Chapter 1). They are also aware of the direction of gaze of other individuals and can follow it (Chapter 1). Finally, they can distinguish intentional from accidental actions (Call and Tomasello 1998). In other words, chimpanzees are aware of the bodily states of themselves and others, and of the goals of bodily action. But they cannot, as far as we know, reflect on their own thoughts and characteristics or of those of others. Does this imply the development of new anterior cingulate strips that are unique to humans? The characteristic of the human paracingulate cortex is that it is a transitional cortex with a dysgranular layer IV, rather than an agranular layer IV as in the anterior cingulate cortex (Vogt et al. 1995). It lies superior to, as well as anterior to, the anterior cingulated area 24. It is labelled area 32 and has subdivisions.

It is true that there is also an area 32 in the macaque brain (Vogt et al. 2005), but it lies anterior and ventral to area 24. Ongur et al. (2003) doubt whether it is homologous with area 32 in the human brain. Unfortunately, no recent cyto-architectonic map has been published of the anterior cingulate cortex in the chimpanzee, and this is particularly regrettable given that it is possible to identify a paracingulate sulcus in the chimpanzee but not macaque brain. It is this sulcus that in the human brain separates the anterior cingulate cortex area 24 from the paracingulate area 32.

Further comparative studies are also needed using immunocyto-chemistry. For example, Hof et al. (2001) have described a population of pyramidal neurones in layer V of the human anterior cingulate cortex that express calretinin. These do not exist in the brains of any monkeys but can be found in smaller numbers in chimpanzees. In humans, a few of these cells were also found in area 32. A close comparison of the paracingulate cortex in humans and great apes is clearly called for.

Cooperation

The reason why there has been pressure for humans to understand the mental states of others is that we have adapted by cooperating. In contrast, chimpanzees are in general competitive, though they do engage in joint hunting of red colobus monkeys in the wild (Mitani and Watts 1999). In the laboratory they can be induced to cooperate in problem solving, but they do not communicate their intentions in the same way that human infants (Tomasello and Carpenter 2005) or young children do (Warneken *et al.* 2006).

The contrast between cooperating and competing has been formalized in the Prisoner's Dilemma. In this game, played for money, there are two players and their options are either to cooperate or defect. In a single run of the game, it pays each player to defect but in iterated runs, it pays to adopt other strategies, such as tit-for-tat, i.e. if the partner defects on the next trial you defect, but if the partner cooperates on the next trial you cooperate (Ridley 1996). An alternative way of assessing cooperation is via the Ultimatum Game. Here a player offers a sum of money and the other player either accepts or rejects the offer. If the offer is rejected, neither player gets any money. Human players typically offer an even split, and reject an unfair offer. Chimpanzees typically accept offers even if they are unfair (Jensen *et al.* 2007). This suggests that they do not understand the concept of 'fairness'.

If cooperation and competition depend on the ability to infer mental states, then it should make a difference whether the players think that they are playing against a human partner or against a computer. For this reason, imaging studies have contrasted these two conditions. Rilling *et al.* (2004*a*) scanned subjects playing both games. In either case there was activity in the paracingulate cortex when the subjects believed that they were playing against human partners.

It should be possible to detect changes in the brain that distinguish whether players experience cooperation or defection in the Prisoner's Dilemma, or fair or unfair offers in the Ultimatum Game. In the Prisoner's Dilemma, activity has been reported in brain areas associated with the processing of rewards when the player cooperates and the partner does the same (Rilling *et al.* 2002). These include the ventral striatum, ventromedial frontal cortex and the anterior cingulate cortex. When the partner fails to reciprocate, there is a negative BOLD signal in the ventral striatum and ventromedial frontal cortex (Rilling *et al.* 2004*b*).

In the Ultimatum Game, unfair proposals by the partner are followed by activity in the anterior insula, and this activity is greater if the proposal is rejected (Sanfey *et al.* 2003). The authors take this activity to reflect the emotional response. The same interpretation is given by Grèzes *et al.* (2004*a*) for the activation they report in the amygdala, when subjects judge that they are being deceived. The amygdala is also activated when subjects judge that faces are untrustworthy (Winston *et al.* 2003). As expected, damage to the amygdala impairs the ability to pick out untrustworthy from trustworthy faces (Adolphs *et al.* 1998).

In everyday life we need to learn who cooperates and who does not. If the partner cooperates, this will change the way in which they are viewed in the future. Singer *et al.* (2004*a*) took subjects who had played the Prisoner's Dilemma and had learned which partners cooperate and which defect. Viewing the faces of those who had cooperated led to activation in areas associated with reward, such as the ventral striatum and orbital frontal cortex. In a subsequent study, Singer *et al.* (2006) investigated whether subjects were more likely to feel empathy towards those that cooperated than towards those that did not. As in their previous study on empathy (Singer *et al.* 2004*b*), the subjects observed painful stimulation being applied to the hand of someone else. As compared with women, men showed less cingulate activity when viewing stimulation of someone who had defected. In other words, they were less likely to empathize with a defector.

Moral judgements

Humans differ from chimpanzees in that adults transmit to their children a set of moral rules and values. These are then internalized by the children (Bandura 1989). These values concern not what pays but what one *ought* to do.

One can ask subjects to make moral judgements in the scanner. Moll *et al.* (2002) presented subjects with sentences such as 'criminals should go to gaol' and asked them to judge whether they were right or wrong. The comparison sentences involved statements with no moral implication, such as 'pregnant women often throw up'. For the moral sentences, there was activity in the superior temporal sulcus and ventromedial frontal cortex. In a related study, Berthoz *et al.* (2006) presented a series of short stories in which social norms were either violated deliberately or accidentally. The subjects were asked to imagine what either they or someone else would feel like in these situations. There was activation in the paracingulate cortex when they imagined deliberate as opposed to accidental violations. However, there was also evidence that the subjects reacted more strongly when they were themselves involved in the moral violation. The amygdala was activated specifically when they were responsible for the violation.

In real life we are sometimes faced with moral dilemmas. For example, is it justified to shoot in war to save others? Greene *et al.* (2001) faced subjects with similar dilemmas. One well-known one involves a moving trolley that threatens to kill several people if it continues on the same track. The question is whether it is worse to push someone off the bridge to stop the trolley, than it is to pull a lever to move the trolley onto a side track where it will kill someone. People across a wide range of cultures have surprisingly similar intuitions about dilemmas of this sort (Hauser 2006).

Pushing someone off the bridge engages the emotions more than pulling the lever. This is evident from the results of the study by Greene *et al.* (2001). They found that the dilemmas induced activity in the medial frontal polar cortex, but that the activity is greater when the person was faced with pushing the person off the bridge. But moral dilemmas may also place demands on reasoning. Greene *et al.* (2004) took difficult dilemmas that took some time to consider and contrasted them with easy ones that were decided quickly. As expected from other studies on reasoning, the difficult dilemmas led to activation in the lateral frontal cortex.

One might therefore expect that lesions of the prefrontal cortex impair the ability to make moral judgements. Eslinger and Damasio (1985) described patient EVR who had surgery to remove a very large frontal meningioma. The removal included the ventral and medial surface bilaterally and extended into the dorsal prefrontal cortex on one side. The surgery had a devastating effect on EVR's life. He divorced, remarried quickly, divorced again, lost his job, did menial jobs and was often fired. The fact that he lived a disordered life does not, however, show that his moral values had changed. So Saver and Damasio (1991) tested him for his knowledge of the actions that would be appropriate in particular situations and for his ability to perform moral reasoning at an advanced level. Surprisingly, he showed normal or superior performance, even though his social conduct in everyday life was greatly disrupted. His problem was not that he did not know the appropriate rules but that in practice he failed to keep them in mind.

Since moral values are learned in childhood, one possibility is that they were acquired normally by EVR when he was young and that the lesion did not prevent retrieval in adulthood. So Anderson *et al.* (1999*b*) looked for patients with early lesions. They report on two adults: one was run over at the age of 15 months and the other had surgery for a tumour at 3 months. Both became very disruptive but, more importantly, when tested in adulthood, the patients were impaired on tests of moral reasoning; for example, failing to identify the primary issues in moral dilemmas.

In both patients the lesion included the polar cortex and the orbital and ventromedial cortex. There are two reasons for thinking that the ventromedial cortex is important. First, patients with ventromedial prefrontal lesions can be shown to be poor at decision-making when they have to evaluate the costs and benefits of their actions (Bechara *et al.* 2000). Second, patients with ventromedial lesions are more likely than control subjects to say that they would kill one person to save the lives of others (Koenigs *et al.* 2007). In other words, they are more likely to make utilitarian judgements. This may be because they feel less anxiety. Patients with bilateral ventromedial lesions fail to show anticipatory autonomic responses in the face of possible punishment (Bechara *et al.* 2000).

Altruism

Not only can humans make moral judgements, they are also capable of genuine altruism. This is defined as providing help to others at risk to oneself. Altruism has been a problem for evolutionary biology, because, if it depends on genetic factors, the relevant genes should die out in the population (Dawkins 1989*b*). The solution proposed to account for altruism in animals is to argue that the altruism is only apparent. Either it benefits kin, and they pass on the relevant genes, or it has a delayed benefit to the helper because it is later paid back in kind. Chimpanzees, for example, are more likely to be generous in sharing if the recipient is known to have been generous in the past (de Waal 1996). This is a case of 'reciprocal altruism'.

Neither explanation will account for the men who go out in the lifeboat. These may be retired fisherman. So not only do they save people to whom they are not related, but they are not themselves later saved. True altruism probably develops from the extension of feelings towards one's kin to members of the group and wider society. In human society this extension is promoted through education by instilling moral values and obligations. We are taught that we should help others, not because they will pay us back, but because that is the right thing to do.

However, altruism is part of a larger problem. This is that humans do not always act in a way so as to ensure that their genes are passed on to later generations. Monks and nuns swear a vow of chastity. The explanation is that humans, unlike animals, can set their own goals and monitor their progress towards them (Bandura 1989). This is probably the consequence of the expansion of the prefrontal cortex. As described in Chapter 7, there is activation in the medial prefrontal cortex when subjects set themselves a particular task (Haynes *et al.* 2007) and we found that activity in the paracingulate cortex when they monitor their behaviour in relation to their self-image (Bengtsson *et al.*, submitted). The prefrontal cortex is also activated when subjects must inhibit a default response, as on a go-no go task (Konishi *et al.* 1999). If the default is provided by genetic mechanisms, humans can overcome it.

One might wonder how this has come about. The reason is that the ability to set goals and monitor progress towards them is of enormous evolutionary advantage. Humans have adapted to such a wide variety of environments because they can pose problems to themselves and solve them via technology. In most cases, the goal of gene survival will be achieved but, as Dawkins (1989*a*) points out, a consequence is that, on occasion, this goal can be subverted.

Conclusions

The ability to reflect on the mental states of others has more leverage than any factor other than language. It is the ability to mentalize that makes communication by language possible (Frith 2007). In speaking to you or in writing a sentence I aim to influence your mental state; for example, by inserting an idea. If this is the aim of language, then I must be able to realize that you have ideas in the same way as I do. In other words, I must be able to reflect on my own mental states and infer that you have similar mental states.

Imaging studies reveal activation in the paracingulate cortex whether I reflect on my own characteristics or on your's (Ochsner *et al.* 2005; Amodio and Frith 2006; Northoff *et al.* 2006). So does this suggest the operation of a mirror neuronal system? The answer is no, if one takes the strict line that mirror neurones are confined to the motor system (Jacob and Jeannerod 2005). But one can generalize the hypothesis to ask if the same cells are active when I reflect on my mental states and on yours.

The problem is that both simulation theory (Gallese and Goldman 1998) and theory–theory (Gopnik and Meltzoff 1997) predict that there is a relation between mechanisms for understanding my own mind and understanding your mind. Simulation theory suggests that I understand your mind by simulating your behaviour, and then reading off my own mental states. Theory–theory suggests that I come to understand and predict your mental states in the same way that I come to understand and predict physical events in the world, i.e. I form theories.

It may not be possible to distinguish empirically between these two hypotheses. The reason is that the only way that I can come to form theories about mental states is through experience of my own mental states and observations of others. So both hypotheses suppose that, in reading your mental states, I refer to my own mental states. Thus, in either case, the same cells might be involved in reflecting on my own mental states and reflecting on those of others. The only difference is that on simulation theory, the simulation occurs on line.

Whichever account is correct, we need to establish what changes occurred in the brain during human evolution that made it possible for humans to mentalize. One lead is provided by the syndrome of autism in which these mechanisms have been impaired. The suggestion is that, since autism is a genetic disorder (Rutter 2000), it may provide clues as to the genetic and neural changes that occurred during the evolution of the hominids. The analogy is with the KE family, where the FoxP2 gene may be one of the genes that changed during the evolution of speech.

The story of the FoxP2 gene is now well-developed (Chapter 5), but this is not currently the case for autism. First, candidate genes have been proposed on several chromosomes, such as 2q (Bacchelli *et al.* 2003), 7q (Bonora *et al.* 2005) and 16p (Barnby *et al.* 2005) but, as so often in such studies, the results are not always replicable (Blasi *et al.* 2006). There are three reasons. One is that we do not have reliable methods for measuring the symptoms (Todd 2005). Another is that the sample sizes may not have been sufficient. In the more recent report by the Autism Genome Project Consortium (Consortium 2007), 1168 families were included, and the data pointed to chromosomes 11 and 15. The final reason is that autism is not a unitary syndrome and different genes may be responsible for different symptoms (Happe *et al.* 2006).

There is a second difference from the FoxP2 story. We know something of the evolution of the FoxP2 gene (Enard *et al.* 2002; Zhang *et al.* 2002; Scharff and Haesler 2005). But we know nothing of the evolution of candidate genes for autism.

Finally, while the pattern of neurological impairment is well-described for the KE family (Watkins *et al.* 2002*b*; Belton *et al.* 2003), this is not yet true for autism. There have been four studies of the brains of subjects with autism that have used automated procedures, but the results differ between the studies (Abell *et al.* 1999; Kwon *et al.* 2004; Waiter *et al.* 2004; Salmond *et al.* 2005). This could, of course, be due in part to differences between the groups of subject that were studied. Subjects with autism have impairments in language and cognition, whereas in subjects with Asperger's syndrome the impairment is confined to one of social understanding. There have been two studies of subjects with Asperger's syndrome, and both identified a decrease in grey matter in the paracingulate and anterior cingulate cortex (Abell *et al.* 1999; Kwon *et al.* 2004).

There are several reports of decreased activity in medial frontal cortex in subjects with autism. Hazlett *et al.* (2004) report less activation in the anterior cingulate and paracingulate cortex while the subjects performed a verbal memory task. Ohnishi *et al.* (2000) scanned subjects at rest and found that the greater the impairment in social interaction, the less the activity at rest in the paracingulate cortex. As already mentioned in Chapter 7, activity at rest in the medial cortex is thought to be associated with self-reflective thoughts (Gusnard *et al.* 2001). When the subjects are given a task to perform, this medial activity decreases. Kennedy *et al.* (2006) have reported a lack of this deactivation in subjects with autism, the implication being that the medial cortex was not activated at rest.

However, perhaps the most significant finding comes from a study by Chiu *et al.* (2008). They scanned subjects with Asperger's syndrome while they took part in an iterated trust game. First the investor proposes an amount of money to invest, and then after this amount has increased in value, the trustee decides how much to repay the investor. Normally, when the investor makes their proposal, there is activity in the anterior cingular cortex, so long as the game is played with another responsive human partner. But that activity was lacking in the subjects with Asperger's syndrome. It was as if they were not playing with a human partner. Frith and Frith (2008) suggest that the implication is that these subjects failed to realize that their proposal would have an effect on their reputation in the eyes of another person.

Apart from evidence from activation studies, there is also data from structural studies. Hadjikhani *et al.* (2005) used an automated procedure to measure cortical thickness and included subjects with autism and Asperger's syndrome. They report very widespread decreases in cortical thickness. These included areas in which there are mirror neurones, the inferior parietal cortex and Broca's area 44, and areas involved in social cognition, such as the anterior cingulate cortex and paracingulate cortex. However, there are two reservations. First, the decreases included many more areas than these. Second, the authors did not analyse the data separately for the four subjects with Asperger's syndrome. The prediction would be that the decreases in cortical thickness would much more focal.

Microstructural differences can only be examined in post-mortem brains. Casanova *et al.* (2002*b*) were able to study the brains of nine autistic subjects and controls. They analysed data for the lateral prefrontal cortex, Tpt and inferotemporal cortex (area 21), and report that, in the autistic subjects, the mini-columns were smaller than normal. They made the same measurements in the brains of two subjects with Asperger's syndrome, and report the same findings (Casanova *et al.* 2002*a*). Later studies by Casanova *et al.* (2006) and Buxhoeveden *et al.* (2006) have shown that this is true of other areas as well. The latter authors examined the mesial frontal cortex and found a non-significant tendency in the same direction as the lateral frontal cortex; but they do not specify from where the medial sections were taken.

There is no doubt that there are widespread abnormalities in microstructure and connectivity in the brains of subjects with autism (Bailey *et al.* 1998; Courchesne *et al.* 2004; Courchesne and Pierce 2005). But then the symptoms of autism are also widespread, including often severe linguistic and intellectual impairments. It is crucial that there now be studies specifically of subjects with Asperger's syndrome, since they tend to have a more specific disorder of social cognition (Abell *et al.* 1999).

In searching for the specializations of the human brain, it is appropriate that we end on social cognition. An important mark of our humanity is that we can reflect on our own mental states and on those of others. Indeed, the aim of the book was to understand ourselves. The next and final chapter will judge how far we have come.

Chapter 10

Conclusions

This book set out to explain the mental gap between humans and their nearest relatives. The human mind can be briefly characterized by saying that humans can speak and rapidly acquire language, are able to deliberate and plan for the distant future, can reason, can reflect on their own mental states and those of others, and can engage in shared intention. So how well have we done in accounting for these abilities?

Brain size

Let us start with the fact that stares us in the face (see front cover). The human brain is over 3.5 times as big as would be predicted for an ape our size (MacLeod *et al.* 2003). To provide a scale, in Chapter 2 we compared the size of the brain to the size of the medulla in the brainstem. The gap between humans and chimpanzees turns out to be larger than the gap between chimpanzees and shrews.

When considering the human brain, the functional importance of brain size is sometimes downgraded because it is assumed that differences in brain size could not produce qualitative differences in function. There are two responses. The first was introduced in Chapter 2. It is that we are less likely to use the same argument when we consider animals. For example, chimpanzees are not clever shrews. Of course, there are many other differences between the brains of chimpanzees and shrews, but in this case we are less likely to discount the importance of size.

The second response is that many of the differences between humans and chimpanzees are actually quantitative. Chapter 1 looked for differences in the abilities of humans and chimpanzees. It is true that some abilities were unique to humans but, in other cases, the differences were quantitative. It was pointed out, for example, that quantitative differences on an IQ scale can produce differences between individuals that one might otherwise wish to describe as qualitative. Enculturated chimpanzees can sometimes do very badly what children do very well indeed.

Brain proportions

Comparisons of overall size conceal differences in brain proportions. For example, the brain is much bigger in the chimpanzee than the bushbaby, but the neocortex together with the white matter forms 76% of the brain in the chimpanzee but only 49% of the brain in a dwarf bushbaby (*Galago demidovii*). Selection pressures towards bigger brains have affected some areas of the brain more than others. It is not just the overall number of cells and interconnections that matter, it also matters where they are.

So what of the proportions in the human brain? First, there has been expansion, in particular, of the neocortex. The neocortex is 35% larger in the human brain than predicted for a monkey or ape with as large a neocortex (Rilling and Insel 1999). This is equivalent to an extra 254 cc. This suggests a positive selection pressure for the neocortex in the human brain. Within this region, the most obvious difference is that the prefrontal cortex forms 28% of the neocortex in the human brain but only 16.9% in the chimpanzee brain (Brodmann 1913). Chapter 2 discussed the controversy over the size of the prefrontal cortex in humans, but concluded by accepting these data. The main reason is that Semendeferi *et al.* (2001) have carried out a much more recent cyto-architectural study, and they report that a similar proportionate difference for the frontal polar area 10.

There are no comparative data on the parietal and temporal association areas as measured by cyto-architecture. We only have data for the parietal and occipital cortex as a whole (Semendeferi and Damasio 2000) and the superior temporal cortex and temporal lobe as a whole (Rilling and Seligman 2002). Chapter 3 pointed out that the middle and inferior temporal gyrus is roughly four times as large in the human as in the chimpanzee brain (Rilling and Seligman 2002). Yet, the amount of information that enters through the eye is little different in the two species. The consequence of the difference in size is a much more sophisticated analysis of that information. Similarly, Chapter 4 pointed out that the parietal and occipital lobe is 4.3 times as large in the human compared with the chimpanzee brain (Semendeferi and Damasio 2000). Yet, the difference between the size of the arm in the two species is very much less than that. The effect is to allow the skill required in tool use.

The prefrontal cortex does not receive inputs directly from the periphery or send connections to the pyramidal tract. Rather, as emphasized in Chapter 7, the information that it receives is already highly processed, such that it sits at the top of the sensory hierarchy. It also lies at the top of the motor hierarchy. The larger the prefrontal cortex for any body size, the more the information that can be taken into account in deciding on and planning the appropriate action. Chapters 7 and 8 reviewed the evidence that there is activation in the frontal polar cortex, in particular, during planning and reasoning; and the medial frontal polar cortex is especially activated when subjects set themselves goals and hold on to their intentions (Haynes *et al.* 2007).

It is unfortunate that we have no quantitative measures of the size of the paracingulate area 32 and anterior cingulate area 24 in the human brain. Chapter 9 reviewed the extensive evidence that there is activation in the paracingulate cortex, both when humans reflect on themselves and reflect on the mental states of others. So it is of particular importance that measurements should now be taken from the MRI scans that already exist for the brains of humans and other primates.

Microstructure

The effects of brain size

Differences in size have consequences for microstructure. Of these the most dramatic concerns the dendrites of pyramidal cells and the number of spines on them. There is a systematic difference between these in different areas. For example, there is an increase in the size of the dendritic tree of layer III pyramidal neurones, the higher one ascends the hierarchy within the ventral visual system (Elston and Rosa 1998). Of particular interest is that there are many more spines on these cells in the prefrontal than in the temporal cortex in both the human and macaque brain (Elston *et al.* 2001). This supports the notion that the prefrontal cortex is specialized for integrating information (Chapter 7).

However, the most critical finding is that the prefrontal pyramidal cells of the human brain have a greater peak branching complexity and are 70% more spinous than in any of the species of monkey that has been examined (Elston *et al.* 2001, 2006; Elston 2007). However, this difference appears to correlate with the difference in the size of the prefrontal cortex. Using Brodmann's (1913) data for the area of the prefrontal cortex, Elston *et al.* (2006; Elston 2007) calculate that the number of spines in the human prefrontal cortex is as predicted for a monkey with as large a prefrontal cortex.

The implication of this finding is that one cannot separate issues of size from issues of microstructure. It is naïve to think that we have to choose between them. What is special about the human brain is not just the total number of cells but also the number of cells in particular areas and the ways in which they are connected.

Language areas

But there are also specializations of the human brain that cannot be related to issues of size. Chapter 6 reviewed the evidence that there are microstructural differences between the left and right hemisphere. For obvious reasons, studies have concentrated on the language areas. Within Wernicke's area, the mini-column width and neuropil space are larger on the left than the right, with differences of the order of 14–17% (Buxhoeveden and Casanova 2002). There are also more magnopyramidal cells in the left than the right superior temporal cortex in the human brain (Hutsler 2003). Within Broca's area, the density of cells is usually higher on the left than the right (Amunts *et al.* 1999), and there are more very large pyramidal cells on the left than the right (Hayes and Lewis 1996).

Comparisons are now needed with the brains of chimpanzees. We already know that there are no differences between the mini-column width in Tpt on the left compared with the right (Buxhoeveden and Casanova 2002). It is highly likely that the other microstructural asymmetries will also turn out to be unique to the human brain.

In other words, it is plausible that they are related to the human specialization for language. This claim should now be tested by carrying out further comparative studies.

It is frustrating that we have no information on the microstructure of Broca's area and Wernicke's area in the brains of the affected members of the KE family. But then we have no information either about microstructural differences between area X or the hyperstriatum ventrale caudale in song birds and other birds. Further progress can be made by studying the expression of FoxP2 in song birds and its operation as a transcription factor during development (Scharff and Haesler 2005). This is not to say that the FOXP2 gene is the sole solution to the question as to how the human brain came to be specialized for speech and language. Children with a mutation in the FOXP2 gene still speak and learn language; it is just that their articulation is poor, their sentences are simplified and there is a developmental delay (Watkins *et al.* 2002*a*). Many other genes are involved in building the microstructure of the language areas, and it is early days.

Paracingulate cortex

We know even less about the neural basis for our ability to reflect on our own mental states and those of others. It is true that children with autism often fail tests of theory of mind, including the Sally Anne task (Grant *et al.* 2001), but they also typically have intellectual and language impairments. That is why it is more relevant to look at the brains of subjects with Asperger's syndrome, who have a more isolated impairment in social cognition. In particular, they are usually impaired at second-order theory of mind (Abell *et al.* 1999).

Further study of individuals with Asperger's syndrome might therefore provide us with a lead as to the neural specializations in the human brain that allow us to reflect on our own mental states and those of others. We know that, as in autism, there are abnormalities in the size of mini-columns and the dispersion of cells, but these are widespread, involving the frontal and temporal lobe (Casanova *et al.* 2002*a*). As yet we have no specific information about the microstructure of the paracingulate cortex. Studies should concentrate on this area because of the extensive evidence that it is activated when subjects reflect on mental states (Amodio and Frith 2006).

Organization of the brain

The specialization of the human brain for speech and language has had a profound effect on the organization of the brain. Even outside the classic language areas, there is a specialization of the left hemisphere for the processing of verbal tasks, and this is true both for the temporal (Price 2004a) and frontal lobes (Owen et al. 1997; Price 2004b). This specialization relates to the performance of verbal operations (Stephan et al. 2003).

It is true that there is evidence for dominance for the discrimination of species-specific calls in macaque monkeys (Heffner and Heffner 1986). But, in their visual system, each hemisphere is specialized for processing inputs from the contralateral visual field and this is the case not only for the temporal lobe (Merigan and Saunders 2004) but also for the frontal lobe (Funahashi et al. 1993). The left and right hemispheres do not differ in terms of the material that they handle; in other words, there is extensive duplication of function. In general, the left and right hemispheres perform the same functions, but for different inputs.

But language brings a new form of representation, and for this the visual field is irrelevant. The left hemisphere has come to be specialized for semantic processing and the right for visuo-spatial processing. Chapter 6 argued that this is a more efficient use of space than duplicating both functions. Duplication would have required the brain to be larger yet, and there are constraints on the size that the brain can be at birth.

Expanding the mental gap

So far, the assumption has been that the mental gap is to be explained wholly terms of specializations of the human brain. But are these enough to account for the immense gap between humans and chimpanzees? Even an enculturated chimpanzee, such as Kanzi, cannot compete in mental capacity with a child of 2 years.

So there must be other factors that can 'ratchet-up' the difference. I take the term from Tomasello (1999). He points to the rapid pace of cultural change, as in the development of science. Compare, for example, the abilities of modern humans 30 000 years ago with the abilities of a trained scientist. Yet, there have been no changes that we know of in the anatomy of the brain during this time. This indicates that cultural transmission is a very potent factor in ratcheting-up the mental gap.

Teaching

Chapter 1 assessed the mental gap by comparing human children and adult chimpanzees; but the comparison is unfair. Human children are deliberately educated, initially by their parents and later by others, whereas chimpanzees in the wild are not. So there are two factors that differ between the species: brain anatomy and education.

The significance of education can be appreciated by looking at the achievements of the chimpanzee, Sarah. From the age of five and a half years until she was seven, Sarah was taught to use plastic symbols (Premack 1976). Then, for over ten years, she was educated three to four hours a day and for five days a week (Premack and Premack 1983). In this time she was set a very great variety of different cognitive problems.

Of what advantage, in terms of mental achievement, is such an education? We need tests that measure intellectual capacity, and one common form of IQ test is that typified by Raven's Matrices. This is a test of analogical reasoning. Chapters 8 has already mentioned that Sarah was set a series of tests along the same lines (Gillan *et al.* 1981). She was able to succeed on items such as 'lock is to key as tin is to?', where she had a choice between paint brush and tin opener. And she could succeed on novel problems given for one trial each.

Sarah has also been presented with many other types of problem, involving number, causality, conservation of mass, and other principles (Premack and Premack 1983). What is remarkable about her performance is that she seems to grasp abstract concepts very easily. On many problems she outclasses chimpanzees who have not had the advantage of a long education (Premack and Premack 1983). In other words, her education has taught her to think.

Sarah was taught by her human carers, but there are few if any accredited examples in which apes have been themselves observed to teach. In the wild there are a few instances in which chimpanzees can be said to provide the opportunity for learning (Boesch 1991), but active facilitation by mothers of the attempts by their offspring have not been observed (Lonsdorf 2006). In captivity, two examples have been reported that suggest active instruction. The first was reported by Fouts *et al.* (1989): the chimpanzee Washoe was seen to mould the hands of another chimpanzee into a sign. The second example comes from Patterson and Linden (1981) who taught the gorilla Koko to use sign language: she was also once observed moulding a sign for a human caretaker who had not learned sign language (Patterson and Linden 1981). In each case the chimpanzee was simply repeating the method that had been used to teach them signs.

Caro and Hauser (1992) have argued that the search for teaching in animals has been held back by using a narrow definition of teaching based on the way in which human adults teach children. They cite, for example, cases in the animal literature in which the behaviour of the young is encouraged or punished, and refer to this as 'coaching'. The point is well taken, but it is still true that humans do much more than this. The teacher deliberately arranges a series of tasks, starting with the simpler ones and building up to the more complex. As in Sarah's case, the more complex achievements are only possible because of this pro-grammed experience. The teacher also modifies the lesson according to how the subject is doing. Thus, the mental gap between humans and chimpanzees is further ratcheted up as result of education throughout childhood.

Teaching in a language

The way in which Sarah was taught is slow and cumbersome. If we wish to educate her in some new concept, we have to expose her to real cases in which that concept applies. Suppose that we wish to teach the mathematical concept of proportions, such as a half or a quarter. This has been done by Woodruff and Premack (1981). The procedure was to show Sarah half a glass of liquid, and then to see whether she appreciated that it was the same as a half a disc. With patience, it should prove possible to tutor such an animal in many concepts by showing it the various situations that exemplify the concepts. But this is not the way in which much of our own education proceeds. New concepts can be introduced by *definition*. We do not need to teach the concept of an eighth or a sixteenth by exposure to real instances of these proportions. A sixteenth can be defined as half of an eighth. The mathematical symbol 'x' is taught by defining it in language as a variable number.

Language is a very powerful tool for setting up conceptual distinctions. In Chapter 8 we have already referred to the work of Plunkett *et al.* (2007), who showed that labels can influence the way in which infants learn category boundaries. But language can do more than that. In asking 'why we are so smart?' both Genter (2003) and Spelke (2003) give a similar answer. They point to the ability of language to combine representations, formulate propositions and represent relations. Thus language provides us with a very powerful method for *teaching* an explicit understanding of concepts, states of affairs, and causal and logical relations. This further ratchets-up the mental gap.

Cultural transmission

There are two other effects of being taught in language. The first is that one can learn about facts and events that are at a *distance* both in space and time. Children learn both geographical and historical facts, whether these are taught informally or in formal education. So the child does not have to visit distant lands to learn about them.

The second effect is that knowledge *cumulates* over the generations. Each society, however small, has its traditions of knowledge that are passed on from one generation to the next. The cumulative effect can be seen both in technology and knowledge. For example, an individual in one generation invents some device and teaches the method to someone in the next generation by demonstration and explanation. That individual then further perfects the invention and so on through the generations. The same process occurs in the passing on of theoretical knowledge. Consider mathematics. Members of one generation do not have, for example, to re-invent calculus. Instead they start with the advantage of being taught it, and this allows further developments in mathematics across the generations. As Newton wrote in a letter to Robert Hooke, we stand on the shoulders of giants.

This is not to deny that chimpanzees can learn simple traditions of tool manufacture and use. Whiten (1999, 2000) describes 39 different behaviour patterns that are found in some chimpanzee communities but not others. These include not only the use or manufacture of tools but also the methods that they use to groom each other. Local repertoires are also described for orang-utans, and these cannot be explained simply by differences between the various habitats (van Schaik *et al.* 2003).

To prove that these could indeed be traditions, Whiten *et al.* (2005) taught two female chimpanzees, from different captive groups, how to operate a mechanism to obtain food. There were two methods, 'poking' and 'lifting', and one female was taught one method and the other female the other. When they were reintroduced to their respective groups, others in the group learned how to operate the apparatus, and there was a very strong tendency for them to use the method that their female had been taught. So, in this case, it is fair to use the term 'cultural tradition'.

But there is a crucial difference from human cultural traditions. As we have emphasized, these are cumulative. Yet this does not seem to be true of the cultural traditions of chimpanzees (Whiten 2005). In other words, there is little evidence of improvement in the technologies over the generations. The only example that Whiten (2005) could provide is the introduction of prop stones to stabilize stone anvils for cracking nuts.

Human culture differs in that each generation can build on the discoveries of previous generations. Thus, we cannot divorce the human mind from the cultural context in which children and adults live. It is this that leads Tomasello (1999) to talk of 'the cultural origins of human cognition'.

Summary

It is time to sum up. I have ten suggestions as to how one can account for the mental gap between humans and our nearest animal relatives.

1. I start with the vast gap opened up by the difference in brain size between humans and chimpanzees. This is widely acknowledged, but there has been a tendency to downplay its effect. The difference in relative size between the human and chimpanzee brain is larger than the difference between the brains of the chimpanzee and shrew.

2. Next, the brain does not simply balloon as it increases in size. There can be marked differences in the proportions of the different parts of the brain, in brains of different size. For example, the neocortex forms 76% of the brain in a chimpanzee but only 12% in a shrew. The human neocortex is 35% larger than predicted from data on monkeys and apes. The human prefrontal cortex forms 28.5% of the neocortex, whereas the figure for the chimpanzee is just 16.9%. The result is that humans can imagine at will, set their own goals and monitor their progress towards them.

3. The expansion of the human prefrontal cortex correlates with an increase in the peak branching complexity and number of spines on pyramidal cells. This has important consequences for the integration of information.

4. The human brain has specializations for speech and language. First, the larynx area projects directly to the motor-neurones. Then there are microstructural specializations in the left Wernicke's and Broca's areas. Just as some birds are specialized as song learners, so humans are specialized as primates that speak. This probably involves an auditory/vocal mirror neuronal system as in song birds. The KE family provides an entrée into understanding how the relevant genes influence the development of the brain.

5. Communication by speech depends on the ability to understand the effect of what one says on the thoughts of others. In other words, it requires the ability to mentalize and thus share thoughts. The

ability to do this depends on the ability to reflect on one's own thoughts. The genetic disorder of Asperger's syndrome shows that the mechanisms for mentalizing can be selectively disrupted. Here the example of KE family encourages further research on this disorder, and in particular on the microstructure of the paracingulate cortex.

6. As the result of the development of language, the human neocortex has been fundamentally reorganized. In other primates, the two hemispheres duplicate functions, but for one side of space. In the human brain, the development of language has led to left-hemisphere specialization for phonological, semantic and grammatical processing, and right-hemisphere specialization for visuo-spatial processing. There is less duplication of function, and thus an increase in efficiency.

7. The mental gap is further ratcheted-up by the remaining four factors. First, children are taught. Education involves a directed and organized series of tasks, starting with the simpler and building up to the more complex. At the same time the teacher monitors progress and supplies feedback. This is true whether one is referring to an apprenticeship or formal education, and whether one is referring to learning the skills of a hunter gatherer or the skills of a scientist.

8. Children are taught in a language. This means that they do not have to be faced with concrete examples of everything that they are to learn. They can simply be told about situations and events that are distant in space and time.

9. The effect is to allow rapid cultural transmission and rapid change by the cumulative effect of the cultural variants that are successful. One has only to think of the change in technology and society that has occurred in the last 30 000 years. During this time there has been, as far as we know, no change in the human brain. Yet the mental gap between humans and apes has widened out of all proportion during this time.

10. I bet on a final effect of language, though the evidence is slight. This concerns the fact that we can become aware of our thoughts via the phonological loop. The bet is that this provides a more efficient system than visual imagery for engaging in mental trial and error, planning for the distant future and considering causal relations. Having tried, throughout this book, to be careful to back up what I say, I am allowed this one speculation.

So is that all? It is appropriate to finish with a touch of humility. Neuroscience is in its infancy, and we know very little even of how a monkey brain supports monkey cognition. Given this ignorance, it would be foolish to think that we have all the answers for human cognition. It is one of the joys of science that further research always overturns complacency.

But I take comfort from a book written on 'Consciousness' by a former colleague, Jeffrey Gray (2005). He gave his book the delightful subtitle 'Creeping up on the hard problem'. It is no less tough to find the key to humanity. But in the spirit of cultural tradition, I hope that others will now be able to creep further.

References

Abell, F., Krams, M., Ashburner, J., Passingham, R., Friston, K., Frackowiak, R., Happe, F., Frith, C. and Frith, U. (1999). The neuroanatomy of autism: a voxel-based whole brain analysis of structural scans. *Neuroreport.* **10,** 1647–1651.

Adcock, J. E., Wise, R. G., Oxbury, J. M., Oxbury, S. M. and Matthews, P. M. (2003). Quantitative fMRI assessment of the differences in lateralization of language-related brain activation in patients with temporal lobe epilepsy. *Neuroimage.* **18,** 423–438.

Addis, D. R., Wong, A. T. and Schacter, D. L. (2007). Remembering the past and imagining the future: common and distinct neural substrates during event construction and elaboration. *Neuropsychologia.* **45,** 1363–1377.

Adolphs, R., Tranel, D. and Damasio, A. R. (1998). The human amygdala in social judgment. *Nature.* **393,** 470–474.

Aitken, M. R., Larkin, M. J. and Dickinson, A. (2000). Super-learning of causal judgements. *Q J Exp Psychol B.* **53,** 59–81.

Alcock, K. J., Passingham, R. E., Watkins, K. E. and Vargha-Khadem, F. (2000). Oral dyspraxia in inherited speech and language impairment and acquired dysphasia. *Brain Lang.* **75,** 17–33.

Alexander, M. P., Benson, D. F. and Stuss, D. T. (1989). Frontal lobes and language. *Brain Lang.* **37,** 656–691.

Alexander, M. P., Naeser, M. A. and Palumbo, C. (1990). Broca's area aphasias: aphasia after lesions including the frontal operculum. *Neurology.* **40,** 353–362.

Allman, J. M. and Kaas, J. H. (1971). A representation of the visual field in the caudal third of the middle temporal gyrus of the owl monkey (*Aotus trivirgatus*). *Brain Res.* **31,** 85–105.

Allman, J., Hakeem, A. and Watson, K. (2002). Two phylogenetic specializations in the human brain. Neuroscientist. **8,** 335–346.

Allman, J. M., Watson, K. K., Tetreault, N. A. and Hakeem, A. Y. (2005). Intuition and autism: a possible role for Von Economo neurons. *Trends Cogn Sci.* **9,** 367–373.

Allport, A. (1983). Langauge and cognition. In: Harris, R. (ed.), *Approaches to Language*, vol.4. Pergamon, Oxford, pp. 61–94.

Amodio, D. M. and Frith, C. D. (2006). Meeting of minds: the medial frontal cortex and social cognition. *Nat Rev Neurosci.* **7,** 268–277.

Amunts, K., Schleicher, A., Burgel, U., Mohlberg, H., Uylings, H. B. M. and Zilles, K. (1999). Broca's region revisited: cytoarchitecture and intersubject variability. *J Comp Neurol.* **412,** 319–341.

Amunts, K., Schleicher, A., Ditterich, A. and **Zilles, K.** (2003). Broca's region: cytoarchitectonic asymmetry and developmental changes. *J Comp Neurol.* **465**, 72–89.

Amunts, K., Schleicher, A. and **Zilles, K.** (2007). Cytoarchitecture of the cerebral cortex—more than localization. *Neuroimage.* **37**, 1061–1065.

Anderson, B., Southern, B. D. and **Powers, R. E.** (1999*a*). Anatomic asymmetries of the posterior superior temporal lobes: a postmortem study. *Neuropsychiatry Neuropsychol Behav Neurol.* **12**, 247–254.

Anderson, S. W., Bechara, A., Damasio, H., Tranel, d. and **Damasio, A. R.** (1999*b*). Impairment of social and moral behavior related to early damage in human prefrontal cortex. *Nature Neuroscience.* **2**, 1032–1037.

Annett, M. (2004). Hand preference observed in large healthy samples: classification, norms and interpretations of increased non-right-handedness by the right shift theory. *Br J Psychol.* **95**, 339–353.

Anwander, A., Tittgemeyer, M., von Cramon, D. Y., Friederici, A. D. and **Knosche, T. R.** (2006). Connectivity-Based Parcellation of Broca's Area. *Cerebral Cortex.*

Arbib, M. A. (2005). From monkey-like action recognition to human language: an evolutionary framework for neurolinguistics. *Behavioral and Brain Sciences.* **28**, 105–124; discussion 125–167.

Armand, J. (1984. [The pyramidal tract. Recent anatomic and physiologic findings]. *Rev Neurol (Paris).* **140**, 309–329.

Avants, B. B., Schoenemann, P. T. and **Gee, J. C.** (2006). Lagrangian frame diffeomorphic image registration: morphometric comparison of human and chimpanzee cortex. *Med Image Anal.* **10**, 397–412.

Baars, B. J. (2002). The conscious access hypothesis: origins and recent evidence. *Trends Cogn Sci.* **6**, 47–52.

Baars, B. J. and **Franklin, S.** (2003). How conscious experience and working memory interact. *Trends Cogn Sci.* **7**, 166–172.

Bacchelli, E., Blasi, F., Biondolillo, M., Lamb, J. A., Bonora, E., Barnby, G., Parr, J., Beyer, K. S., Klauck, S. M., Poustka, A., Bailey, A. J., Monaco, A. P. and **Maestrini, E.** (2003). Screening of nine candidate genes for autism on chromosome 2q reveals rare nonsynonymous variants in the cAMP-GEFII gene. *Mol Psychiatry.* **8**, 916–924.

Baciu, M. V., Watson, J. M., Maccotta, L., McDermott, K. B., Buckner, R. L., Gilliam, F. G. and **Ojemann, J. G.** (2005). Evaluating functional MRI procedures for assessing hemispheric language dominance in neurosurgical patients. *Neuroradiology.* **47**, 835–844.

Baddeley, A. (1986). *Working Memory.* Oxford University Press, Oxford.

Baddeley, A. (2003). Working memory: looking back and looking forward. *Nat Rev Neurosci.* **4**, 829–839.

Baddeley, A. D. and **Hitch, G.** (1974). Working memory. In: Bower, G. H. (ed.), *The Psychology of Learning and Motivation*, vol.8. Academic Press, New York, pp. 47–90.

Bailey, P., von Bonin, G. and McCullogh, W. S. (1950). The Isocortex of the Chimpanzee. University of Illinois Press, Urbana.

Bailey, A., Luthert, P., Dean, A., Harding, B., Janota, I., Montgomery, M., Rutter, M. and Lantos, P. (1998). A clinicopathological study of autism. *Brain.* 121, (Pt 5), 889–905.

Baizer, J. S., Ungerleider, L. G. and Desimone, R. (1991). Organization of visual inputs to the inferior temporal and posterior parietal cortex in macaques. *J Neurosci.* 11, 168–190.

Baker, S. C., Rogers, R. D., Owen, A. M., Frith, C. D., Dolan, R. J., Frackowiak, R. S. J. and Robbins, T. W. (1996. Neural systems engaged by planning: a PET study of the Tower of London task. *Neuropsychologia.* 34, 515–526.

Bandura, A. (1989). Self-regulation of motivation and actioin through internal standards and goals systems. In: Pervin, L. A. (ed.), *Goal Concepts in Personality and Social Psychology.* Erlbaum, Hillsdale, pp. 19–85.

Barbas, H. (2000). Connections underlying the synthesis of cognition, memory, and emotion in primate prefrontal cortices. *Brain Res Bull.* 52, 319–330.

Barnby, G., Abbott, A., Sykes, N., Morris, A., Weeks, D. E., Mott, R., Lamb, J., Bailey, A. J. and Monaco, A. P. (2005). Candidate-gene screening and association analysis at the autism-susceptibility locus on chromosome 16p: evidence of association at GRIN2A and ABAT. *Am J Hum Genet.* 76, 950–966.

Baron-Cohen, S. (1995). *Mindblindness: an Essay on Autism and Theory of Mind.* MIT press, Cambridge.

Baron-Cohen, S., Leslie, A. M. and Frith, U. (1985). Does the autistic child have a 'theory of mind'? *Cognition.* 21, 37–46.

Barraclough, D. J., Conroy, M. L. and Lee, D. (2004). Prefrontal cortex and decision making in a mixed-strategy game. *Nat Neurosci.* 7, 404–410.

Bartels, A. and Zeki, S. (2000). The architecture of the colour centre in the human visual brain: new results and a review. *EurJ Neurosci.* 12, 172–193.

Barton, R. A. (2007). Mosaic evolution of brain structure in mammals. In: Kaas, J. and Krubitzer, L. (ed.), *Evolutioin of Nervous Systems: a Comprehensive Reference,* vol.3. Elsevier, New York, pp. 97–102.

Barton, R. A. and Harvey, P. H. (2000). Mosaic evolution of brain structure in mammals. *Nature.* 405, 1055–1058.

Bates, E. and Elman, J. (1996). Learning rediscovered. *Science.* 274, 1849–1850.

Bechara, A., Damasio, H. and Damasio, A. R. (2000). Emotion, decision making and the orbitofrontal cortex. *Cerebral Cortex.* 10, 295–307.

Beecher, M. D., Petersen, M. R., Zoloth, S. R., Moody, D. B. and Stebbins, W. C. (1979). Perception of conspecific vocalizations by Japanese macaques. Evidence for selective attention and neural lateralization. *Brain Behav Evol.* 16, 443–460.

Belton, E., Salmond, C. H., Watkins, K. E., Vargha-Khadem, F. and Gadian, D. G. (2003). Bilateral brain abnormalities associated with dominantly inherited verbal and orofacial dyspraxia. *Hum Brain Mapp.* 18, 194–200.

Bengtsson, S. L., Ehrsson, H. H., Forssberg, H. and Ullen, F. (2004). Dissociating brain regions controlling the temporal and ordinal structure of learned movement sequences. *EurJ Neurosci.* **19**, 2591–2602.

Bengtsson, S. L., Nagy, Z., Skare, S., Forsman, L., Forssberg, H. and Ullen, F. (2005). Extensive piano practicing has regionally specific effects on white matter development. *Nat Neurosci.* **8**, 1148–1150.

Bengtsson, S. L. and Ullen, F. (2006). Dissociation between melodic and rhythmic processing during piano performance from musical scores. *Neuroimage.* **30**, 272–284.

Bengtsson, S. L., Csikszentmihalyi, M. and Ullen, F. (2007). Cortical regions involved in the generation of musical structures during improvisation in pianists. *J Cogn Neurosci.* **19**, 830–842.

Bengtsson, S. L., Lau, H. C. and Passingham, R. E., submitted. Motivation to do well enhances responses to errors and self-monitoring. *Cer. Cort.*

Beninger, R. J., Kendall, S. B. and Vanderwolf, C. H. (1974). The ability of rats to discriminate their own behaviors. *Canad J Psychol.* **28**, 79–91.

Berthoz, S., Grezes, J., Armony, J. L., Passingham, R. E. and Dolan, R. J. (2006). Affective response to one's own moral violations. *Neuroimage.* **31**, 945–950.

Bhatt, R. S., Wasserman, E. A., W.F., R. and Knauss, K. S. (1988). Conceptual behavior in pigeons: categorization of both familiar and novel examples from four classes of natural categories. *J Exp Psychol: Anim Beh Process.* **14**, 219–234.

Binder, J. R., Swanson, S. J., Hammeke, T. A., Morris, G. L., Mueller, W. M., Fischer, M., Benbadis, S., Frost, J. A., Rao, S. M. and Haughton, V. M. (1996). Determination of language dominance using functional MRI: a comparison with the Wada test. *Neurology.* **46**, 978–984.

Binder, J. R., Frost, J. A., Hammeke, T. A., Bellgowan, P. S., Springer, J. A., Kaufman, J. N. and Possing, E. T. (2000). Human temporal lobe activation by speech and nonspeech sounds. *Cerebral Cortex.* **10**, 512–528.

Blaisdell, A. P., Sawa, K., Leising, K. J. and Waldmann, M. R. (2006). Causal reasoning in rats. *Science.* **311**, 1020–1022.

Blake, R. and Logothetis, N. K. (2002). Visual competition. *Nat Rev Neurosci.* **3**, 13–21.

Blasi, F., Bacchelli, E., Carone, S., Toma, C., Monaco, A. P., Bailey, A. J. and Maestrini, E. (2006). SLC25A12 and CMYA3 gene variants are not associated with autism in the IMGSAC multiplex family sample. *Eur J Hum Genet.* **14**, 123–126.

Bloom, P. (2000). *How Children Learn the Meaning of Words.* MIT Press, Cambridge.

Boesch, C. (1991). Teaching in wild chimpanzees. *Anim Behav.* **41**, 530–532.

Bond, J., Scott, S., Hampshire, D. J., Springell, K., Corry, P., Abramowicz, M. J., Mochida, G. H., Hennekam, R. C., Maher, E. R., Fryns, J. P., Alswaid, A., Jafri, H., Rashid, Y., Mubaidin, A., Walsh, C. A., Roberts, E. and Woods, C. G. (2003). Protein-truncating mutations in ASPM cause variable reduction in brain size. *Am J Hum Genet.* **73**, 1170–1177.

Bonora, E., Lamb, J. A., Barnby, G., Sykes, N., Moberly, T., Beyer, K. S., Klauck, S. M., Poustka, F., Bacchelli, E., Blasi, F., Maestrini, E., Battaglia, A., Haracopos, D., Pedersen, L., Isager, T., Eriksen, G., Viskum, B., Sorensen, E. U., Brondum-Nielsen, K., Cotterill, R., Engeland, H., Jonge, M., Kemner, C., Steggehuis, K., Scherpenisse, M., Rutter, M., Bolton, P. F., Parr, J. R., Poustka, A., Bailey, A. J. and Monaco, A. P. (2005). Mutation screening and association analysis of six candidate genes for autism on chromosome 7q. *Eur J Hum Genet.* **13**, 198–207.

Booth, J. R., Burman, D. D., Meyer, J. R., Gitelman, D. R., Parrish, T. B. and Mesulam, M. M. (2002). Modality independence of word comprehension. *Hum Brain Mapp.* **16**, 251–261.

Bottini, G., Cappa, S. F. and Vignolo, L. A. (1991). Somesthetic-visual matching disorders in right and left hemisphere-damaged patients. *Cortex.* **27**, 223–228.

Botvinick, M. and Cohen, J. (1998). Rubber hands 'feel' touch that eyes see. *Nature.* **391**, 756.

Botvinick, M., Jha, A. P., Bylsma, L. M., Fabian, S. A., Solomon, P. E. and Prkachin, K. M. (2005). Viewing facial expressions of pain engages cortical areas involved in the direct experience of pain. *Neuroimage.* **25**, 312–319.

Boysen, S. T. and Berntson, G. G. (1989. Numerical competence in a chimpanzee (*Pan troglodytes*). *J Comp Psychol.* **103**, 23–31.

Boysen, S. T., Berntson, G. G., Shreyer, T. A. and Hannan, M. B. (1995. Indicating acts during counting by a chimpanzee (*Pan troglodytes*). *J Comp Psychol.* **109**, 47–51.

Bozeat, S., Lambon Ralph, M. A., Patterson, K., Garrard, P. and Hodges, J. R. (2000). Non-verbal semantic impairment in semantic dementia. *Neuropsychologia.* **38**, 1207–1215.

Braine, M. D. S. (1998). Steps towards a mental predicate logic. In: Braine, M. D. S. and O'Brien, D. P. (ed.), *Mental Logic.* Erlbaum, Mahwah, pp. 273–331.

Brass, M. and Haggard, P. (2007). To do or not to do: the neural signature of self-control. *J Neurosci.* **27**, 9141–9145.

Bremmer, F., Schlack, A., Shah, N. J., Zafiris, O., Kubischik, M., Hoffmann, K., Zilles, K. and Fink, G. R. (2001). Polymodal motion processing in posterior parietal and premotor cortex: a human fMRI study strongly implies equivalencies between humans and monkeys. *Neuron.* **29**, 287–296.

Brewer, A. A., Press, W. A., Logothetis, N. K. and Wandell, B. A. (2002). Visual areas in macaque cortex measured using functional magnetic resonance imaging. *J Neurosci.* **22**, 10416–10426.

Brewer, A. A., Liu, J., Wade, A. R. and Wandell, B. A. (2005). Visual field maps and stimulus selectivity in human ventral occipital cortex. *Nat Neurosci.* **8**, 1102–1109.

Broca, P., (1861). Remarques sur le siege del la faculte du language articule, suives d'une observation d'aphasie. *Bulletin de la Societe Anatomique.* **6**, 330–357.

Brodmann, K. (1909). *Vergleichende Lokalisationlehre der Grosshirnrinde*. Barth, Leipzig.

Brodmann, K. (1912). Neue ergebnisse uber die verleichende histologische localisation der grosshirnrinde mit besonderer berucksichtigung des stirnhirns. *Anat Anz. spllp* **41**, 157–216.

Brodmann, K. (1913). Neue Forchungsergebnisse der Grosshirnrindeanatomische mit besonderer Berucksichtung anthropologischer Fragen. *Gesselch Deuts Naturf Artze*. **85**, 200–240.

Brodmann, K. (1925). *Vergleichende Localisationslehre der Grosshirnrinde*. Barth, Leipzig.

Brunet, E., Sarfati, Y., Hardy-Bayle, M. C. and **Decety, J.** (2000). A PET investigation of the attribution of intentions with a nonverbal task. *Neuroimage*. **11**, 157–166.

Buccino, G., Binkofski, F., Fink, G. R., Fadiga, L., Fogassi, L., Gallcsc, V., Scitz, R. J., Zilles, K., Rizzolatti, G. and **Freund, H. J.** (2001). Action observation activates premotor and parietal areas in a somatotopic manner: an fMRI study. *EurJ Neurosci*. **13**, 400–404.

Buccino, G., Vogt, S., Ritzl, A., Fink, G. R., Zilles, K., Freund, H. J. and **Rizzolatti, G.** (2004). Neural circuits underlying imitation learning of hand actions: an event-related fMRI study. *Neuron*. **42**, 323–334.

Buckley, M. J. and **Gaffan, D.** (1998). Perirhinal cortex ablation impairs visual object identification. *J Neurosci*. **18**, 2268–2275.

Bunge, S. A., Wendelken, C., Badre, D. and **Wagner, A. D.** (2005). Analogical reasoning and prefrontal cortex: evidence for separable retrieval and integration mechanisms. *Cerebral Cortex*. **15**, 239–249.

Burgess, P., Scott, S. K. and **Frith, C.** (2003). The role of the rostral frontal cortex (area 10) in prospective memory: a lateral versus medial dissociation. *Neuropsychol*. **41**, 906–918.

Bussey, T., Wise, S. and **Marray, E.** (2001). The role of ventral and orbital prefrontal cortex in conditional visuomotor learning and strategy use in rhesus monkeys (*Macaca mulatta*). *Behav Neurosci*. **115**, 971–982.

Buxhoeveden, D. P., Switala, A. E., Litaker, M., Roy, E. and **Casanova, M. F.** (2001*a*). Lateralization of minicolumns in human planum temporale is absent in nonhuman primate cortex. *Brain Behav Evol*. **57**, 349–358.

Buxhoeveden, D. P., Switala, A. E., Roy, E., Litaker, M. and **Casanova, M. F.** (2001*b*). Morphological differences between minicolumns in human and nonhuman primate cortex. *Am J Phys Anthropol*. **115**, 361–371.

Buxhoeveden, D. P. and **Casanova, M. F.** (2002). The minicolumn and evolution of the brain. *Brain Behav Evol*. **60**, 125–151.

Buxhoeveden, D. P., Semendeferi, K., Buckwalter, J., Schenker, N., Switzer, R. and **Courchesne, E.** (2006). Reduced minicolumns in the frontal cortex of patients with autism. *Neuropathol Appl Neurobiol*. **32**, 483–491.

Cajal, R. (1917. *Recuerdos de mi Vida: Histoire de mi Labour Cientifica Madrid, Moya*. Moya, Madrid.

Calder, A. J., Keane, J., Manes, F., Antoun, N. and **Young, A. W.** (2000). Impaired recognition and experience of disgust following brain injury. *Nat Neurosci.* **3**, 1077–1078.

Call, J. and **Tomasello, M.** (1998). Distinguishing intentional from accidental actions in orangutans (*Pongo pygmaeus*), chimpanzees (*Pan troglodytes*), and human children (*Homo sapiens*). *J Comp Psychol.* **112**, 192–206.

Call, J. and **Tomasello, M.** (1999). A nonverbal false belief task: the performance of children and great apes. *Child Development.* **70**, 381–395.

Call, J., Hare, B., Carpenter, M. and **Tomasello, M.** (2004). 'Unwilling' versus 'unable': chimpanzees' understanding of human intentional action. *Dev Sci.* **7**, 488–498.

Call, J., Carpenter, M. and **Tomasello, M.** (2005). Copying results and copying actions in the process of social learning: chimpanzees (*Pan troglodytes*) and human children (*Homo sapiens*). *Anim Cogn.* **8**, 151–163.

Callan, A. M., Callan, D. E. and **Masaki, S.** (2005). When meaningless symbols become letters: Neural activity change in learning new phonograms. *Neuroimage.* **28**, 553–562.

Calvo-Merino, B., Glaser, D. E., Grezes, J., Passingham, R. E. and **Haggard, P.** (2005). Action observation and acquired motor skills: an FMRI study with expert dancers. *Cerebral Cortex.* **15**, 1243–1249.

Calvo-Merino, B., Grezes, J., Glaser, D. E., Passingham, R. E. and **Haggard, P.** (2006). Seeing or doing? Influence of visual and motor familiarity in action observation. *Curr Biol.* **16**, 1905–1910.

Cantalupo, C. and **Hopkins, W. D.** (2001). Asymmetric Broca's area in great apes. *Nature.* **414**, 505.

Cantalupo, C., Pilcher, D. L. and **Hopkins, W. D.** (2003). Are planum temporale and sylvian fissure asymmetries directly related? A MRI study in great apes. *Neuropsychologia.* **41**, 1975–1981.

Caplan, D., Alpert, N., Waters, G. and **Olivieri, A.** (2000). Activation of Broca's area by syntactic processing under conditions of concurrent articulation. *Hum Brain Mapp.* **9**, 65–71.

Carlson, S. M. and **Moses, L. J.** (2001). Individual differences in inhibitory control and children's theory of mind. *Child Development.* **72**, 1032–1053.

Caro, T. M. and **Hauser, M. D.** (1992). Is there teaching in nonhuman animals? *Q Rev Biol.* **67**, 151–174.

Carpenter, K., Berti, A., Oxbury, S., Molyneux, A. J., Biseach, E. and **Oxbury, J. M.** (1995). Awareness of an memory for arm weakness during intracarotid sodium amytal testing. *Brain.* **118**, 243–251.

Carpenter, M., Nagell, K. and **Tomasello, M.** (1998). Social cognition, joint attention, and communicative competence from 9 to 15 months of age. *Monogr Soc Res Child Development.* **63**, i-vi, 1–143.

Casanova, M. F., Buxhoeveden, D. P., Switala, A. E. and **Roy, E.** (2002*a*). Asperger's syndrome and cortical neuropathology. *J Child Neurol.* **17**, 142–145.

Casanova, M. F., Buxhoeveden, D. P., Switala, A. E. and Roy, E. (2002*b*). Minicolumnar pathology in autism. *Neurology*. **58**, 428–432.

Casanova, M. F., van Kooten, I. A., Switala, A. E., van Engeland, H., Heinsen, H., Steinbusch, H. W., Hof, P. R., Trippe, J., Stone, J. and Schmitz, C. (2006). Minicolumnar abnormalities in autism. *Acta Neuropathol (Berl)*. **112**, 287–303.

Caspers, S., Geyer, S., Schleicher, A., Mohlberg, H., Amunts, K. and Zilles, K. (2006). The human inferior parietal cortex: cytoarchitectonic parcellation and interindividual variability. *Neuroimage*. **33**, 430–448.

Castelli, F., Happe, F., Frith, U. and Frith, C. (2000). Movement and mind: a functional imaging study of perception and interpretation of complex intentional movement patterns. *Neuroimage*. **12**, 314–325.

Castelli, F., Frith, C., Happe, F. and Frith, U. (2002). Autism, Asperger syndrome and brain mechanisms for the attribution of mental states to animated shapes. *Brain*. **125**, 1839–1849.

Chen, F. C. and Li, W. H. (2001). Genomic divergences between humans and other hominoids and the effective population size of the common ancestor of humans and chimpanzees. *Am J Hum Genet*. **68**, 444–456.

Chen, F. C., Vallender, E. J., Wang, H., Tzeng, C. S. and Li, W. H. (2001). Genomic divergence between human and chimpanzee estimated from large-scale alignments of genomic sequences. *J Hered*. **92**, 481–489.

Chiu, P. H., Kayali, M. A., Kishida, K. T., Tomlin, D., Klinger, L. G., Klinger, M. R. and Montague, P. R. (2008). Self responses along cingulate cortex reveal quantitative neural phenotype for high-functioning autism. *Neuron*. **57**, 463–473.

Christoff, K., Prabhakaran, V., Dorfman, J., Zhao, Z., Kroger, J. K., Holyoak, K. J. and Gabrieli, J. D. E. (2001). Rostrolateral prefrontal cortex involvement in relational integration during reasoning. *Neuroimage*. **14**, 1136–1149.

Cisek, P. and Kalaska, J. F. (2002). Simultaneous encoding of multiple potential reach directions in dorsal premotor cortex. *J Neurophysiol*. **87**, 1149–1154.

Cisek, P. and Kalaska, J. F. (2004). Neural correlates of mental rehearsal in dorsal premotor cortex. *Nature*. **431**, 993–996.

Clarke, S. (1994). Association and intrinsic connections of human extrastriate visual cortex. *Proc Roy Soc Lond B Biol Sci*. **257**, 87–92.

Clayton, N. S., Griffiths, D. P., Emery, N. J. and Dickinson, A. (2001). Elements of episodic-like memory in animals. *Phil Trans Roy Soc Lond*. B **356**, 1483–1491.

Clayton, N. S., Bussey, T. J. and Dickinson, A. (2003). Can animals recall the past and plan for the future? *Nat Rev Neurosci*. **4**, 685–691.

Clements, W. A. and Perner, J. (1994). Implicit understanding of belief. *Cogn Dev*. **9**, 377–395.

Clower, D. M., West, R. A., Lynch, J. C. and Strick, P. L. (2001). The inferior parietal lobule is the target of output from the superior colliculus, hippocampus, and cerebellum. *J Neurosci*. **21**, 6283–6291.

Colby, C. L., Duhamel, J. R. and **Goldberg, M. E.** (1996). Visual, presaccadic, and cognitive activation of single neurons in monkey lateral intraparietal area. *J Neurophysiol.* **76**, 2841–2852.

Conrad, R. (1972). Short-term memory in the deaf: a test for speech coding. *Br J Psychol.* **63**, 173–180.

Conrad, R. (1973). Some correlates of speech coding in the short-term memory of the deaf. *J Speech Hear Res.* **16**, 375–384.

Consortium (2007). Mapping autism risk loci using genetic linkage and chromosomal rearrangements. *Nature Genetics.* **39**, 319–328.

Conturo, T. E., Lori, N. F., Cull, T. S., Akbudak, E., Snyder, A. Z., Shimony, J. S., McKinstry, R. C., Burton, H. and **Raichle, M. E.** (1999). Tracking neuronal fiber pathways in the living human brain. *Proc Nat Acad Sci.* **96**, 10422–10427.

Cooney, J. W. and **Gazzaniga, M. S.** (2003). Neurological disorders and the structure of human consciousness. *Trends Cogn Sci.* **7**, 161–165.

Corballis, M. C. (1991). *The Lopsided Ape.* Oxford University Press, Oxford.

Corbetta, M., Miezin, F. M., Shulman, G. L. and **Petersen, S. E.** (1993). A PET study of visuospatial attention. *J Neuroscience.* **13**, 1202–1226.

Corfield, D. R., Murphy, K., Josephs, O., Fink, G. R., Frackowiak, R. S., Guz, A., Adams, L. and **Turner, R.** (1999). Cortical and subcortical control of tongue movement in humans: a functional neuroimaging study using fMRI. *J Appl Physiol.* **86**, 1468–1477.

Corina, D. P., McBurney, S. L., Dodrill, C., Hinshaw, K., Brinkley, J. and **Ojemann, G.** (1999). Functional roles of Broca's area and SMG: evidence from cortical stimulation mapping of a deaf signer. *Neuroimage.* **10**, 570–581.

Courchesne, E., Redcay, E. and **Kennedy, D. P.** (2004). The autistic brain: birth through adulthood. *Curr Opin Neurol.* **17**, 489–496.

Courchesne, E. and **Pierce, K.** (2005). Brain overgrowth in autism during a critical time in development: implications for frontal pyramidal neuron and interneuron development and connectivity. *Int J Dev Neurosci.* **23**, 153–170.

Cowey, A. and **Stoerig, P.** (1995). Blindsight in monkeys. *Nature.* **373**, 247–249.

Cowey, A. and **Stoerig, P.** (1997). Visual detection in monkeys with blindsight. *Neuropsychologia.* **35**, 929–939.

Cowey, A., Dean, A. and **Weiskrantz, L.** (1998). Ettlinger at Bay: can visual agnosias be explained by low-level visual impairments? In: Milner, A. D. (ed.), *Comparative Neuropsychology.* Oxford University Press, Oxford, pp. 30–50.

Creutzfeldt, O., Ojemann, G. and **Lettich, E.** (1989). *Neuronal* activity in the human lateral temporal lobe. I. Responses to speech. *Exp Brain Res.* **77**, 451–475.

Crick, F. and **Jones, E.** (1993). Backwardness of human neuroanatomy. *Nature.* **361**, 109–110.

Crow, T. (1998a). Why cerebral asymmetry is the key to the origin of homosapiens: How to find the gene or eliminate the theory. *Current Psychology of Cognition.* **17**, 1237–1277.

Crow, T. J. (1998b). Why cerebral asymmetry is the key to the origin of *Homo sapiens*: how to find the gene or eliminate the theory. *Current Psychology of Cognition.* **17**, 1237–1277.

Crow, T. J. (2002). Sexual selection, timing and an X-Y homologous gene: did *Homo sapiens* speciate on the Y chromosome? In: Crow, T. J. (ed.), *The Speciation of Modern Homo sapiens.* Oxford University Press, Oxford.

Crow, T. J. (2004). Directional asymmetry is the key to the origin of modern *Homo sapiens* (the Broca-Annett axiom): a reply to Rogers' review of *The Speciation of Modern* Homo sapiens. *Laterality.* **9**, 233–242.

Crow, T. J. (2007). Nuclear schizophrenic symptoms as a key to the evolution of the human brain. In: Kaas, J. and Preuss, T. M. (ed.), *Evolution of Nervous Systems: a Comprehensive Reference*, vol.4. Elsevier, New York, pp. 549–568.

Croxson, P. L., Johansen-Berg, H., Behrens, T. E., Robson, M. D., Pinsk, M. A., Gross, C. G., Richter, W., Richter, M. C., Kastner, S. and Rushworth, M. F. (2005). Quantitative investigation of connections of the prefrontal cortex in the human and macaque using probabilistic diffusion tractography. *J Neurosci.* **25**, 8854–8866.

Cui, X., Jeter, C. B., Yang, D., Montague, P. R. and Eagleman, D. M. (2007). Vividness of mental imagery: individual variability can be measured objectively. *Vision Res.* **47**, 474–478.

Culham, J. C. and Kanwisher, N. G. (2001). Neuroimaging of cognitive functions in human parietal cortex. *Curr Opin Neurobiol.* **11**, 157–163.

Culham, J. C., Danckert, S. L., DeSouza, J. F., Gati, J. S., Menon, R. S. and Goodale, M. A. (2003). Visually guided grasping produces fMRI activation in dorsal but not ventral stream brain areas. *Exp Brain Res.* **153**, 180–189.

Dagher, A., Owen, A. M., Boecker, H. and Brooks, D. J. (1999). Mapping the network for planning: a correlational PET activation study with the Tower of London. *Brain.* **122**, 1973–1987.

Damasio, H. and Damasio, A. R. (1989). *Lesion Analysis in Neuropsychology.* Oxford University Press, New York.

D'Amato, M. R. and Sant, P. V. (1988). The person concept in monkeys (*Cebus apella*). *Animal Behaviour Processes.* **14**, 43–55.

Dapretto, M. and Bookheimer, S. Y. (1999). Form and content: dissociating syntax and semantics in sentence comprehension. *Neuron.* **24**, 427–432.

Davies, R. R., Graham, K. S., Xuereb, J. H., Williams, G. B. and Hodges, J. R. (2004). The human perirhinal cortex and semantic memory. *EurJ Neurosci.* **20**, 2441–2446.

Dawkins, R. (1989a. Darwinism and human purpose. In: Durant, J. R. (ed.), Human Origins. Oxford University Press, Oxford, pp. 137–143.

Dawkins, R. (1989b. The Selfish Gene. Oxford University Press, Oxford.

de Waal, F. (1996). Good *Natured.* Harvard, Boston.

DeFelipe, J., Alonso-Nanclares, L., Arellano, J., Ballesteros-Yanez, I., Benavides-Piccione, R. and Munoz, A. (2007). Specializations of the cortical microstructure of humans. In: Kaas, J. and Preuss, T. M. (ed.), *Evolution of Nervous Systems*, vol.4. Academic Press, New York, pp. 167–190.

Dehaene, S. and **Changeux, J.-P.** (2004). Neural Mechanisms for Access to Consciousness. In: Gazzaniga, M. S. (ed.), *The Cognitive Neuroscience*s. MIT Press, Cambridge.

Dehaene, S. and **Naccache, L.** (2001). Towards a cognitive neuroscience of consciousness: basic evidence and a workspace framework. *Cognition.* **79,** 1–37.

Dehaene, S., Kerszberg, M. and **Changeux, J.-P.** (1998). A neuronal model of a global workspace in effortful cognitive tasks. *Proc Nat Acad Sci.* **95,** 14529–14534.

Dehaene, S., Spelke, E., Pinel, P., Stanescu, R. and **Tsivkin, S.** (1999). Sources of mathematical thinking: behavioral and brain-imaging evidence. *Science.* **284,** 970–974.

Dehaene, S., Le Clec, H. G., Poline, J. B., Le Bihan, D. and **Cohen, L.** (2002). The visual word form area: a prelexical representation of visual words in the fusiform gyrus. *Neuroreport.* **13,** 321–325.

Dehaene, S., Molko, N., Cohen, L. and **Wilson, A. J.** (2004). Arithmetic and the brain. *Curr Opin Neurobiol.* **14,** 218–224.

Deiber, M.-P., Passingham, R. E., Colebatch, J. G., Friston, K. J., Nixon, P. D. and **Frackowiak, R. S. J.** (1991). Cortical areas and the selection of movement: a study with positron emission tomography. *Experimental Brain Research.* **84,** 393–402.

Demonet, J. F., Chollet, F., Ramsay, S., Cardebat, D., Nespoulous, J. L., Wise, R., Rascol, A. and **Frackowiak, R.** (1992). The anatomy of phonological and semantic processing in normal subjects. *Brain.* **115,** (Pt 6), 1753–1768.

Dennett, D. C. (1991). *Consciousness Explained.* Allen Lane, London.

Dennett, D. C. (2003). *Freedom Evolves.* Allen Lane, London.

Denys, K., Vanduffel, W., Fize, D., Nelissen, K., Sawamura, H., Georgieva, S., Vogels, R., Van Essen, D. and **Orban, G. A.** (2004). Visual activation in prefrontal cortex is stronger in monkeys than in humans. *J Cogn Neurosci.* **16,** 1505–1516.

De Renzi, E. and **Lucchelli, F.** (1988). Ideational apraxia. *Brain.* **111,** 1173–1185.

De Renzi, E., Faglioni, P., Lodesani, M. and **Vecchi, A.** (1983). Performance of left brain-damaged patients on imitation of single movements and motor sequences. Frontal and parietal-injured patients compared. *Cortex.* **19,** 333–343.

Descartes, R. (1644). *Principia Philosophiae.* Elzevier, Amsterdam.

Desimone, R. and **Schein, S. J.** (1987). Visual properties of neurons in area V4 of the macaque: sensitivity to stimulus form. *J Neurophysiol.* **57,** 835–868.

Desimone, R., Schein, S. J., Moran, J. and **Ungerleider, L. G.** (1985). Contour, color and shape analysis beyond the striate cortex. *Vision Res.* **25,** 441–452.

Desimone, R. and **Ungerleider, L.** (1989). Neural mechanisms of visual processing in monkeys. In: Boller, F. and Graffman, J. (ed.), *Handbook of Neuropsychology*, vol.2. Elsevier, New York, pp. 267-.

Desmond, A. and **Moore, J.** (1991). *Darwin.* Michael Joseph, London.

Desmond, J. E. and **Fiez, J.** (1998). Neuroimaging studies of the cerebellum: language, learning and memory. *Trends in Cognitive Sciences.* **2**, 355–361.

De Valois, R. L. and **Jacobs, G. H.** (1971). Vision. In: Schrier, A. M. and Stollnitz, F. (ed.), *Behavior of Nonhuman Primates*, vol.3. Academic Press, New York, pp. 107–157.

DeValois, R. L. and **Jacobs, G. H.** (1998). Primate color vision. *Science.* **162**, 533–540.

de Veer, M. W., Gallup, G. G., Jr., Theall, L. A., van den Bos, R. and **Povinelli, D. J.** (2003). An 8-year longitudinal study of mirror self-recognition in chimpanzees (*Pan troglodytes*). *Neuropsychologia.* **41**, 229–234.

Devlin, J. T., Moore, C. J., Mummery, C. J., Gorno-Tempini, M. L., Phillips, J. A., Noppeney, U., Frackowiak, R. S., Friston, K. J. and **Price, C. J.** (2002). Anatomic constraints on cognitive theories of category specificity. *Neuroimage.* **15**, 675–685.

Devoogd, T. J., Krebs, J. R., Healy, S. D. and **Purvis, A.** (1993). Relations between song repertoire size and the volume of brain nuclei related to song: comparative evolutionary analyses amongst oscine birds. *Proc Biol Sci.* **254**, 75–82.

Dewson, J. H., 3rd, Cowey, A. and **Weiskrantz, L.** (1970). Disruptions of auditory sequence discrimination by unilateral and bilateral cortical ablations of superior temporal gyrus in the monkey. *Exp Neurol.* **28**, 529–548.

Dewson, J. H., Pribram, K. H. and **Lynch, J. C.** (1969). Effects of ablations of temporal cortex upon speech sound discrimination in the monkey. Experimental *Neurology.* **24**, 579–591.

DeYoe, E. A. and **van Essen, D. C.** (1988). Concurrent processing streams in monkey visual cortex. *TINS.* **11**, 219–226.

Dickinson, A. (1980). *Contemporary Animal Learning Theory.* Cambridge University Press, Cambridge.

Dierks, T., Linden, D. E., Jandl, M., Formisano, E., Goebel, R., Lanfermann, H. and **Singer, W.** (1999). Activation of Heschl's gyrus during auditory hallucinations. *Neuron.* **22**, 615–621.

Dijksterhuis, A., Bos, M. W., Nordgren, L. F. and **van Baaren, R. B.** (2006). On making the right choice: the deliberation-without-attention effect. *Science.* **311**, 1005–1007.

di Pellegrino, G., Fadiga, L., Fogassi, L., Gallese, V. and **Rizzolatti, G.** (1992). Understanding motor events: a neurophysiological study. *Exp Brain Res.* **91**, 176–180.

Dorsaint-Pierre, R., Penhune, V. B., Watkins, K. E., Neelin, P., Lerch, J. P., Bouffard, M. and **Zatorre, R. J.** (2006). Asymmetries of the planum temporale and Heschl's gyrus: relationship to language lateralization. *Brain,* **129**, 1164–1176.

Dronkers, N. F. (1996). A new brain region for coordinating speech articulation. *Nature.* **384**, 159–161.

Dronkers, N. F., Plaisant, O., Iba-Zizen, M. T. and **Cabanis, E. A.** (2007). Paul Broca's historic cases: high resolution MR imaging of the brains of Leborgne and Lelong. *Brain,* **130**, 1432–1445.

Duncan, J., Seitz, R. J., Kolodny, J., Bor, D., Herzog, H., Ahmed, A., Newell, F. N. and Emslie, H. (2000). A neural basis for general intelligence. *Science*. **289**, 457–460.

Eddy, T. J., Gallup, G. G., Jr. and Povinelli, D. J. (1996). Age differences in the ability of chimpanzees to distinguish mirror-images of self from video images of others. *J Comp Psychol*. **110**, 38–44.

Ehrsson, H. H., Spence, C. and Passingham, R. E. (2004). That's my hand! Activity in premotor cortex reflects feeling of ownership of a limb. *Science*. **305**, 875–877.

Eickhoff, S., Walters, N. B., Schleicher, A., Kril, J., Egan, G. F., Zilles, K., Watson, J. D. and Amunts, K. (2005a). High-resolution MRI reflects myeloarchitecture and cytoarchitecture of human cerebral cortex. *Hum Brain Mapp*. **24**, 206–215.

Eickhoff, S. B., Stephan, K. E., Mohlberg, H., Grefkes, C., Fink, G. R., Amunts, K. and Zilles, K. (2005b). A new SPM toolbox for combining probabilistic cytoarchitectonic maps and functional imaging data. *Neuroimage*. **25**, 1325–1335.

Eickhoff, S. B., Schleicher, A., Scheperjans, F., Palomero-Gallagher, N. and Zilles, K. (2007). Analysis of neurotransmitter receptor distribution patterns in the cerebral cortex. *Neuroimage*. **34**, 1317–1330.

Eidelberg, D. and Galaburda, A. M. (1984). Inferior parietal lobule: divergent architectonic asymmetries of the human brain. *Archives of Neurology*. **41**, 843–852.

Eldridge, L. L., Knowlton, B. J., Furmanski, C. S., Bookheimer, S. Y. and Engel, S. A. (2000). Remembering episodes: a selective role for the hippocampus during retrieval. *Nat Neurosci*. **3**, 1149–1152.

Elman, J. L. (1993). Learning and development in neural networks: the importance of starting small. *Cognition*. **48**, 71–99.

Elman, J. L. (2005). Connectionist models of cognitive development: where next? *Trends Cogn Sci*. **9**, 111–117.

Elston, G. N. (2003). *Cortex*, cognition and the cell: new insights into the pyramidal neuron and prefrontal function. *Cerebral Cortex*. **13**, 1124–1138.

Elston, G. N. (2007). Specialization of the neocortical pyramidal cell during primate evolution. In: Kaas, J. and Preuss, T. M. (ed.), *Evolution of Nervous Systems: a Comprehensive Reference*, vol.4. Elsevier, New York, pp. 191–242.

Elston, G. N. and Rosa, M. G. (1998). Morphological variation of layer III pyramidal neurones in the occipitotemporal pathway of the macaque monkey visual cortex. *Cerebral Cortex*. **8**, 278–294.

Elston, G. N., Benavides-Piccione, R. and DeFelipe, J. (2001). The pyramidal cell in cognition: a comparative study in human and monkey. *J Neurosci*. **21**, RC163.

Elston, G. N., Benavides-Piccione, R., Elston, A., Zietsch, B., Defelipe, J., Manger, P., Casagrande, V. and Kaas, J. H. (2006). Specializations of the granular prefrontal cortex of primates: implications for cognitive processing. *Anat Rec A Discov Mol Cell Evol Biol*. **288**, 26–35.

Embick, D., Marantz, A., Miyashita, Y., O'Neil, W. and Sakai, K. L. (2000a). A syntactic specialization for Broca's area. *Proc Natl Acad Sci USA*. **97**, 6150–6154.

Embick, D., Marantz, A., Miyashita, Y., O'Neill, W. and Sakai, K. L. (2000b). A syntactic specialization for Broca's area. PNAS. **97**, 6150–6154.

Emmorey, K., Grabowski, T., McCullough, S., Damasio, H., Ponto, L. L., Hichwa, R. D. and Bellugi, U. (2003). Neural systems underlying lexical retrieval for sign language. *Neuropsychologia*. **41**, 85–95.

Enard, W., Przeworski, M., Fisher, S. E., Lai, C. S., Wiebe, V., Kitano, T., Monaco, A. P. and Paabo, S. (2002). Molecular evolution of FOXP2, a gene involved in speech and language. *Nature*. **418**, 869–872.

Erdler, M., Beisteiner, R., Mayer, D., Kaindl, T., Edward, V., Windischberger, C., Lindiger, G. and Deecke, L. (2001). Supplementary motor area activating preceding voluntary movement is detectable with a whole-scalp magnetoencephalography system. *Neuroimage*. **11**, 697–707.

Eslinger, P. J. and Damasio, A. R. (1985). Severe disturbance of higher cognition after bilateral frontal lobe ablation: patient EVR. *Neurology*. **35**, 1731–1741.

Fadiga, L., Craighero, L., Buccino, G. and Rizzolatti, G. (2002). Speech listening specifically modulates the excitability of tongue muscles: a TMS study. *EurJ Neurosci*. **15**, 399–402.

Felleman, D. J., Nelson, R. J., Sur, M. and Kaas, J. H. (1983). Representations of the body surface in areas 3b and 1 of postcentral parietal cortex of Cebus monkeys. *Brain Res*. **268**, 15–26.

Fernandez-Carriba, S., Loeches, A., Morcillo, A. and Hopkins, W. D. (2002). Asymmetry in facial expression of emotions by chimpanzees. *Neuropsychologia*. **40**, 1523–1533.

Ferrari, P. F., Gallese, V., Rizzolatti, G. and Fogassi, L. (2003). Mirror neurons responding to the observation of ingestive and communicative mouth actions in the monkey ventral premotor cortex. *EurJ Neurosci*. **17**, 1703–1714.

Ferrari, P. F., Rozzi, S. and Fogassi, L. (2005). Mirror neurons responding to observation of actions made with tools in monkey ventral premotor cortex. *J Cogn Neurosci*. **17**, 212–226.

Fiebach, C. J., Schlesewsky, M., Lohmann, G., von Cramon, D. Y. and Friederici, A. D. (2005). Revisiting the role of Broca's area in sentence processing: syntactic integration versus syntactic working memory. *Hum Brain Mapp*. **24**, 79–91.

Finlay, B. L. and Brodsky, P. (2007). Cortical evolution as the expression of a program for disproportionate growth and the proliferation of areas. In: Kaas, J. and Krubitzer, L. (ed.), *Evolution of Nervous Systems: a Comprehensive Reference*, vol.3. Elsevier, New York, pp. 73–96.

Fish, J. L., Kosodo, Y., Enard, W., Paabo, S. and Huttner, W. B. (2006). Aspm specifically maintains symmetric proliferative divisions of neuroepithelial cells. *Proc Natl Acad Sci USA*. **103**, 10438–10443.

Fitch, W. T. (2000). The phonetic potential of human vocal tracts: comparative cineradiographic observations of vocalizing animals. *Phonetica*. **57**, 205–218.

Fletcher, P. C., Happe, F., Frith, U., Baker, S. C., Dolan, R. J., Frackowiak, R. S. J. and Frith, C. D. (1995). Other minds in the brain: a functional imaging study of 'theory of mind' in story comprehension. *Cognition.* **57**, 109–128.

Fletcher, P. C., Anderson, J. M., Shanks, D. R., Honey, R., Carpenter, T. A., Donovan, T., Papadakis, N. and Bullmore, E. T. (2001). Responses of human frontal cortex to surprising events are prediced by formal associative learning theory. *Nat Neurosci.* **4**, 1043–1048.

Flombaum, J. I., Junge, J. A. and Hauser, M. D. (2005). Rhesus monkeys (*Macaca mulatta*) spontaneously compute addition operations over large numbers. *Cognition.* **97**, 315–325.

Floyer-Lea, A. and Matthews, P. M. (2004). Changing brain networks for visuomotor control with increased movement automaticity. *J Neurophysiol.* **92**, 2405–2412.

Fogassi, L., Ferrari, P. F., Gesierich, B., Rozzi, S., Chersi, F. and Rizzolatti, G. (2005). Parietal lobe: from action organization to intention understanding. *Science.* **308**, 662–667.

Forstmann, B. U., Brass, M., Koch, I. and von Cramon, D. Y. (2006). Voluntary selection of task sets revealed by functional magnetic resonance imaging. *J Cogn Neurosci.* **18**, 388–398.

Fortin, N. J., Wright, S. P. and Eichenbaum, H. (2004). Recollection-like memory retrieval in rats is dependent on the hippocampus. *Nature.* **431**, 188–191.

Foundas, A. L., Leonard, C. M., Gilmore, R., Fennell, E. and Heilman, K. M. (1994). Planum temporale asymmetry and language dominance. *Neuropsychologia.* **32**, 1225–1231.

Foundas, A. L., Leonard, C. M., Gilmore, R. L., Fennell, E. B. and Heilman, K. M. (1996). Pars triangularis asymmetry and language dominance. *Proc Natl Acad Sci USA.* **93**, 719–722.

Foundas, A. L., Eure, K. F., Luevano, L. F. and Weinberger, D. R. (1998). MRI asymmetries of Broca's area: the pars triangularis and pars opercularis. *Brain Lang.* **64**, 282–296.

Foundas, A. L., Leonard, C. M. and Hanna-Pladdy, B. (2002). Variability in the anatomy of the planum temporale and posterior ascending ramus: do right- and left handers differ? *Brain Lang.* **83**, 403–424.

Fouts, R. S., Fouts.D.H. and van Cantfort, T. E. (1989). The infant Loulis learns signs from cross-fostered chimpanzees. In: Gardner, R. A. *et al.* (ed.), *Teaching Sign Lanugage to Chimpanzees.* SUNY Press, Albany, pp. 280–292.

Freedman, D. J., Riesenhuber, M., Poggio, T. and Miller, E. K. (2001). Categorical representation of visual stimuli in the primate prefrontal cortex. *Science.* **291**, 312–316.

Freedman, D. J., Riesenhuber, M., Poggio, T. and Miller, E. K. (2002). Visual categorization and the primate prefrontal cortex: neurophysiology and behavior. *J Neurophysiol.* **88**, 929–941.

Freund, H. J. (1987). Differential effects of cortical lesions in humans. Ciba Found Symp. **132**, 269–281.

Friederici, A. D., Fiebach, C. J., Schlesewsky, M., Bornkessel, I. D. and von Cramon, D. Y. (2006). Processing linguistic complexity and grammaticality in the left frontal cortex. *Cerebral Cortex*. **16**, 1709–1717.

Frith, C. (1996). The role of the prefrontal cortex in self-consciousness: the case of auditory hallucinations. *Phil Trans Roy Soc Lond B Biol Sci*. **351**, 1505–1512.

Frith, C. D. (2000). The role of dorsolateral prefrontal cortex in the selection of action. In: Monsell, S. and Driver, J. (ed.), Control of Cognitive Processes: Attention and Performance XVIII. MIT press, Cambridge, pp. 549–565.

Frith, C. (2007). *Making Up The Mind*. Blackwell's, Oxford.

Frith, C. D. and Frith, U. (2006). The neural basis of mentalizing. *Neuron*. **50**, 531–534.

Frith, C. D. and Frith, U. (2008). The self and its reputation in autism. *Neuron*. **57**, 331–332.

Frith, C. D., Friston, K., Liddle, P. F. and Frackowiak, R. S. J. (1991). Willed action and the prefrontal cortex in man: a study with PET. Proceeding of the Royal Society of London, series B. **244**, 241–246.

Funahashi, S., Bruce, C. J. and Goldman-Rakic, P. S. (1989. Mnemonic coding of visual space in monkey dorsolateral prefrontal cortex. *J Neurophysiol*. **61**, 331–349.

Funahashi, S., Bruce, C. J. and Goldman-Rakic, P. S. (1993). Dorsolateral prefrontal lesions and oculomotor delayed-response performance: evidence for mnemonic 'scotomas'. *J Neuroscience*. **13**, 1479–1497.

Fuster, J. M. (1973). Unit activity in prefrontal cortex during delayed-response performance: neuronal correlates of transient memory. *J Neurophysiol*. **36**, 61–78.

Fuster, J. (1997). *The Prefrontal Cortex*. Lippincott-Raven, Philadelphia.

Fuster, J. M. and Alexander, G. E. (1971). Neuron activity related to short term memory. *Science*. **173**, 652–654.

Gaffan, D. (1992). Amnesia for complex naturalistic scenes and for objects following fornix transection in the rhesus monkey. *EurJ Neurosci*. **4**, 381–388.

Gaffan, D. and Eacott, M. J. (1995). Visual learning for an auditory secondary reinforcer by macaques is intact after uncinate fascicle section: indirect evidence for the involvement of the corpus striatum. *Eur J Neuroscience*. **7**, 1866–1871.

Gaffan, D. and Hornak, J. (1997). Visual neglect in the monkey. Representation and disconnection. *Brain*. **120**, (Pt 9), 1647–1657.

Gaffan, D., Harrison, S. and Gaffan, E. A. (1986). Visual identification following inferotemporal ablation in the monkey. *Q J Exp Psychol B*. **38**, 5–30.

Galaburda, A. M. (1980. La region de Broca. *Revue Neurol*. **136**, 609–616.

Galaburda, A. M. and Pandya, D. N. (1983). The intrinsic architectonic and connectional organization of the superior temporal region of the rhesus monkey. *J Comp Neurol*. **221**, 169–184.

Galaburda, A. and Sanides, F. (1980). Cytoarchitectonic organization of the human auditory cortex. *J Comp Neurol*. **190**, 597–610.

Galaburda, A. M., Sanides, F. and Geschwind, N. (1978). Human brain. Cytoarchitectonic left–right asymmetries in the temporal speech region. *Arch Neurol.* **35**, 812–817.

Gallagher, H. L. and Frith, C. D. (2003). Functional imaging of 'theory of mind'. *Trends Cogn Sci.* **7**, 77–83.

Gallagher, H. L., Happe, F., Brunswick, N., Fletcher, P. C., Frith, U. and Frith, C. D. (2000). Reading the mind in cartoons and stories: an fMRI study of 'theory of mind' in verbal and nonverbal tasks. *Neuropsychologia.* **38**, 11–21.

Gallese, G. and Goldman, A. (1998). Mirror neurons and the simulation theory of mind reading. *Trends in Cognitive Sciences.* **2**, 493–500.

Gallese, V., Fadiga, L., Fogassi, L. and Rizzolatti, G. (1996). Action recognition in the premotor cortex. *Brain.* **119**, 593–610.

Gallup, G. G. (1970). Chimpanzee self-recognition. *Science.* **167**, 86–87.

Galton, C. J., Patterson, K., Graham, K., Lambon-Ralph, M. A., Williams, G., Antoun, N., Sahakian, B. J. and Hodges, J. R. (2001a). Differing patterns of temporal atrophy in Alzheimer's disease and semantic dementia. *Neurology.* **57**, 216–225.

Galton, C. J., Patterson, K., Graham, K., Lambon-Ralph, M. A., Williams, G., Antoun, N., Sahakian, B. J. and Hodges, J. R. (2001b). Differing patterns of temporal atrophy in Alzheimer's disease and semantic dementia. *Neurology.* **57**, 216–225.

Galuske, R. A., Schlote, W., Bratzke, H. and Singer, W. (2000). Interhemispheric asymmetries of the modular structure in human temporal cortex. *Science.* **289**, 1946–1949.

Gannon, P. J., Holloway, R. L., Broadfield, D. C. and Braun, A. R. (1998). Asymmetry of chimpanzee planum temporale: humanlike pattern of Wernicke's brain language area homolog. *Science.* **279**, 220–222.

Gardner, R. A. and Gardner, B. T. (1969). Teaching sign language to a chimpanzee. *Science.* **187**, 752–753.

Gardner, R. A. and Gardner, B. T. (1975). Early signs of language in child and chimpanzee. *Science.* **187**, 752–753.

Gardner, B. T. and Gardner, R. A. (1985). Signs of intelligence in cross-fostered chimpanzees. *Phil Trans Roy Soc London, series B.* **308**, 159–176.

Gardner, T. J., Naef, F. and Nottebohm, F. (2005). Freedom and rules: the acquisition and reprogramming of a bird's learned song. *Science.* **308**, 1046–1049.

Garnham, W. and Perner, J. (2001). Actions really do speak louder than words – but only implicitly: young children's understanding of false belief in action. *Br J Developmental Psychology.* **19**, 413–432.

Garrard, P. and Hodges, J. R. (2000). Semantic dementia: clinical, radiological and pathological perspectives. *J Neurol.* **247**, 409–422.

Gattass, R., Nascimento-Silva, S., Soares, J. G., Lima, B., Jansen, A. K., Diogo, A. C., Farias, M. F., Botelho, M. M., Mariani, O. S., Azzi, J. and Fiorani, M. (2005). Cortical visual areas in monkeys: location, topography, connections, columns, plasticity and cortical dynamics. *Phil Trans Roy Soc Lond B Biol Sci.* **360**, 709–731.

Gelfand, J. R. and **Bookheimer, S. Y.** (2003). Dissociating neural mechanisms of temporal sequencing and processing phonemes. *Neuron*. **38**, 831–842.

Gentilucci, M. and **Corballis, M. C.** (2006). From manual gesture to speech: a gradual transition. *Neurosci Biobehav Rev*. **30**, 949–960.

Gentner, D. (2003). Why we're so smart. In: Gentner, D. and Goldin-Meadow, S. (ed.), *Language in Mind*. MIT Press, Cambridge, pp. 195–236.

Gerardin, A., Sirigu, A., Lehericy, S., Poline, J.-B., Gaymard, B., Marsault, C., Agid, Y. and **Le Bihan, D.** (2000). Partially overlapping neural networks for real and imagined hand movements. *Cerebral Cortex*. **10**, 1093–1104.

Geschwind, N. (1965). Disconnection syndromes in animals and man. *Brain*. **88**, 585–644.

Geschwind, N. (1979). Specializations of the human brain. *Scientific American*. **241**, 180–199.

Geschwind, N. and **Levitsky, W.** (1968). Human brain: left-right asymmetries in temporal speech region. *Science*. **161**, 186–187.

Geyer, S., Luppino, G., Ekamp, H. and **Zilles, K.** (2005). The macaque inferior parietal lobule: cytoarchitecture and distribution pattern of serotonin 5-HT1A binding sites. *Anat Embryol (Berl)*. **210**, 353–362.

Gil-da-Costa, R. and **Hauser, M. D.** (2006). Vervet monkeys and humans show brain asymmetries for processing conspecific vocalizations, but with opposite patterns of laterality. *Proc Biol Sci*. **273**, 2313–2318.

Gil-da-Costa, R., Braun, A., Lopes, M., Hauser, M. D., Carson, R. E., Herscovitch, P. and **Martin, A.** (2004). Toward an evolutionary perspective on conceptual representation: species-specific calls activate visual and affective processing systems in the macaque. *Proc Natl Acad Sci USA*. **101**, 17516–17521.

Gil-da-Costa, R., Martin, A., Lopes, M. A., Munoz, M., Fritz, J. B. and **Braun, A. R.** (2006). Species-specific calls activate homologs of Broca's and Wernicke's areas in the macaque. *Nat Neurosci*. **9**, 1064–1070.

Gilbert, S. J., Simons, J. S., Frith, C. D. and **Burgess, P. W.** (2006). Performance-related activity in medial rostral prefrontal cortex (area 10) during low-demand tasks. *J Exp Psychol Hum Percept Perform*. **32**, 45–58.

Gillan, D. J., Premack, D. and **Woodruff, G.** (1981). Reasoning in the chimpanzee: I. Analogical reasoning. *J Exp Psychol Anim Beh Proc*. **7**, 1–17.

Gillisen, E. (2001). Structural symmetries and asymmetries in human and chimpanzee brains. In: Falk, D. and Gibson, K. R. (ed.), *Evolutionary Anatomy of the Primate Cerebral Cortex*. Cambridge University Press, Cambridge, pp. 187–215.

Goel, V. and **Dolan, R. J.** (2004). Differential involvement of left prefrontal cortex in inductive and deductive reasoning. *Cognition*. **93**, B109–121.

Goel, V., Grafman, J., Tajik, J., Gana, S. and **Danto, D.** (1997). A study of the performance of patients with frontal lobe lesions in a financial planning task. *Brain*. **120**, (Pt 10), 1805–1822.

Goel, V., Buchel, C., Frith, C. and **Dolan, R. J.** (2000). Dissociation of mechanisms underlying syllogistic reasoning. *Neuroimage.* **12,** 504–514.

Goldin-Meadow, S. and **Mylander, C.** (1983). Gestural communication in deaf children: noneffect of parental input on language development. *Science.* **221,** 372–374.

Goldin-Meadow, S. and **Mylander, C.** (1998). Spontaneous sign systems created by deaf children in two cultures. *Nature.* **391,** 279–281.

Goldman-Rakic, P. (1987). Circuitry of primate prefrontal cortex and regulation of behaviour by representational memory. In: Plum, F. and Mountcastle, V. (ed.), *Handbook of Physiology: the Nervous System,* vol.5. American Physiological Society, Bethesda, pp. 373–417.

Goldman-Rakic, P. S. (1990). Cellular and circuit basis of working memory in prefrontal cortex of nonhuman primates. *Prog Brain Res.* **85,** 325–335.

Goldman-Rakic, P. (1992). Working memory and the mind. *Scientific American.* **267,** 110–117.

Goldman-Rakic, P. S. (1998). The prefrontal landscape: implications of functional architecture for understanding human mentation and the central executive. In: Roberts, A. C. *et al.* (ed.), *The Prefrontal Cortex.* Oxford University Press, Oxford, pp. 117–130.

Goldman-Rakic, P. and **Leung, H.-C.** (2002). Functional architecture of the dorsolateral prefrontal cortex in monkeys and humans. In: Stuss, D. T. and Knight, R. T. (ed.), *Principles of Frontal Lobe Function.* Oxford University Press, New York, pp. 85–95.

Goldman, P. S., Rosvold, H. E., Vest, B. and **Galkin, T. W.** (1971). Analysis of the delayed-alternation deficit produced by dorsolateral prefrontal lesions in the rhesus monkey. Journal of Comparative and *Physiological Psychology.* **77,** 212–220.

Goodwin, G. P. and **Johnson-Laird, P. N.** (2005). Reasoning about relations. *Psychol Rev.* **112,** 468–493.

Gopnik, M. (1990). Genetic basis of grammar defect. *Nature.* **347,** 26.

Gopnik, M. and **Crago, M. B.** (1991). Familial aggregation of a developmental language disorder. *Cognition.* **39,** 1–50.

Gopnik, M. and **Meltzoff, A.** (1997). *Words, Thoughts and Theories.* MIT Press, Cambridge.

Gottfried, J. A., O'Doherty, J. and **Dolan, R. J.** (2003). Encoding predictive reward value in human amygdala and orbitofrontal cortex. *Science.* **301,** 1104–1107.

Gough, P. M., Nobre, A. C. and **Devlin, J. T.** (2005). Dissociating linguistic processes in the left inferior frontal cortex with transcranial magnetic stimulation. *J Neurosci.* **25,** 8010–8016.

Grafton, S. T., Tyszka, M. and **Colletti, P. M.** (1993). Longitudinal changes of regional cerebral blood flow during procedural motor learning in humans. *J. Cereb. Blood Flow Metab.* **13,** S497.

Grant, C. M., Grayson, A. and Boucher, J. (2001). Using tests of false belief with children with autism: how valid and reliable are they? *Autism*. **5**, 135–145.

Gray, J. (2005). *Consciousness: Creeping up on the Hard Problem*. Oxford University Press, Oxford.

Gray, J. R., Chabris, C. F. and Braver, T. S. (2003). Neural mechanisms of general fluid intelligence. *Nat Neurosci*. **6**, 316–322.

Graziano, M. S., Taylor, C. S. and Moore, T. (2002). Complex movements evoked by microstimulation of precentral cortex. *Neuron*. **34**, 841–851.

Greene, J. D., Sommerville, R. B., Nystrom, L. E., Darley, J. M. and Cohen, J. D. (2001). An fMRI investigation of emotional engagement in moral judgement. *Science*. **293**, 2105–2108.

Greene, J. D., Nystrom, L. E., Engell, A. D., Darley, J. M. and Cohen, J. D. (2004). The neural bases of cognitive conflict and control in moral judgment. *Neuron*. **44**, 389–400.

Grefkes, C. and Fink, G. R. (2005). The functional organization of the intraparietal sulcus in humans and monkeys. *J Anat*. **207**, 3–17.

Gregoriou, G. G., Borra, E., Matelli, M. and Luppino, G. (2006). Architectonic organization of the inferior parietal convexity of the macaque monkey. *J Comp Neurol*. **496**, 422–451.

Grèzes, J., Armony, J. L., Rowe, J. and Passingham, R. E. (2003). Activations related to 'mirror' and 'canonical' neurones in the human brain: an fMRI study. *Neuroimage*. **18**, 928–937.

Grèzes, J., Frith, C. and Passingham, R. E. (2004a). Brain mechanisms for inferring deceit in the actions of others. *J Neurosci*. **24**, 5500–5505.

Grèzes, J., Frith, C. D. and Passingham, R. E. (2004b). Inferring false beliefs from the actions of oneself and others: an fMRI study. *Neuroimage*. **21**, 744–750.

Grill-Spector, K., Kourtzi, Z. and Kanwisher, N. (2001). The lateral occipital complex and its role in object recognition. *Vision Res*. **41**, 1409–1422.

Gross, C. G. (1993). Hippocampus minor and man's place in *Nature*: a case study in the social construction of neuroanatomy. *Hippocampus*. **3**, 403–415.

Gruber, O., Indefrey, P., Steinmetz, H. and Kleinschmidt, A. (2001). Dissociating neural correlates of cognitive components in mental calculation. *Cerebral Cortex*. **11**, 350–359.

Gusnard, D. A., Akbudak, E., Shulman, G. L. and Raichle, M. E. (2001). Medial prefrontal cortex and self-referential mental activity: relation to a default mode of brain function. *Proc Natl Acad Sci USA*. **98**, 4259–4264.

Habib, M., Robichon, F., Levrier, O., Khalil, R. and Salamon, G. (1995). Diverging asymmetries of temporo-parietal cortical areas: a reappraisal of Geschwind/Galaburda theory. *Brain Lang*. **48**, 238–258.

Hackett, T. A. (2007). Organization and correspondence of the auditory cortex of humans and nonhuman primates. In: Kaas, J. and Preuss, T. M. (ed.), *Evolution of Nervous Systems: a Comprehensive Reference*, vol.4. Elsevier, New York, pp. 109–119.

Hackett, T. A., Preuss, T. M. and Kaas, J. H. (2001). Architectonic identification of the core region in auditory cortex of macaques, chimpanzees, and humans. *J Comp Neurol.* 441 197–222.

Hadjikhani, N., Liu, A. K., Dale, A. M., Cavanagh, P. and Tootell, R. B. (1998). Retinotopy and color sensitivity in human visual cortical area V8. *Nat Neurosci.* **1**, 235–241.

Hadjikhani, N., Joseph, R. M., Snyder, J. and Tager-Flusberg, H. (2005). Anatomical differences in the mirror neuron system and social cognition network in autism. *Cer. Cort.* **16**, 1276–1282.

Haesler, S., Wada, K., Nshdejan, A., Morrisey, E. E., Lints, T., Jarvis, E. D. and Scharff, C. (2004). FoxP2 expression in avian vocal learners and non-learners. *J Neurosci.* **24**, 3164–3175.

Haesler, S., Rochefort, C., BGeolrgi, B., Licznerski, P., Osten, P. and Scharff, C., (2007). Incomplete and inaccurate vocal imitation after knockdown of FoxF2 in Songbird Basal Ganglia Nucleus Area X. *PLoS Biol.* **5**, 2885–2897.

Haggard, P. and Eimer, M. (1999). On the relation between brain potentials and the awareness of voluntary movements. *Exper Brain Res.* **126**, 128–133.

Hagler, D. J., Jr., Riecke, L. and Sereno, M. I. (2007). Parietal and superior frontal visuospatial maps activated by pointing and saccades. *Neuroimage.* **35**, 1562–1577.

Hagoort, P., Indefrey, P., Brown, C., Herzog, H., Steinmetz, H. and Seitz, R. J. (1999). The neural circuitry involved in the reading of German words and pseudowords: a PET study. *J Cogn Neurosci.* **11**, 383–398.

Halgren, E., Dale, A. M., Sereno, M. I., Tootell, R. B. H., Marinkovic, K. and Rosen, B. R. (1999). Location of human face-selective cortex with respect to retinotopic areas. *Human Brain Mapping.* **7**, 29–27.

Halpern, A. R. and Zatorre, R. J. (1999). When that tune runs through your head: a PET investigation of auditory imagery for familiar melodies. *Cerebral Cortex.* **9**, 697–704.

Halsband, U. and Freund, H.-J. (1990. Premotor cortex and conditional motor learning in man. *Brain.* **113**, 207–222.

Halsband, U. and Passingham, R. E. (1985). Premotor cortex and the conditions for movement in monkeys (*Macaca mulatta*). Behavioral *Brain Research.* **18**, 269–276.

Hampton, R. R. (2001). Rhesus monkeys know when they remember. *Proc Natl Acad Sci USA.* **98**, 5359–5362.

Hampton, R. R. (2005). Can rhesus monkeys discriminate between remembering and forgetting? In: Terrace, H. S. and Metcalfe, J. (ed.), *The Missing Link in Cognition.* Oxford University Press, Oxford, pp. 272–295.

Hamzei, F., Rijntjes, M., Dettmers, C., Glauche, V., Weiller, C. and Buchel, C. (2003). The human action recognition system and its relationship to Broca's area: an fMRI study. *Neuroimage.* **19**, 637–644.

Hansen, K. A., Kay, K. N. and Gallant, J. L. (2007). Topographic organization in and near human visual area V4. *J Neurosci.* **27**, 11896–11911.

Happe, F., Ronald, A. and Plomin, R. (2006). Time to give up on a single explanation for autism. *Nat Neurosci.* **9**, 1218–1220.

Hare, B. and Tomasello, M. (2005). Human-like social skills in dogs? *Trends Cogn Sci.* **9**, 439–444.

Hare, B., Call, J., Agnetta, B. and Tomasello, M. (2000). Chimpanzees know what conspecifics do and do not see. *Animal Behaviour.* **59**, 771–785.

Hare, B., Call, J. and Tomasello, M. (2001). Do chimpanzees know what conspecifics know? *Animal Behaviour.* **61**, 139–151.

Hassabis, D., Kumaran, D., Vann, S. D. and Maguire, E. A. (2007). Patients with hippocampal amnesia cannot imagine new experiences. *Proc Natl Acad Sci USA.* **104**, 1726–1731.

Hast, M. H., Fischer, J. M., Wetzela, B. and Thompson, V. E. (1974). Cortical motor representation of the laryngeal muscles in (*Macaca mulatta*). *Brain Research.* **73**, 229–240.

Hauser, M. D. (2003). Knowing about knowing: dissociations between perception and action systems over evolution and during development. *Ann N Y Acad Sci.* **1001**, 79–103.

Hauser, M. (2006). *Moral Minds.* Little Brown, London.

Hauser, M. D. and Andersson, K. (1994). Left hemisphere dominance for processing vocalizations in adult, but not infant, rhesus monkeys: field experiments. *Proc Natl Acad Sci USA.* **91**, 3946–3948.

Hauser, M., Agnetta, B. and Perez, C. (1998). Orienting asymmetries in rhesus monkeys: the effect of time-domain changes on acoustic perception. *Anim Behav.* **56**, 41–47.

Hauser, M. D., Newport, E. L. and Aslin, R. N. (2001). Segmentation of the speech stream in a non-human primate: statistical learning in cotton-top tamarins. *Cognition.* **78**, B53–64.

Hauser, M. D., Chomsky, N. and Fitch, W. T. (2002). The faculty of language: what is it, who has it, and how did it evolve? *Science.* **298**, 1569–1579.

Hayes, K. J. (1951). *The Ape in Our House.* Harper, New York.

Hayes, T. L. and Lewis, D. A. (1993). Hemispheric differences in layer III pyramidal neurons of the anterior language area. *Arch Neurol.* **50**, 501–505.

Hayes, T. L. and Lewis, D. A. (1995). Anatomical specialization of the anterior motor speech area: hemispheric differences in magnopyramidal neurons. *Brain Lang.* **49**, 289–308.

Hayes, T. L. and Lewis, D. A. (1996). Magnopyramidal neurons in the anterior motor speech region. Dendritic features and interhemispheric comparisons. *Arch Neurol.* **53**, 1277–1283.

Haynes, J. D., Sakai, K., Rees, G., Gilbert, S., Frith, C. and Passingham, R. E. (2007). Reading hidden intentions in the human brain. *Curr Biol.* **17**, 323–328.

Hazlett, E. A., Buchsbaum, M. S., Hsieh, P., Haznedar, M. M., Platholi, J., LiCalzi, E. M., Cartwright, C. and Hollander, E. (2004). Regional glucose metabolism within cortical Brodmann areas in healthy individuals and autistic patients. *Neuropsychobiology.* **49,** 115–125.

Heffner, H. and Heffner, S. (1986). Effect of unilateral and bilateral auditory cortex lesions on the discriminaiton of vocalizations by Japanese macaques. *J Neurophysiol.* **56,** 683–690.

Heffner, R. and Masterton, B. (1975). Variation in form of the pyramidal tract and its relationship to digital dexterity. *Brain Behav Evol.* **12,** 161–200.

Heffner, R. S. and Masterton, R. B. (1983). The role of the corticospinal tract in the evolution of human digital dexterity. *Brain Behav Evol.* **23,** 165–183.

Hegde, J. and Van Essen, D. C. (2006). A comparative study of shape representation in macaque visual areas V2 and V4. *J. Exper. Child Psychol.* **95,** 27–55.

Heim, S., Opitz, B. and Friederici, A. D. (2003). Distributed cortical networks for syntax processing: Broca's area as the common denominator. *Brain Lang.* **85,** 402–408.

Henson, R. N. A., Rugg, M. D., Shallice, T., Josephs, O. and Dolan, R. J. (1999). Recollection and familiarity in recognition memory: an event-related functional magnetic resonance imaging study. *J Neurosci.* **19,** 3962–3972.

Henson, R. N., Burgess, N. and Frith, C. D. (2000). Recoding, storage, rehearsal and grouping in verbal short-term memory: an fMRI study. *Neuropsychologia.* **38,** 426–440.

Hernstein, R. J., Loveland, D. H. and Cable, C. (1976). Natural concepts in pigeons. *J Exp Psychol Anim Behav Process.* **2,** 285–302.

Herrmann, E., Call, J., Hernandez-Lloreda, M. V., Hare, B. and Tomasello, M. (2007). Humans have evolved specialized skills of social cognition: the cultural intelligence hypothesis. *Science.* **317,** 1360–1366.

Heywood, C. A. and Cowey, A. (1987). On the role of cortical area V4 in the discrimination of hue and pattern in macaque monkeys. *J Neurosci.* **7,** 2601–2617.

Hihara, S., Yamada, H., Iriki, A. and Okanoya, K. (2003). Spontaneous vocal differentiation of coo-calls for tools and food in Japanese monkeys. Neurosci Res. **45,** 383–389.

Hill, R. S. and Walsh, C. A. (2005). Molecular insights into human brain evolution. *Nature.* **437,** 64–67.

Hodges, J. R. and Patterson, K. (1995). Is semantic memory consistently impaired early in the course of Alzheimer's disease? Neuroanatomical and diagnostic implications. *Neuropsychologia.* **33,** 441–459.

Hoen, M., Pachot-Clouard, M., Segebarth, C. and Dominey, P. F. (2006). When Broca experiences the Janus syndrome: an ER-fMRI study comparing sentence comprehension and cognitive sequence processing. *Cortex.* **42,** 605–623.

Hof, P. R., Nimchinsky, E. A., Perl, D. P. and Erwin, J. M. (2001). An unusual population of pyramidal neurons in the anterior cingulate cortex of hominids contains the calcium-binding protein calretinin. *Neurosci Lett.* **307,** 139–142.

Hoffman, D. S. and Strick, P. L. (1995). Effects of a primary motor cortex lesion on step-tracking movements of the wrist. *J Neurophysiol.* **73**, 891–895.

Honderich, T. (1993). *How Free are You? The Determinism Problem.* Oxford University Press, Oxford.

Hood, B., Carey, S. and Prasada, S. (2000). Predicting the outcomes of physical events: two-year-olds fail to reveal knowledge of solidity and support. *Child Development.* **71**, 1540–1554.

Hopkins, W. D. (1994). Hand preferences for bimanual feeding in 140 captive chimpanzees (*Pan troglodytes*): rearing and ontogenetic determinants. *Dev Psychobiol.* **27**, 395–407.

Hopkins, W. D. (1995). Hand preferences for a coordinated bimanual task in 110 chimpanzees (*Pan troglodytes*): cross-sectional analysis. *J Comp Psychol.* **109**, 291–297.

Hopkins, W. D. (1996). Chimpanzee handedness revisited: 55 years since Finch (1941). *Psychonom Bull Rev.* **3**, 449–457.

Hopkins, W. D. and Cantalupo, C. (2003). Does variation in sample size explain individual differences in hand preferences of chimpanzees (*Pan troglodytes*)? An empirical study and reply to Palmer (2002). *Am J Phys Anthropol.* **121**, 378–381; author's reply 382–374.

Hopkins, W. D. and Morris, R. D. (1989). Laterality for visual-spatial processing in two language-trained chimpanzees (*Pan troglodytes*). *Behav Neurosci.* **103**, 227–234.

Hopkins, W. D. and Pearson, K. (2000). Chimpanzee (*Pan troglodytes*) handedness: variability across multiple measures of hand use. *J Comp Psychol.* **114**, 126–135.

Hopkins, W. D., Fernandez-Carriba, S., Wesley, M. J., Hostetter, A., Pilcher, D. and Poss, S. (2001). The use of bouts and frequencies in the evaluation of hand preferences for a coordinated bimanual task in chimpanzees (*Pan troglodytes*): an empirical study comparing two different indices of laterality. *J Comp Psychol.* **115**, 294–299.

Hopkins, W. D., Wesley, M. J., Izard, M. K., Hook, M. and Schapiro, S. J. (2004). Chimpanzees (*Pan troglodytes*) are predominantly right-handed: replication in three populations of apes. *Behav Neurosci.* **118**, 659–663.

Hopkins, W. D., Russell, J. L., Cantalupo, C., Freeman, H. and Schapiro, S. J. (2005). Factors influencing the prevalence and handedness for throwing in captive chimpanzees (*Pan troglodytes*). *J Comp Psychol.* **119**, 363–370.

Horner, V. and Whiten, A. (2005). Causal knowledge and imitation/emulation switching in chimpanzees (*Pan troglodytes*) and children (*Homo sapiens*). *Anim Cogn.* **8**, 164–181.

Houde, O. and Tzourio-Mazoyer, N. (2003). Neural foundations of logical and mathematical cognition. *Nature Reviews Neuroscience.* **4**, 507–514.

Houston-Price, C., Plunkett, K. and Harris, P. (2005). 'Word-learning wizardry' at 1;6. *J Child Lang.* **32**, 175–189.

Houston-Price, C., Plunkett, K. and Duffy, H. (2006). The use of social and salience cues in early word learning. *J. Exper. Child Psychol.* **95**, 27–55.

Hubbard, E. M., Piazza, M., Pinel, P. and Dehaene, S. (2005). Interactions between number and space in parietal cortex. *Nat Rev Neurosci.* **6**, 435–448.

Humphrey, N. K. (1974). Vision in a monkey without striate cortex: a case study. *Perception.* **3**, 241–255.

Hutchison, W. D., Davis, K. D., Lozano, A. M., Tasker, R. R. and Dostrovsky, J. O. (1999). Pain-related neurons in the human cingulate cortex. *Nat Neurosci.* **2**, 403–405.

Hutsler, J. J. (2003). The specialized structure of human language cortex: pyramidal cell size asymmetries within auditory and language-associated regions of the temporal lobes. *Brain Lang.* **86**, 226–242.

Huttner, W. B. and Kosodo, Y. (2005). Symmetric versus asymmetric cell division during neurogenesis in the developing vertebrate central nervous system. *Curr Opin Cell Biol.* **17**, 648–657.

Huxley, T. H. (1895). *Man's Place in Nature.* MacMillan, London.

Huxlin, K. R. and Merigan, W. H. (1998). Deficits in complex visual perception following unilateral temporal lobectomy. *J Cogn Neurosci.* **10**, 395–407.

Huxlin, K. R., Saunders, R. C., Marchionini, D., Pham, H. A. and Merigan, W. H. (2000). Perceptual deficits after lesions of inferotemporal cortex in macaques. *Cerebral Cortex.* **10**, 671–683.

Iacoboni, M., Woods, R. P., Brass, M., Bekkering, H., Mazziotta, J. C. and Rizzolatti, G. (1999). Cortical mechanisms of human imitation. *Science.* **286**, 2526–2528.

Indefrey, P., Brown, C. M., Hellwig, F., Amunts, K., Herzog, H., Seitz, R. J. and Hagoort, P. (2001a). A neural correlate of syntactic encoding during speech production. *Proc Natl Acad Sci USA.* **98**, 5933–5936.

Indefrey, P., Hagoort, P., Herzog, H., Seitz, R. J. and Brown, C. M. (2001b). Syntactic processing in left prefrontal cortex is independent of lexical meaning. *Neuroimage.* **14**, 546–555.

Indovina, I. and Sanes, J. N. (2001). On somatotopic representation centers for finger movements in human primary motor cortex and supplementary motor area. *Neuroimage.* **13**, 1027–1034.

Inoue, K., Kawashima, R., Sugiura, M., Ogawa, A., Schormann, T., Zilles, K. and Fukuda, H. (2001). Activation in the ipsilateral posterior parietal cortex during tool use: a PET study. *Neuroimage.* **14**, 1469–1475.

Inoue, S. and Matsuzawa, T. (2007). Working memory of numerals in chimpanzees. *Curr. Biol.* **17**, R1004–1005.

Iriki, A., Tanaka, M. and Iwamura, Y. (1996). Coding of modified body schema during tool use by macaque postcentral neurones. *Neuroreport.* **7**, 2325–2330.

Ishai, A., Ungerleider, L. G., Martin, A., Schouten, J. L. and Haxby, J. V. (1999). Distributed representation of objects in the human ventral visual pathway. *Proc Natl Acad Sci USA.* **96**, 9379–9384.

Ishai, A., Ungerleider, L. G. and Haxby, J. V. (2000). Distributed neural systems for the generation of visual images. *Neuron.* **28**, 979–990.

Ishai, A., Haxby, J. V. and Ungerleider, L. G. (2002). Visual imagery of famous faces: effects of memory and attention revealed by fMRI. *Neuroimage.* **17**, 1729–1741.

Iwaniuk, A. N., Pellis, S. M. and Whishaw, I. Q. (1999). Is digital dexterity really related to corticospinal projections?: a re-analysis of the Heffner and Masterton data set using modern comparative statistics. *Behav Brain Res.* **101**, 173–187.

Iwatsubo, T., Kuzuhara, S., Kanemitsu, A., Shimada, H. and Toyokura, Y. (1990). Corticofugal projections to the motor nuclei of the brainstem and spinal cord in humans. *Neurology.* **40**, 309–312.

Jackendoff, R. (1997). *The Architecture of the Language Faculty.* MIT Press, Cambridge.

Jackendoff, R. (1999). Possible stages in the evolution of the language capacity. *Trends Cogn Sci.* **3**, 272–279.

Jackendoff, R. (2007). *Language, Consciousness, Culture: Essays on Mental Structure.* MIT Press, Cambridge.

Jackson, P. L., Meltzoff, A. N. and Decety, J. (2005). How do we perceive the pain of others? A window into the neural processes involved in empathy. *Neuroimage.* **24**, 771–779.

Jacob, P. and Jeannerod, M. (2005). The motor theory of social cognition: a critique. *Trends Cogn Sci.* **9**, 21–25.

Jahanshahi, M. and Dirnberger, G. (1999). The left dorsolateral prefrontal cortex and random generation of responses: studies with transcranial magnetic stimulation. *Neuropsychologia.* **37**, 181–190.

Jahanshahi, M., Jenkins, I. H., Brown, R. G., Marsden, C. D., Passingham, R. E. and Brooks, D. J. (1995). Self-initiated versus externally-triggered movements: I. An investigation using regional cerebral blood flow and movement-related potentials in normals and Parkinson's disease. *Brain.* **118**, 913–934.

Jahanshahi, M., Dirnberger, G., Fuller, R. and Frith, C. D. (2000). The role of the dorsolateral prefrontal cortex in random number generation: a study with positron emission tomography. *Neuroimage.* **12**, 713–725.

James, W. (1890). *The Principles of Psychology.* Holt, New York.

James, T. W., Humphrey, G. K., Gati, J. S., Menon, R. S. and Goodale, M. A. (2002). Differential effects of viewpoint on object-driven activation in dorsal and ventral streams. *Neuron.* **35**, 793–801.

Jancke, L., Wustenberg, T., Scheich, H. and Heinze, H. J. (2002). Phonetic perception and the temporal cortex. *Neuroimage.* **15**, 733–746.

Jarvelainen, J., Schurmann, M. and Hari, R. (2004). Activation of the human primary motor cortex during observation of tool use. *Neuroimage.* **23**, 187–192.

Jarvis, E. D., Gunturkun, O., Bruce, L., Csillag, A., Karten, H., Kuenzel, W., Medina, L., Paxinos, G., Perkel, D. J., Shimizu, T., Striedter, G., Wild, J. M., Ball, G. F., Dugas-Ford, J., Durand, S. E., Hough, G. E., Husband, S., Kubikova, L., Lee, D. W., Mello, C. V., Powers, A., Siang, C., Smulders, T. V., Wada, K., White, S. A., Yamamoto, K., Yu, J., Reiner, A. and Butler, A. B. (2005). Avian brains and a new understanding of vertebrate brain evolution. *Nat Rev Neurosci.* **6**, 151–159.

Jeannerod, M. (1994). The representing brain: neural correlates of motor intention and imagery. *Behavioral and Brain Sciences.* **17**, 187–245.

Jeannerod, M. (2006). Motor *Cognition.* Oxford University Press, Oxford.

Jellema, T. and **Perrett, D. I.** (2003). Cells in monkey STS responsive to articulated body motions and consequent static posture: a case of implied motion? *Neuropsychologia.* **41**, 1728–1737.

Jenkins, I. H., Brooks, D. J., Nixon, P. D., Frackowiak, R. S. J. and **Passingham, R. E.** (1994). Motor sequence learning: a study with positron emission tomography. Journal of *Neuroscience.* **14**, 3775–3790.

Jensen, K., Call, J. and **Tomasello, M.** (2007). Chimpanzees are rational maximizers in an ultimatum game. *Science.* **318**, 107–109.

Jerison, H. (1973). *Evolution of the Brain and Intelligence.* Academic Press, New York.

Johnson-Frey, S. H. (2003). What's so special about human tool use? *Neuron.* **39**, 201–204.

Johnson-Frey, S. H., Newman-Norlund, R. and **Grafton, S. T.** (2005). A distributed left hemisphere network active during planning of everyday tool use skills. *Cerebral Cortex.* **15**, 681–695.

Johnson-Laird, P. N. (1999). Deductive reasoning. *Ann Rev Psychol.* **50**, 109–135.

Johnson-Laird, P. N. (2001). Mental models and deduction. *Trends Cogn Sci.* **5**, 434–442.

Jurgens, U. (1970). Cerebral representation of vocalization in the squirrel monkey. *Experimental Brain Research.* **10**, 532–554.

Kaada, B. R. (1960). Cingulate, posterior orbital, anterior insular and temporal pole cortex. In: Field, J. (ed.), *Handbook of Physiology*, vol.1. American Physiological Society, Bethesda, pp. 1345–1372.

Kaas, J. (2000). Why is brain size so important: design problems and solutions as neocortex gets bigger or smaller. *Brain and Mind.* **1**, 7–23.

Kaas, J. (2007). The evolution of sensory and motor systems in primates. In: Kaas, J. and Preuss, T. M. (ed.), *Evolution of Nervous Systems: a Comprehensive Reference*, vol.4. Elsevier, New York, pp. 34–57.

Kaas, J. and **Preuss, T.** (2002). Human brain evolution. In: Squire, L. E. A. (ed.), *Fundamental Neuroscience.* Academic Press, London, pp. Chapter 45.

Kaas, J. H. and **Preuss, T. M.** (ed.) 2007. *Evolution of Nervous Systems: a Comprehensive Reference*, vol.4. Academic Press, New York.

Kaminski, J., Call, J. and **Fischer, J.** (2004). Word learning in a domestic dog: evidence for 'fast mapping'. *Science.* **304**, 1682–1683.

Kanwisher, N., McDermott, J. and **Chun, M. M.** (1997). The fusiform face area: a module in human extrastriate cortex specialized for face perception. *J Neurosci.* **17**, 4302–4311.

Karmiloff-Smith, A. (1992). *Beyond Modularity.* MIT Press, Cambridge.

Kegl, J., Senghas, A. and **Coppola, M.** (1999). Creation through contact: sign language emergence and sign language change in Nicaragua. In: Degraff, M. (ed.), *Language*

Creation and Language Change: Creolization, Diachrony, and Development. MIT press, Cambridge, pp. 179–237.

Kellenbach, M. L., Brett, M. and Patterson, K. (2003). Actions speak louder than functions: the importance of manipulability and action in tool representation. *J Cogn Neurosci.* **15**, 30–46.

Kelley, J. (1992. Evolution of the apes. In: Jones, S. *et al.* (ed.), *The Cambridge Encylopedia of Human Evolution.* Cambridge University Press, Cambridge, pp. 223–230.

Kelly, R. M. and Strick, P. L. (2003). Cerebellar loops with motor cortex and prefrontal cortex of a nonhuman primate. *J Neurosci.* **23**, 8432–8444.

Kennedy, D. P., Redcay, E. and Courchesne, E. (2006). Failing to deactivate: resting functional abnormalities in autism. *Proc Natl Acad Sci USA.* **103**, 8275–8280.

Kennedy, D. P., Semendeferi, K. and Courchesne, E. (2007). No reduction of spindle neuron number in frontoinsular cortex in autism. *Brain Cogn.* **64**, 124–129.

Kertesz, A. and Ferro, J. M. (1984). Lesion size and location in ideomotor apraxia. *Brain.* **107**, 921–933.

Kim, S. G., Ugurbil, K. and Strick, P. L. (1994). Activation of a cerebellar output nucleus during cognitive processing. *Science.* **265**, 949–951.

Kimura, D. (1993). *Neuromotor Mechanisms in Human Communication.* Oxford University Press, Oxford.

Kirzinger, A. and Jurgens, U. (1982). Cortical lesion effects and vocalization in the squirrel monkey. *Brain Res.* **233**, 299–315.

Knight, R. T., Grabowecky, M. F. and Scabini, D. (1995). Role of human prefrontal cortex in attention control. *Adv Neurol.* **66**, 21–34; discussion 34–26.

Koehler, O. (1950). The ability of birds to count. *Bull Anim Beh.* **9**, 41–45.

Koenigs, M., Young, L., Adolphs, R., Tranel, D., Cushman, F., Hauser, M. and Damasio, A. (2007). Damage to the prefrontal cortex increases utilitarian moral judgements. *Nature.* **446**, 908–911.

Konishi, S., Nakajima, K., Uchida, I., Kikyo, H., Kameyama, M. and Miyashita, Y. (1999). Common inhibitory mechanism in human inferior prefrontal cortex revealed by event-related functional MRI. *Brain.* **122**, 981–991.

Kornell, N., Son, L. K. and Terrace, H. S. (2007). Transfer of metacognitive skills and hint seeking in monkeys. *Psychol Sci.* **18**.

Kosslyn, S. M. (1994). *Image and Brain: the Resolution of the Imagery Debate.* MIT Press, Cambridge.

Kosslyn, S. M., Thompson, W. L. and Alpert, N. M. (1997). Neural systems shared by visual imagery and visual perception: a positron emission tomography study. *Neuroimage.* **6**, 320–334.

Kosslyn, S. M., Ganis, G. and Thompson, W. L. (2001). Neural foundations of imagery. *Nature Neuroscience Reviews.* **2**, 635–642.

Kotter, R., Stephan, K. E., Palomero-Gallagher, N., Geyer, S., Schleicher, A. and Zilles, K. (2001). Multimodal characterisation of cortical areas by multivariate analyses of receptor binding and connectivity data. *Anat Embryol (Berl).* **204**, 333–350.

Kreiman, G., Koch, C. and Fried, I. (2000). Imagery neurons in the human brain. *Nature.* **408**, 357–361.

Kringelbach, M. L., O'Doherty, J., Rolls, E. T. and Andrews, C. (2003). Activation of the human orbitofrontal cortex to a liquid food stimulus is correlated with its subjective pleasantness. *Cerebral Cortex.* **13**, 1064–1071.

Krubitzer, L. and Huffman, K. J. (2000). Arealization of the neocortex in mammals: genetic and epigenetic contributions to the phenotype. *Brain Behav Evol.* **55**, 322–335.

Krubitzer, L. and Hunt, D. L. (2007). Captured in the net of space and time: understanding cortical field evolution. In: Kaas, J. and Krubitzer, L. (ed.), *Evolution of Nervous Systems: a Comprehensive Reference*, vol.3. Elsevier, New York, pp. 49–72.

Kumar, S. and Hedges, S. B. (1998). A molecular timescale for vertebrate evolution. *Nature.* **392**, 917–920.

Kumashiro, M., Ishibashi, H., Uchiyama, Y., Itakura, S., Murata, A. and Iriki, A. (2003). Natural imitation induced by joint attention in Japanese monkeys. *Int J Psychophysiol.* **50**, 81–99.

Kurata, K. and Hoffman, D. S. (1994). Differential effects of muscimol microinjection into dorsal and ventral aspects of the premotor cortex of monkeys. *J Neurophysiol.* **64**, 1151–1164.

Kuypers, H. G. (1958). Corticobular connexions to the pons and lower brain-stem in man: an anatomical study. *Brain.* **81**, 364–388.

Kuypers, H. G. J. M. (1981). Anatomy of the descending pathways. In: Brooks, V. (ed.), *Handbook of Physiology*, vol.2. American Physiological Society, Bethesda, pp. 597–666.

Kwon, H., Ow, A. W., Pedatella, K. E., Lotspeich, L. J. and Reiss, A. L. (2004). Voxel-based morphometry elucidates structural neuroanatomy of high-functioning autism and Asperger syndrome. *Dev Med Child Neurol.* **46**, 760–764.

Lai, C. S., Fisher, S. E., Hurst, J. A., Vargha-Khadem, F. and Monaco, A. P. (2001). A forkhead-domain gene is mutated in a severe speech and language disorder. *Nature.* **413**, 519–523.

Lai, C. S., Gerrelli, D., Monaco, A. P., Fisher, S. E. and Copp, A. J. (2003). FOXP2 expression during brain development coincides with adult sites of pathology in a severe speech and language disorder. *Brain.* **126**, 2455–2462.

Larsson, J. and Heeger, D. J. (2006). Two retinotopic visual areas in human lateral occipital cortex. *J Neurosci.* **26**, 13128–13142.

Lau, H. C., Rogers, R. D., Haggard, P. and Passingham, R. E. (2004). Attention to intention. *Science.* **303**, 1208–1210.

Lau, H. C., Rogers, R. D. and Passingham, R. E. (2006). On measuring the perceived onsets of spontaneous actions. *J Neurosci.* **26**, 7265–7271.

Lawrence, D. G. and Kuypers, H. G. J. M. (1968). The functional organization of the motor system in the monkey. I The effects of bilateral pyramidal lesions. *Brain.* **91**, 1–14.

Lefebvre, L., Reader, S. M. and **Sol, D.** (2004). Brains, innovations and evolution in birds and primates. *Brain Behav Evol.* **63**, 233–246.

Lerner, Y., Hendler, T., Ben-Bashat, D., Harel, M. and **Malach, R.** (2001). A hierarchical axis of object processing stages in the human visual cortex. *Cerebral Cortex.* **11**, 287–297.

Levine, S. C. and **Levy, J.** (1986). Perceptual asymmetry for chimeric faces across the life span. *Brain Cogn.* **5**, 291–306.

Levine, D. N., Calvanio, R. and **Popovics, A.** (1982). Language in the absence of inner speech. *Neuropsychol.* **20**, 391–409.

Levy, J. (1977). The mammalian brain and the adaptive advantage of cerebral asymmetry. *Ann N Y Acad Sci.* **299**, 264–272.

Levy, J., Heller, W., Banich, M. T. and **Burton, L. A.** (1983). Asymmetry of perception in free viewing of chimeric faces. *Brain Cogn.* **2**, 404–419.

Lewis, J. W. (2006). Cortical networks related to human use of tools. *Neuroscientist.* **12**, 211–231.

Libet, B., Gleason, C. A., Wright, E. W. and **Pearl, D. K.** (1983*a*). Time of conscious intention to act in relation to onset of cerebral activity (readiness-potential). The unconscious initiation of a freely voluntary act. *Brain.* **106**, 623–642.

Libet, B., Wright, E. W., Jr. and **Gleason, C. A.** (1983*b*). Preparation- or intention-to-act, in relation to pre-event potentials recorded at the vertex. *Electroencephalogr Clin Neurophysiol.* **56**, 367–372.

Liebenthal, E., Binder, J. R., Spitzer, S. M., Possing, E. T. and **Medler, D. A.** (2005). Neural substrates of phonemic perception. *Cerebral Cortex.* **15**, 1621–1631.

Lieberman, P. (1975). *On the Origins of Language.* MacMillan, New York.

Lieberman, P. (2002). On the *Nature* and evolution of the neural bases of human language. *Am J Phys Anthropol.* Suppl **35**, 36–62.

Lieberman, P. (2006). *Towards an Evolutionary Biology of Language.* Harvard University Press, Cambridge.

Liegeois, F., Baldeweg, T., Connelly, A., Gadian, D. G., Mishkin, M. and **Vargha-Khadem, F.** (2003). Language fMRI abnormalities associated with FOXP2 gene mutation. *Nat Neurosci.* **6**, 1230–1237.

Liu, Y. and **Rouiller, E. M.** (1999). Mechanisms of recovery of dexterity following unilateral lesion of the sensorimotor cortex in adult monkeys. *Exp Brain Res.* **128**, 149–159.

Liu, W. C., Gardner, T. J. and **Nottebohm, F.** (2004). Juvenile zebra finches can use multiple strategies to learn the same song. *Proc Natl Acad Sci USA.* **101**, 18177–18182.

Locke, J. (1689). *An Essay on Human Understanding.* Republished by Penguin Books, London.

Lonsdorf, E. V. (2006). What is the role of mothers in the acquisition of termite-fishing behaviors in wild chimpanzees (*Pan troglodytes schweinfurthii*)? *Anim Cogn.* **9**, 36–46.

Lonsdorf, E. V. and **Hopkins, W. D.** (2005). Wild chimpanzees show population-level handedness for tool use. *Proc Natl Acad Sci USA*. **102**, 12634–12638.

Lu, X., Hikosaka, O. and **Miyachi, S.** (1998). Role of monkey cerebellar nuclei in skill for sequential movement. *J Neurophysiol*. **79**, 2245–2254.

Lund, J. S., Yoshioka, T. and **Levitt, J. B.** (1993). Comparison of intrinsic connectivity in different areas of macaque monkey cerebral cortex. *Cerebral Cortex*. **3**, 148–162.

Lynch, J. C. and **McLaren, J. W.** (1989). Deficits of visual attention and saccadic eye movements after lesions of parietooccipital cortex in monkeys. *J Neurophysiol*. **61**, 74–90.

Macdermot, K. D., Bonora, E., Sykes, N., Coupe, A. M., Lai, C. S., Vernes, S. C., Vargha-Khadem, F., McKenzie, F., Smith, R. L., Monaco, A. P. and **Fisher, S. E.** (2005). Identification of FOXP2 truncation as a novel cause of developmental speech and language deficits. *Am J Hum Genet*. **76**, 1074–1080.

MacLarnon, A. M. and **Hewitt, G. P.** (1999). The evolution of human speech: the role of enhanced breathing control. *Am J Phys Anthropol*. **109**, 341–363.

MacLeod, C. E., Zilles, K., Schleicher, A., Rilling, J. K. and **Gibson, K. R.** (2003). Expansion of the neocerebellum in Hominoidea. *J Hum Evol*. **44**, 401–429.

MacNeilage, P. F. (1998). The frame/content theory of evolution of speech production. *Behavioral and Brain Sciences*. **21**, 499–511; discussion 511–446.

MacNeilage, P. F. and **Davis, B. L.** (2000). Deriving speech from nonspeech: a view from ontogeny. *Phonetica*. **57**, 284–296.

MacSweeney, M., Woll, B., Campbell, R., McGuire, P. K., David, A. S., Williams, S. C., Suckling, J., Calvert, G. A. and **Brammer, M. J.** (2002). Neural systems underlying British Sign Language and audio-visual English processing in native users. *Brain*. **125**, 1583–1593.

Maguire, E. A. and **Mummery, C. J.** (1999). Differential modulation of a common memory retrieval network revealed by positron emission tomography. *Hippocampus*. **9**, 54–61.

Malach, R., Reppas, J. B., Benson, R. R., Kwong, K. K., Jiang, H., Kennedy, W. A., Ledden, P. J., Brady, T. J., Rosen, B. R. and **Tootell, R. B.** (1995). Object-related activity revealed by functional magnetic resonance imaging in human occipital cortex. *Proc Natl Acad Sci USA*. **92**, 8135–8139.

Maravita, A. and **Iriki, A.** (2004). Tools for the body (schema). *Trends Cogn Sci*. **8**, 79–86.

Maravita, A., Spence, C., Kennett, S. and **Driver, J.** (2002). Tool-use changes multi-modal spatial interactions between vision and touch in normal humans. *Cognition*. **83**, B25–34.

Marcus, G. F. and **Fisher, S. E.** (2003). FOXP2 in focus: what can genes tell us about speech and language? *Trends Cogn Sci*. **7**, 257–262.

Marin-Padilla, M. (1992). Ontogenesis of the pyramidal cell of the mammalian neocortex and developmental cytoarchitectonics: a unifying theory. *J Comp Neurol*. **321**, 223–240.

Matano, S. and **Hirasaki, E.** (1997). Volumetric comparisons in the cerebellar complex of anthropoids, with special reference to locomotor types. *Am J Phys Anthropol.* **103**, 173–183.

Matsuzawa, T. (1985). Use of numbers by a chimpanzee. *Nature.* **315**, 57–59.

McDermott, K. B., Petersen, S. E., Watson, J. M. and **Ojemann, J. G.** (2003). A procedure for identifying regions preferentially activated by attention to semantic and phonological relations using functional magnetic resonance imaging. *Neuropsychologia.* **41**, 293–303.

McGrew, W. C. and **Marchant, L. F.** (1997). On the other hand: current issues in and meta-analysis of the behavioral laterality of hand function in non-human primates. *Yrbok Phys Anthrop.* **40**, 201–232.

McGuire, P. K., Paulesu, E., Frackowiak, R. S. and **Frith, C. D.** (1996*a*). Brain activity during stimulus independent thought. *Neuroreport.* **7** 2095–2099.

McGuire, P. K., Silbersweig, D. A., Murray, R. M., David, A. S., Frackowiak, R. S. and **Frith, C. D.** (1996*b*). Functional anatomy of inner speech and auditory verbal imagery. *Psychol Med.* **26**, 29–38.

McLeod, P., Plunkett, P. K. and **Rolls, E.** (1998). *Introduction to Connectionist Modelling of Cognitive Processes.* Oxford University Press, Oxford.

Meador, K. J., Loring, D. W., Feinberg, T. E., Lee, G. P. and **Nichols, M. E.** (2000). Anosognosia and asomatognosia during intracarotid amobarbital inactivation. *Neurology.* **55**, 816–820.

Mechelli, A., Price, C. J., Friston, K. J. and **Ishai, A.** (2004). Where bottom-up meets top-down: neuronal interactions during perception and imagery. *Cerebral Cortex.* **14**, 1256–1265.

Melis, A. P., Call, J. and **Tomasello, M.** (2006). Chimpanzees (*Pan troglodytes*) conceal visual and auditory information from others. *J Comp Psychol.* **120**, 154–162.

Menzel, C. (2005). Progress in the study of chimpanzee recall and episodic memory. In: Terrace, H. S. and Metcalfe, J. (ed.), The Missing Link in *Cognition.* Oxford University Pres, Oxford, pp. 188–224.

Mercader, J., Panger, M. and **Boesch, C.** (2002). Excavation of a chimpanzee stone tool site in the African rainforest. *Science.* **296**, 1452–1455.

Merigan, W. H. and **Saunders, R. C.** (2004). Unilateral deficits in visual perception and learning after unilateral inferotemporal cortex lesions in macaques. *Cerebral Cortex.* **14**, 863–871.

Mesulam, M. M. (2002). The human frontal lobes: transending the default mode through contingent encoding. In: Stuss, D. T. and Knight, R. T. (ed.), *Principles of Frontal Lobe Function.* Oxford University Press, Oxford, pp. 8–30.

Miall, R. C., Reckess, G. Z. and **Imamizu, H.** (2001). The cerebellum coordinates eye and hand tracking movements. *Nat Neurosci.* **4**, 638–644.

Middleton, F. A. and **Strick, P. L.** (2000). Basal ganglia and cerebellar loops: motor and cognitive circuits. *Brain Res Brain Res* Rev. **31**, 236–250.

Middleton, F. A. and **Strick, P. L.** (2001). Cerebellar projections to the prefrontal cortex of the primate. *J Neurosci.* **21**, 700–712.

Miller, E. K. and **Cohen, J. D.** (2001). An integrative theory of prefrontal cortex function. *Ann Rev Neurosci.* **24,** 167–202.

Milner, B. (1975). Psychological aspects of focal epilepsy and its neurosurgical management. *Adv Neurol.* **8,** 299–321.

Milner, A. D. and **Goodale, M. A.** (2007). *The Visual Brain in Action.* Oxford University Press, Oxford.

Mishkin, M. (1957). Effects of small frontal lesions on delayed alternation in monkeys. *J Neurophysiol.* **20,** 615–622.

Mishkin, M. (1972). Cortical visual areas and their interactions. In: Karczmar, A. G. (ed.), *The Brain and Human Behavior.* Springer-Verlag, Berlin, pp. 187–208.

Mitani, J. C. and **Watts, D. P.** (1999). Demographic influences on the hunting behavior of chimpanzees. *Am J Phys Anthropol.* **109,** 439–454.

Mitz, A. R., Godschalk, M. and **Wise, S. P.** (1991). Learning-dependent neuronal activity in the premotor cortex: activity during acquisition of conditional motor associations. Journal of *Neuroscience.* **11,** 1855–1872.

Miyashita, Y. and **Hayashi, T.** (2000). Neural representation of visual objects: encoding and top-down activation. *Curr Opin Neurobiol.* **10,** 187–194.

Miyashita, Y., Okuno, H., Tokuyama, W., Ihara, T. and **Nakajima, K.** (1996). Feedback signal from medial temporal lobe mediates visual associative mnemonic codes of inferotemporal neurons. *Brain Res* Cogn *Brain Res.* **5,** 81–86.

Mohr, J. P., Pessin, M. S., Finkelstein, S. and **Funkenstein, H. H.** (1978). Broca's aphasia: pathology and clinical. *Neurology.* **28,** 311–324.

Moll, J., de Oliveira-Souza, R., Bramati, I. E. and **Grafman, J.** (2002). Functional networks in emotional moral and nonmoral social judgments. *Neuroimage.* **16,** 696–703.

Morgan, M. J. and **Nicholas, D. J.** (1979). Discrimination between reinforced action patterns in the rat. *Learning and Motivation.* **10,** 1–22.

Moro, A., Tettamanti, M., Perani, D., Donati, C., Cappa, S. F. and **Fazio, F.** (2001). Syntax and the brain: disentangling grammar by selective anomalies. *Neuroimage.* **13,** 110–118.

Morris, R. D. and **Hopkins, W. D.** (1993). *Perception* of human chimeric faces by chimpanzees: evidence for a right hemisphere advantage. *Brain Cogn.* **21,** 111–122.

Morris, R. G., Downes, J. J., Sahakian, B. J., Evenden, J. L., Heald, A. and **Robbins, T. W.** (1988). Planning and spatial working memory in Parkinson's disease. *J Neurol Neurosurg Psychiatry.* **51,** 757–766.

Mulcahy, N. J. and **Call, J.** (2006). Apes save tools for future use. *Science.* **312,** 1038–1040.

Muller-Preuss, P. and **Jurgens, U.** (1976). Projections from the 'cingular' vocalization area in the squirrel monkey. *Brain Res.* **103,** 29–43.

Mummery, C. J., Patterson, K., Hodges, J. R. and **Wise, R. J.** (1996). Generating 'tiger' as an animal name or a word beginning with T: differences in brain activation. *Proc Roy Soc Lond B Biol Sci.* **263,** 989–995.

Muncer, S. J. and **Ettlinger, G.** (1981). Communication by a chimpanzee: first-trial mastery of word order that is critical for meaning, but failure to negate conjunctions. *Neuropsychologia.* **19**, 73–78.

Murata, A., Gallese, V., Luppino, G., Kaseda, M. and **Sakata, H.** (2000). Selectivity for the shape, size and orientation of objects for grasping in neurones of monkey parietal AIP. *J Neurophysiol.* **83**, 2580–2601.

Murphy, K., Corfield, D. R., Guz, A., Fink, G. R., Wise, R. J. S., Harrison, J. and **Adams, L.** (1997). Cerebral areas associated with motor control of speech in humans. *J Appl Physiology.* **83**, 1438–1447.

Mushiake, H., Saito, N., Sakamoto, K., Sato, Y. and **Tanji, J.** (2001). Visually based path-planning by Japanese monkeys. *Brain Res Cogn Brain Res.* **11**, 165–169.

Mushiake, H., Saito, N., Sakamoto, K., Itoyama, Y. and **Tanji, J.** (2006). Activity in the lateral prefrontal cortex reflects multiple steps of future events in action plans. *Neuron.* **50**, 631–641.

Musso, M., Moro, A., Glauche, V., Rijntjes, M., Reichenbach, J., Buchel, C. and **Weiller, C.** (2003). Broca's area and the language instinct. *Nat Neurosci.* **6**, 774–781.

Myowa-Yamakoshi, M. and **Matsuzawa, T.** (2000). Imitation of intentional manipulatory actions in chimpanzees (*Pan troglodytes*). *J Comp Psychol.* **114**, 381–391.

Naesser, M. A. (1994). NeuroImaging and recovery of auditory comprehension and spontaneous speech in aphasia with some implications for treatment in severe aphasia. In: Kertesz, A. (ed.), *Localization and NeuroImaging in Neuropsychology.* Academic Press, New York, pp. 245–296.

Nakahara, K., Adachi, Y., Osada, T. and **Miyashita, Y.** (2007). Exploring the neural basis of cognition: multi-modal links between human fMRI and macaque neurophysiology. *Trends Cogn Sci.* **11**, 84–92.

Nakajima, K., Maier, M. A., Kirkwood, P. A. and **Lemon, R. N.** (2000). Striking differences in transmission of corticospinal excitation to upper limb motoneurons in two primate species. *J Neurophysiol.* **84**, 698–709.

Napier, J. R. (1961). Prehensility and opposability in the hands of primates. *Symposium of the Zoological Society of London.* **5**, 115–132.

Narain, C., Scott, S. K., Wise, R. J., Rosen, S., Leff, A., Iversen, S. D. and **Matthews, P. M.** (2003). Defining a left-lateralized response specific to intelligible speech using fMRI. *Cerebral Cortex.* **13**, 1362–1368.

Nathaniel-James, D. A. and **Frith, C. D.** (2002). The role of the dorsolateral prefrontal cortex: evidence from the effects of contextual constraint in a sentence completion task. *Neuroimage.* **16**, 1094–1102.

Naya, Y., Sakai, K. and **Miyashita, Y.** (1996). Activity of primate inferotemporal neurons related to a sought target in pair-association task. *Proc Natl Acad Sci USA.* **93**, 2664–2669.

Naya, Y., Yoshida, M. and **Miyashita, Y.** (2001). Backward spreading of memory-retrieval signal in the primate temporal cortex. *Science.* **291**, 661–664.

Nelissen, K., Luppino, G., Vanduffel, W., Rizzolatti, G. and **Orban, G. A.** (2005). Observing others: multiple action representation in the frontal lobe. *Science.* **310**, 332–336.

Newbury, D. F., Bishop, D. V. and Monaco, A. P. (2005). Genetic influences on language impairment and phonological short-term memory. *Trends Cogn Sci.* **9**, 528–534.

Newsome, W. T. and Pare, E. B. (1988). A selective impairment of motion perception following lesions of the middle temporal visual area (MT). *J Neurosci.* **8**, 2201–2211.

Nieder, A. (2005). Counting on neurons: the neurobiology of numerical competence. *Nat Rev Neurosci.* **6**, 177–190.

Nieder, A. and Miller, E. K. (2004). A parieto-frontal network for visual numerical information in the monkey. *Proc Natl Acad Sci USA.* **101**, 7457–7462.

Nieder, A., Freedman, D. J. and Miller, E. K. (2002). Representation of the quantity of visual items in the primate prefrontal cortex. *Science.* **297**, 1708–1711.

Nimchinsky, E. A., Gillisen, E., Almann, J. M., Perl, D. P., Erwin, J. M. and Hof, P. R. (1999). A neuronal morphological type unique to humans and great apes. *Proc Nat Acad Sci.* **96**, 5268–5273.

Nishimura, T., Mikami, A., Suzuki, J. and Matsuzawa, T. (2006). Descent of the hyoid in chimpanzees: evolution of face flattening and speech. *J Hum Evol.* **51**, 244–254.

Nixon, P., Lazarova, J., Hodinott-Hill, I., Gough, P. and Passingham, R. (2004). The inferior frontal gyrus and phonological processing: an investigation using rTMS. *J Cogn Neurosci.* **16**, 289–300.

Nobre, A. C., Sebestyen, G. N., Gitelman, D. R., Mesulam, M. M., Frackowiak, R. S. and Frith, C. D. (1997). Functional localization of the system for visuospatial attention using positron emission tomography. *Brain.* **120**, (Pt 3), 515–533.

Northoff, G., Heinzel, A., de Greck, M., Bermpohl, F., Dobrowolny, H. and Panksepp, J. (2006). Self-referential processing in our brain–a meta-analysis of imaging studies on the self. *Neuroimage.* **31**, 440–457.

Nottebohm, F. (1977). Asymmetries in neural control of vocalization in the canary. In: Harnad, S. *et al.* (ed.), *Handbook of Behavioral Neurobiology.* Plenum Press, New York, pp. 295–344.

Nottebohm, F. (1991). Reassessing the mechanisms and origins of vocal learning in birds. *Trends Neurosci.* **14**, 206–211.

Nottebohm, F., Stokes, T. M. and Leonard, C. M. (1976). Central control of song in the canary, Serinus canarius. *J Comp Neurol.* **165**, 457–486.

Noveck, I. A., Goel, V. and Smith, K. W. (2004). The neural basis of conditional reasoning with arbitrary content. *Cortex.* **40**, 613–622.

O'Craven, K. M. and Kanwisher, N. (2000). Mental imagery of faces and places activates corresponding stiimulus-specific brain regions. *J Cogn Neurosci.* **12**, 1013–1023.

O'Doherty, J., Kringelbach, M. L., Rolls, E. T., Hornak, J. and Andrews, C. (2001). Abstract reward and punishment representations in human orbitofrontal cortex. *Nat Neurosci.* **4**, 95–102.

Obayashi, S., Suhara, T., Kawabe, K., Okauchi, T., Maeda, J., Akine, Y., Onoe, H. and Iriki, A. (2001). Functional brain mapping of monkey tool use. *Neuroimage.* **14**, 853–861.

Obayashi, S., Suhara, T., Nagai, Y., Maeda, J., Hihara, S. and Iriki, A. (2002). Macaque prefrontal activity associated with extensive tool use. *Neuroreport.* **13**, 2349–2354.

Ochsner, K. N., Beer, J. S., Robertson, E. R., Cooper, J. C., Gabrieli, J. D., Kihsltrom, J. F. and D'Esposito, M. (2005). The neural correlates of direct and reflected self-knowledge. *Neuroimage.* **28**, 797–814.

Ohnishi, T., Matsuda, H., Hashimoto, T., Kunihiro, T., Nishikawa, M., Uema, T. and Sasaki, M. (2000). Abnormal regional cerebral blood flow in childhood autism. *Brain.* **123**, (Pt 9), 1838–1844.

Ojemann, G. (1983). Brain organization for language from the perspective of electrical stimulation mapping. *Beh. and Brain Sci.* **2**, 189–230.

Ojemann, G. A. (1994). Cortical stimulation and recording in language. In: Kertesz, A. (ed.), *Localization and Neuroimaging in Psychology.* Academic Press, New York, pp. 35–56.

Ojemann, G. A. and Schoenfield-McNeill, J. (1998). Neurons in human temporal cortex active with verbal associative learning. *Brain Lang.* **64**, 317–327.

Ojemann, G. A., Schoenfield-McNeill, J. and Corina, D. P. (2002). Anatomic subdivisions in human temporal cortical neuronal activity related to recent verbal memory. *Nat Neurosci.* **5**, 64–71.

Okamoto, S., Tomonaga, M., Ishii, K., Kawai, N., Tanaka, M. and Matsuzawa, T. (2002). An infant chimpanzee (*Pan troglodytes*) follows human gaze. *Anim Cogn.* **5**, 107–114.

Okano, K. and Tanji, J. (1987). *Neuronal* activity in the primate motor fields of the agranular frontal cortex preceding visually triggered and self-paced movements. *Experimental Brain Research.* **66**, 155–166.

Okuno, H. and Miyashita, Y. (1996). Expression of the transcription factor Zif268 in the temporal cortex of monkeys during visual paired associate learning. *EurJ Neurosci.* **8**, 2118–2128.

Oldfield, C. (1971). The assessment and analysis of handedness: the Edinburgh Inventory. *Neuropsychol.* **9**, 97–100.

Ongur, D., Ferry, A. T. and Price, J. L. (2003). Architectonic subdivision of the human orbital and medial prefrontal cortex. *J Comp Neurol.* **460**, 425–449.

Onishi, K. H. and Baillargeon, R. (2005). Do 15-month-old infants understand false beliefs? *Science.* **308**, 255–258.

Orban, G. A., Fize, D., Peuskens, H., Denys, K., Nelissen, K., Sunaert, S., Todd, J. and Vanduffel, W. (2003). Similarities and differences in motion processing between the human and macaque brain: evidence from fMRI. *Neuropsychologia.* **41**, 1757–1768.

Orban, G. A., Van Essen, D. and Vanduffel, W. (2004). Comparative mapping of higher visual areas in monkeys and humans. *Trends Cogn Sci.* **8**, 315–324.

Orban, G. A., Claeys, K., Nelissen, K., Smans, R., Sunaert, S., Todd, J. T., Wardak, C., Durand, J. B. and Vanduffel, W. (2006). Mapping the parietal cortex of human and non-human primates. *Neuropsychologia.* **44**, 2647–2667.

Ormerod, I. E., Harding, A. E., Miller, D. H., Johnson, G., MacManus, D., du Boulay, E. P., Kendall, B. E., Moseley, I. F. and McDonald, W. I. (1994. Magnetic resonance imaging in degenerative ataxic disorders. *J Neurol Neurosurg Psychiatry*. **57**, 51–57.

Owen, R. (1858). On the characters, principles of division, and primary groups of the class Mammalia. *Proc Linn Soc Lond*. **2**, 1–17.

Owen, A. M., Downes, J. J., Sahakian, B. J., Polkey, C. E. and Robbins, T. W. (1990). Planning and spatial working memory following frontal lobe lesions in man. *Neuropsychologia*. **28**, 1021–1034.

Owen, A. M., Doyon, J., Petrides, M., and Evans, A. C. (1996). Planning and spatial working memory: a positron emission tomography study in humans. *Eur. J. Neurosci*. **8**, 353–364.

Owen, A. M., Iddon, J. L., Hodges, J. R., Summers, B. A. and Robbins, T. W. (1997). Spatial and non-spatial working memory at different stages of Parkinson's disease. *Neuropsychologia*. **35**, 519–532.

Owen, A. M., Menon, D. K., Johnsrude, I. S., Bor, D., Scott, S. K., Manly, T., Williams, E. J., Mummery, C. and Pickard, J. D. (2002). Detecting residual cognitive function in persistent vegetative state. *Neurocase*. **8**, 394–403.

Padoa-Schioppa, C. and Assad, J. A. (2006). Neurons in the orbitofrontal cortex encode economic value. *Nature*. **441**, 223–226.

Paillard, J., Michel, F. and Stelmarch, G. (1983). Localization without content: a tactile analogue of 'blind sight'. *Archiv Neurol*. **40**, 548–551.

Palmer, A. R. (2002). Chimpanzee right-handedness reconsidered: Evaluating the evidence with funnel plots. *Am J Phys Anthropol*. **118**, 191–199.

Pandya, D. N. and Seltzer, B. (1982). Intrinsic connections and architectonics of posterior parietal cortex in the rhesus monkey. *J Comp Neurol*. (204 196–210.

Pandya, D. N. and Yeterian, E. H. (1985). Architecture and connections of cortical association areas. In: Jones, E. G. (ed.), *Association and Auditory Cortices*. Plenum, New York, pp. 3–61.

Parsons, L. M. (2001). Exploring the functional neuroanatomy of music performance, perception, and comprehension. *Ann N Y Acad Sci*. **930**, 211–231.

Passingham, R. E. (1973). Anatomical differences between the neocortex of man and other primates. *Brain Behav Evol*. **7**, 337–359.

Passingham, R. E. (1975a). The brain and intelligence. *Brain Behav Evol*. **11**, 1–15.

Passingham, R. E. (1975b). Changes in the size and organization of the brain in man and his ancestors. *Brain, Behavior and Evolution*. **11**, 73–90.

Passingham, R. E. (1982). *The Human Primate*. Freeman, Oxford.

Passingham, R. E. (1985). Premotor cortex: sensory cues and movement. *Behavioral Brain Research*. **18**, 175–186.

Passingham, R. E. (1993). *The Frontal Lobes and Voluntary Action*. Oxford University Press, Oxford.

Passingham, R. E., Perry, H. and Wilkinson, F. (1983). The long-term effects of removal of sensorimotor cortex in infant and adult rhesus monkeys. *Brain*. **106**, 675–705.

Passingham, R. E., Toni, I., Schluter, N. and Rushworth, M. F. S. (1998). How do visual instructions influence the motor system? In: Bok, G. R. and Goode, J. (ed.), *Sensory Guidance of Movement*, pp. 129–141.

Passingham, R. E., Rowe, J. B. and Sakai, K. (2005). Prefrontal cortex and attention to action. In: Humphreys, G. W. and Riddoch, M. J. (ed.), *Attention in Action*. Psychology Press, Hove, pp. 263–286.

Passingham, R. E., Stephan, K. E. and Kotter, R. (2002). The anatomical basis of functional localization in the cortex. *Nat Rev Neurosci.* **3**, 606–616.

Patterson, F. and Linden, E. (1981). *The Education of Koko*. Owl Books, New York.

Paulesu, E., Frith, C. D. and R.S.J., F. (1993). The neural correlates of the verbal component of working memory. *Nature.* **362**, 342–345.

Paulesu, E., Goldacre, B., Scifo, P., Cappa, S. F., Gilardi, M. C., Castiglioni, I., Perani, D. and Fazio, F. (1997). Functional heterogeneity of left inferior frontal cortex as revealed by fMRI. *Neuroreport.* 8 2011–2017.

Paus, T., Zijdenbos, A., Worsley, K., Collins, D. L., Blumenthal, J., Giedd, J. N., Rapoport, J. L. and Evans, A. C. (1999). Structural maturation of neural pathways in children and adolescents: in vivo study. *Science.* **283**, 1908–1911.

Pearson, R. C. A. and Powell, T. P. S. (1985). The projection of the primary somatic sensory cortex upon area 5 in the monkey. *Brain Research Reviews.* **9**, 89–107.

Pelphrey, K. A., Morris, J. P. and McCarthy, G. (2005*a*). Neural basis of eye gaze processing deficits in autism. *Brain.* **128**, 1038–1048.

Pelphrey, K. A., Morris, J. P., Michelich, C. R., Allison, T. and McCarthy, G. (2005*b*). Functional Anatomy of Biological Motion *Perception* in Posterior Temporal *Cortex*: An fMRI Study of Eye, Mouth and Hand Movements. *Cer. Cort.* **15**, 1866–1876.

Penfield, W. and Jaspar, H. (1954). *Epilepsy and the Functional Anatomy of the Human Brain*. Little Brown, Boston.

Penfield, W. and Roberts, L. (1959). *Speech and Brain Mechanisms*. Princeton University Press, Princeton.

Pepperberg, J. M. (1987). Evidence for conceptual quantitative abilities in the African Grey Parrot: labelling of cardinal sets. *Ethology.* **75**, 37–61.

Pepperberg, I. M. (2002). In search of king Solomon's ring: cognitive and communicative studies of Grey parrots (*Psittacus erithacus*). *Brain Behav Evol.* **59**, 54–67.

Pepperberg, I. M. (2006). Grey parrot numerical competence: a review. *Anim Cogn.* **9**, 377–391.

Pepperberg, I. M. and McLaughlin, M. A. (1996). Effect of avian-human joint attention on allospecific vocal learning by grey parrots (*Psittacus erithacus*). *J Comp Psychol.* **110**, 286–297.

Petersen, M. R., Beecher, M. D., Zoloth, S. R., Moody, D. B. and Stebbins, W. C. (1978). Neural lateralization of species-specific vocalizations by Japanese macaques (*Macaca fuscata*). *Science.* **202**, 324–327.

Petersen, M. R., Beecher, M. D., Zoloth, S. R., Green, S., Marler, P. R., Moody, D. B. and Stebbins, W. C. (1984). Neural lateralization of vocalizations by Japanese macaques: communicative significance is more important than acoustic structure. *Behav Neurosci*. **98**, 779–790.

Petersen, S. E., Fox, P. T., Posner, M. I., Mintun, M. and Raichle, M. E. (1988). Positron emission tomographic studies of the cortical anatomy of single-word processing. *Nature*. **331**, 585–589.

Petitto, L. A., Zatorre, R. J., Gauna, K., Nikelski, E. J., Dostie, D. and Evans, A. C. (2000). Speech-like cerebral activity in profoundly deaf people processing signed languages: implications for the neural basis of human language. *Proc Natl Acad Sci USA*. **97**, 13961–13966.

Petrides, M. (1985). Deficits in non-spatial conditional associative learning after periarcuate lesions in the monkey. *Behav Brain Res*. **16**, 95–101.

Petrides, M. (1987). Conditional learning and primate frontal lobes. In: Perecman, E. (ed.), *The Frontal Lobes Revisited*. IBRN Press, New York, pp. 91–108.

Petrides, M. and Pandya, D. N. (1995). Comparative architectonic analysis of the human and macaque frontal cortex. In: Grafman, J. and Boller, F. (ed.), *Handbook of Neuropsychology*, vol.9. Elsevier, Amsterdam, pp. 17–58.

Petrides, M. and Pandya, D. N. (1999). Dorsolateral prefrontal cortex: comparative cytoarchitectonic analysis in the human and the macaque brain and corticocortical connection patterns. *Europ J Neurosc*. **11**, 1011–1036.

Petrides, M. and Pandya, D. N. (2006). Efferent association pathways originating in the caudal prefrontal cortex in the macaque monkey. *J Comp Neurol*. **498**, 227–251.

Petrides, M., Cadoret, G. and Mackey, S. (2005). Orofacial somatomotor responses in the macaque monkey homologue of Broca's area. *Nature*. **435**, 1235–1238.

Peuskens, H., Vanrie, J., Verfaillie, K. and Orban, G. A. (2005). Specificity of regions processing biological motion. *EurJ Neurosci*. **21**, 2864–2875.

Pinker, S. (1994). *The Language Instinct*. Allen Lane, London.

Pinker, S. (2007). *The Stuff of Thought*. Allen Lane, London.

Pinker, S. and Jackendoff, R. (2005). The faculty of language: what's special about it? *Cognition*. **95**, 201–236.

Pinsk, M. A., DeSimone, K., Moore, T., Gross, C. G. and Kastner, S. (2005). Representations of faces and body parts in macaque temporal cortex: a functional MRI study. *Proc Natl Acad Sci USA*. **102**, 6996–7001.

Plunkett, K. and Marchman, V. (1993). From rote learning to system building: acquiring verb morphology in children and connectionist nets. *Cognition*. **48**, 21–69.

Pochon, J.-B., Levy, R., Poline, J.-B., Crozier, S., Lehericy, S., Pillon, B., Deweer, B., Bihan, D. L. and Dubois, B. (2001). The role of dorsolateral prefrontal cortex in the preparation of forthcoming actions: an fMRI study. *Cerebral Cortex*. **11**, 260–266.

Poldrack, R. A., Wagner, A. D., Prull, M. W., Desmond, J. E., Glover, G. H. and Gabrieli, J. D. (1999). Functional specialization for semantic and phonological processing in the left inferior prefrontal cortex. *Neuroimage*. **10**, 15–35.

Polyn, S. M., Natu, V. S., Cohen, J. D. and Norman, K. A. (2005). Category-specific cortical activity precedes retrieval during memory search. *Science*. **310**, 1963–1966.

Poremba, A., Malloy, M., Saunders, R. C., Carson, R. E., Herscovitch, P. and Mishkin, M. (2004). Species-specific calls evoke asymmetric activity in the monkey's temporal poles. *Nature*. **427**, 448–451.

Porter, R. and Lemon, R. (1993). *Corticospinal Functioin and Voluntary Movement*. Oxford University Press, Oxford.

Povinelli, D. J. (2000). Folk Physics for Apes. Oxford University Press, Oxford.

Povinelli, D. J. and Eddy, T. J. (1996). What young chimpanzees know about seeing. *Monogr Soc Res Child Development*. **61**, i-vi, 1–152; discussion 153–191.

Povinelli, D. and O'Neil, D. (2000). Do chimpanzees use their gestures to instruct each other? In: Baron-Cohen, S. *et al.* (ed.), *Understanding Other Minds: Perspectives from Developmental Cognitive Neuroscience*. Oxford University Press, Oxford, pp. 459–487.

Povinelli, D. J. and Vonk, J. (2003). Chimpanzee minds: suspiciously human? *Trends Cogn Sci*. **7**, 157–160.

Povinelli, D. J. and Vonk, J. (2006). We don't need a microscope to explore the chimpanzee's mind. In: Hurley, S. and Nudds, M. (ed.), *Rational Animals?* Oxford University Press, Oxford, pp. 385–412.

Povinelli, D., Bering, J. and Giambrone, S. (2000). Toward a science of other minds: escaping the argument by analogy. *Cognitive Science*. **24**, 509–541.

Prather, J. F., Peters, S., Nowicki, S. and Mooney, R. (2008). Precise auditory-vocal mirroring in neurons for learned vocal communication. *Nature*. **451**, 305–310.

Premack, D. (1976). *Intelligence in Ape and Man*. Erlbaum, Hillsale.

Premack, D. (2004). Is language the key to human intelligence? *Science*. **303**, 318–320.

Premack, D. (2007). Human and animal cognition: continuity and discontinuity. *Proc Natl Acad Sci USA*. **104**, 13861–13867.

Premack, D. and Premack, A. J. (1983). *The Mind of an Ape*. Norton, New York.

Premack, D. and Premack, A. J. (1994). Levels of causal understanding in chimpanzees and children. *Cognition*. **50**, 347–362.

Premack, D. and Premack, A. J. (2003). *Original Intelligence*. McGraw-Hill, New York.

Premack, D. and Woodruff, G. (1978). Does the chimpanzee have a theory of mind? *Beh Brain Sci*. **4**, 515–526.

Press, W. A., Brewer, A. A., Dougherty, R. F., Wade, A. R. and Wandell, B. A. (2001). Visual areas and spatial summation in human visual cortex. *Vision Res*. **41**, 1321–1332.

Preston, S. D. and **de Waal, F. B.** (2002). Empathy: Its ultimate and proximate bases. *Behavioral and Brain Sciences.* **25**, 1–20; discussion 20–71.

Preuss, T. (2001). The discovery of cerebral diversity: an unwelcome scientific revolution. In: Falk, D. and Gibson, K. (ed.), *Evolutionary Anatomy of Primate Cerebral Cortex.* Cambridge University Press, Cambridge, pp. 138–164.

Preuss, T. M. (2004). Specializations of the visual system: the monkey model meets human reality. In: Kaas, J. and Collins, C. E. (ed.), *The Primate Visual System.* CRC Press, pp. 231–259.

Preuss, T. M. and **Coleman, G. Q.** (2002*a*). Human-specific organization of primary visual cortex: alternating compartments of dense Cat-301 and calbindin immunoreactivity in layer 4A. *Cerebral Cortex.* **12**, 671–691.

Preuss, T. M. and **Coleman, G. Q.** (2002*b*). Human-specific organization of primary visual cortex: alternating compartments of dense Cat-301 and calbindin immunoreactivity in layer 4A. *Cerebral Cortex.* **12**, 671–691.

Preuss, T. M. and **Goldman-Rakic, P. S.** (1991*a*). Ipsilateral cortical connections of granular frontal cortex in the strepsirhine primate Galago, with comparative comments on anthropoid primates. *J Comp Neurol.* **310**, 507–549.

Preuss, T. M. and **Goldman-Rakic, P. S.** (1991b). Myelo- and cytoarchitecture of the granular frontal cortex and surrounding regions in the strepsirhine primate Galago and the anthropoid primate Macaca. *J Comparative Neurology.* **310**, 429–474.

Preuss, T. M., Qi, H. and **Kaas, J. H.** (1999). Distinctive compartmental organization of human primary visual cortex. *Proc Natl Acad Sci USA.* **96**, 11601–11606.

Price, C. (2004*a*). The functional anatomy of reading. In: Frackowiack, R. S. J. (ed.), *Human Brain Function.* Elsevier, London, pp. 547–562.

Price, C. (2004*b*). An overview of speech comprehension and production. In: Frackowiack, R. S. J. (ed.), *Human Brain Function.* Academic Pres, New York, pp. 517–533.

Price, C. J. and **Devlin, J. T.** (2003). The myth of the visual word form area. *Neuroimage.* **19**, 473–481.

Price, C. J., Wise, R. J., Warburton, E. A., Moore, C. J., Howard, D., Patterson, K., Frackowiak, R. S. and **Friston, K. J.** (1996). Hearing and saying. The functional neuro-anatomy of auditory word processing. *Brain.* **119**, (Pt 3), 919–931.

Price, C., Moore, C., Humphreys, G. and **Wise, R.** (1997). Segregating semantic from phonological processes during reading. *J CognitiveNeuroscience.* **9**, 727–733.

Price, C. J., Mummery, C. J., Moore, C. J., Frakowiak, R. S. and **Friston, K. J.** (1999). Delineating necessary and sufficient neural systems with functional imaging studies of neuropsychological patients. *J Cogn Neurosci.* **11**, 371–382.

Price, C., Thierry, G. and **Griffiths, T.** (2005). Speech-specific auditory processing: where is it? *Trends Cogn Sci.* **9**, 271–276.

Procyk, E. and **Goldman-Rakic, P. S.** (2006). Modulation of dorsolateral prefrontal delay activity during self-organized behavior. *J Neurosci.* **26**, 11313–11323.

Provine, R. R. (1996). Laughter. *Scientific American*. **84**, 38–45.

Quiroga, R. Q., Reddy, L., Kreiman, G., Koch, C. and Fried, I. (2005). Invariant visual representation by single neurons in the human brain. *Nature*. **435**, 1102–1107.

Raby, C. R., Alexis, D. M., Dickinson, A. and Clayton, N. S. (2007). Planning for the future by western scrub-jays. *Nature*. **445**, 919–921.

Rademacher, J., Burgel, U., Geyer, S., Schormann, T., Schleicher, A., Freund, H. J. and Zilles, K. (2001). Variability and asymmetry in the human precentral motor system. A cytoarchitectonic and myeloarchitectonic brain mapping study. *Brain*. **124**, 2232–2258.

Raichle, M. E., Fiez, J. A., Videen, T. O., MacLeod, A. K., Pardo, J. V., Fox, P. T. and Petersen, S. E. (1994). Practice-related changes in human brain functional anatomy during non-motor learning. *Cerebral Cortex*. **4**, 8–26.

Raichle, M. E., MacLeod, A. M., Snyder, A. Z., Powers, W. J., Gusnard, D. A. and Shulman, G. L. (2001). A default mode of brain function. *Proc Natl Acad Sci USA*. **98**, 676–682.

Rainer, G., Augath, M., Trinath, T. and Logothetis, N. K. (2002). The effect of image scrambling on visual cortical BOLD activity in the anesthetized monkey. *Neuroimage*. **16**, 607–616.

Rakic, P. (1995). Corticogenesis in human and nonhuman primates. In: Gazzaniga, M. S. (ed.), *The Cognitive Neuroscience*s. MIT Press, Cambridge, pp. 127–146.

Rakic, P. and Kornack, D. R. (2007). The development and evolutionary expansion of the cerebral cortex in primates. In: Kaas, J. and Preuss, T. M. (ed.), *Evolution of Nervous Systems: a Comprehensive Reference*, vol.4. Elsevier, New York, pp. 243–260.

Ramnani, N. (2006). The primate cortico-cerebellar system: anatomy and function. *Nat Rev Neurosci*. **7**, 511–522.

Ramnani, N. and Passingham, R. E. (2001). Changes in the human brain during rhythm learning. *J Cogn Neurosci*. **13**, 952–966.

Ramnani, N., Toni, I., Passingham, R. E. and Haggard, P. (2001). The cerebellum and parietal cortex play a specific role in coordination: a PET study. *Neuroimage*. **14**, 899–911.

Ramnani, N., Behrens, T. E., Johansen-Berg, H., Richter, M. C., Pinsk, M. A., Andersson, J. L., Rudebeck, P., Ciccarelli, O., Richter, W., Thompson, A. J., Gross, C. G., Robson, M. D., Kastner, S. and Matthews, P. M. (2006). The evolution of prefrontal inputs to the cortico-pontine system: diffusion imaging evidence from Macaque monkeys and humans. *Cerebral Cortex*. **16**, 811–818.

Ramsay, S. C., Adams, L., Murphy, K., Corfield, D. R., Grootoonk, S., Bailey, D. L., Frackowiak, R. S. and Guz, A. (199). Regional cerebral blood flow during volitional expiration in man: a comparison with volitional inspiration. *J Physiol*. **461**, 85–101.

Raos, V., Umilta, M. A., Murata, A., Fogassi, L. and Gallese, V. (2006). Functional properties of grasping-related neurons in the ventral premotor area F5 of the macaque monkey. *J Neurophysiol*. **95**, 709–729.

Rasmussen, T. and Milner, B. (1977). The role of early left-brain injury in determining lateralization of cerebral speech functions. *Ann N Y Acad Sci*. **299**, 355–369.

Rauschecker, J. P., Tian, B. and Hauser, M. (1995). Processing of complex sounds in the macaque nonprimary auditory cortex. *Science*. **268,** 111–114.

Reader, S. M. and Laland, K. N. (2002). Social intelligence, innovation, and enhanced brain size in primates. *Proc Natl Acad Sci USA*. **99,** 4436–4441.

Ridley, M. (1996). *The Origins of Virtue*. Viking, New York.

Rilling, J. (2006). Human and nonhuman primate brains: are they allometrically scaled versions of the same design? *Evol Anthropol*. **15,** 65–77.

Rilling, J. K. and Insel, T. R. (1999). The primate neocortex in comparative perspective using magnetic resonance imaging. *J Hum Evol*. 37 191–223.

Rilling, J. K. and Seligman, R. A. (2002). A quantitative morphometric comparative analysis of the primate temporal lobe. *J Hum Evol*. **42,** 505–533.

Rilling, J., Gutman, D., Zeh, T., Pagnoni, G., Berns, G. and Kilts, C. (2002). A neural basis for social cooperation. *Neuron*. **35,** 395–405.

Rilling, J. K., Sanfey, A. G., Aronson, J. A., Nystrom, L. E. and Cohen, J. D. (2004*a*). The neural correlates of theory of mind within interpersonal interactions. *Neuroimage*. **22,** 1694–1703.

Rilling, J. K., Sanfey, A. G., Aronson, J. A., Nystrom, L. E. and Cohen, J. D. (2004*b*). Opposing BOLD responses to reciprocated and unreciprocated altruism in putative reward pathways. *Neuroreport*. **15,** 2539–2543.

Rilling, J. Glaser, M. F., Preuss, T. M., Ma, X., Zhao, T., Hu, X. and Behrens, T. in press. The evolution of human language pathways revealed by comparative DTI. *Nat Neurosci*.

Ringman, J. M., Saver, J. L., Woolson, R. F., Clarke, W. R. and Adams, H. P. (2004). Frequency, risk factors, anatomy, and course of unilateral neglect in an acute stroke cohort. *Neurology*. **63,** 468–474.

Ringo, J. L. (1991). Neuronal interconnection as a function of brain size. *Brain Behav Evol*. **38,** 1–6.

Ringo, J. L., Doty, R. W., Demeter, S. and Simard, P. Y. (1994). Time is of the essence: a conjecture that hemispheric specialization arises from interhemispheric conduction delay. *Cerebral Cortex*. **4,** 331–343.

Rizzolatti, G. and Arbib, M. A. (1998). Language within our grasp. *Trends Neurosci*. **21,** 188–194.

Rizzolatti, G. and Luppino, G. (2001). The cortical motor system. *Neuron*. **31,** 889–901.

Rizzolatti, G., Fogassi, L. and Gallese, V. (2001). Neurophysiological mechanisms underlying the understanding and imitation of action. *Nat Rev Neurosci*. **2,** 661–670.

Rolls, E. T., Sienkiewicz, Z. J. and Yaxley, S. (1989). Hunger modulates the response to gustatory stimuli of single neurons in the caudolateral orbitofrontal cortex of the macaque monkey. *Eur J Neuroscience*. **1,** 53–60.

Romero, L., Walsh, V. and Papagno, C. (2006). The neural correlates of phonological short-term memory: a repetitive transcranial magnetic stimulation study. *J Cogn Neurosci*. **18,** 1147–1155.

Roser, M. E. and Gazzaniga, M. S. (2007). The interpreter in human psychology. In: Kaas, J. and Preuss, T. M. (ed.), *Evolution of Nervous Systems: a Comprehensive Reference*, vol.4. Elsevier, New York, pp. 503–509.

Rothi, L. J., Heilman, K. M. and Watson, R. T. (1985). Pantomime comprehension and ideomotor apraxia. *J Neurol Neurosurg Psychiatry.* **48**, 207–210.

Rothi, L. J. G., Ochipa, C. and Heilman, K. (1997). A cognitive neuropsychological model of limb praxis and apraxia. In: Rothi, L. J. G. and Heilman, K. M. (ed.), *Apraxia: the Neuropsychology of Action*. Psychology Press, Hove, pp. 29–50.

Roux, F. E., Boetto, S., Sacko, O., Chollet, F. and Tremoulet, M. (2003). Writing, calculating, and finger recognition in the region of the angular gyrus: a cortical stimulation study of Gerstmann syndrome. *J Neurosurg.* **99**, 716–727.

Rowe, J. B., Owen, A. M., Johnsrude, I. S. and Passingham, R. E. (2001). Imaging the mental components of a planning task. *Neuropsychologia.* **39**, 315–327.

Rowe, J., Friston, K., Frackowiak, R. and Passingham, R. (2002). Attention to action: specific modulation of corticocortical interactions in humans. *Neuroimage.* **17**, 988–998.

Rowe, J. B., Stephan, K. E., Friston, K., Frackowiak, R. S. and Passingham, R. E. (2005). The prefrontal cortex shows context-specific changes in effective connectivity to motor or visual cortex during the selection of action or colour. *Cerebral Cortex.* **15**, 85–95.

Ruffman, T., Garnham, W., Import, A. and Connolly, D. (2001). Does eye gaze indicate implicit knowledge of false belief? Charting transitions in knowledge. *J Exp Child Psychol.* **80**, 201–224.

Rumiati, R. I., Weiss, P. H., Shallice, T., Ottoboni, G., Noth, J., Zilles, K. and Fink, G. R. (2004). Neural basis of pantomiming the use of visually presented objects. *Neuroimage.* **21**, 1224–1231.

Rushworth, M. F., Nixon, P. D., Wade, D. T., Renowden, S. and Passingham, R. E. (1998). The left hemisphere and the selection of learned actions. *Neuropsychologia.* **36**, 11–24.

Rushworth, M. F., Ellison, A. and Walsh, V. (2001). Complementary localization and lateralization of orienting and motor attention. *Nat Neurosci.* **4**, 656–661.

Rushworth, M. F., Behrens, T. E. and Johansen-Berg, H. (2005). Connection patterns distinguish 3 regions of human parietal cortex. *Cerebral Cortex.* **16**, 1418–1430.

Rutter, M. (2000). Genetic studies of autism: from the 1970s into the millennium. *J Abnorm Child Psychol.* **28**, 3–14.

Saarela, M. V., Hlushchuk, Y., Williams, A. C., Schurmann, M., Kalso, E. and Hari, R. (2007). The compassionate brain: humans detect intensity of pain from another's face. *Cerebral Cortex.* **17**, 230–237.

Sakai, K. and Miyashita, Y. (1991). Neural organization for the long-term memory of paired associates. *Nature.* **354**, 152–155.

Sakai, K. and Passingham, R. E. (2003). Prefrontal interactions reflect future task operations. *Nat Neurosci.* **6**, 75–81.

Sakai, K. and Passingham, R. E. (2006). Prefrontal set activity predicts rule-specific neural processing during subsequent cognitive performance. *J Neurosci.* **26**, 1211–1218.

Sakai, K., Hikosaka, O., Miyauchi, S., Takino, R., Sasaki, Y. and Putz, B. (1998). Transition of brain activation from frontal to parietal areas in visuomotor sequence learning. *J Neurosci.* **18**, 1827–1840.

Sakai, K. L., Homae, F. and Hashimoto, R. (2003). Sentence processing is uniquely human. *Neurosci Res.* **46**, 273–279.

Saleem, K. S., Pauls, J. M., Augath, M., Trinath, T., Prause, B. A., Hashikawa, T. and Logothetis, N. K. (2002). Magnetic resonance imaging of neuronal connections in the macaque monkey. *Neuron.* **34**, 685–700.

Salmond, C. H., Ashburner, J., Connelly, A., Friston, K. J., Gadian, D. G. and Vargha-Khadem, F. (2005). The role of the medial temporal lobe in autistic spectrum disorders. *EurJ Neurosci.* **22**, 764–772.

Sanfey, A. G., Rilling, J. K., Aronson, J. A., Nystrom, L. E. and Cohen, J. D. (2003). The neural basis of economic decision-making in the Ultimatum Game. *Science.* **300**, 1755–1758.

Satpute, A. B., Fenker, D. B., Waldmann, M. R., Tabibnia, G., Holyoak, K. J. and Lieberman, M. D. (2005). An fMRI study of causal judgments. *EurJ Neurosci.* **22**, 1233–1238.

Savage-Rumbaugh, E. S. (1986). *Ape Language*. Oxford University Press, Oxford.

Savage-Rumbaugh, E. S. and Lewin, R. (1994). *Kanzi: the Ape on the Brink of the Human Mind*. Doubleday, London.

Savage-Rumbaugh, E. S., Rumbaugh, D. M., Smith, S. T. and Lawson, J. (1980). Reference: the linguistic essential. *Science.* **210**, 922–925.

Saver, J. L. and Damasio, A. R. (1991). Preserved access and processing of social knowledge in a patient with acquired sociopathy due to ventromedial frontal damage. *Neuropsychologia.* **29**, 1241–1249.

Scharff, C. and Haesler, S. (2005). An evolutionary perspective on FoxP2: strictly for the birds? *Curr Opin Neurobiol.* **15**, 694–703.

Schenker, N. M., Desgouttes, A. M. and Semendeferi, K. (2005). Neural connectivity and cortical substrates of cognition in hominoids. *J Hum Evol.* **49**, 547–569.

Scheperjans, F., Palomero-Gallagher, N., Grefkes, C., Schleicher, A. and Zilles, K. (2005*a*). Transmitter receptors reveal segregation of cortical areas in the human superior parietal cortex: relations to visual and somatosensory regions. *Neuroimage.* **28**, 362–379.

Scheperjans, F., Palomero-Gallagher, N., Grefkes, C., Schleicher, A. and Zilles, K. (2005*b*). Transmitter receptors reveal segregation of cortical areas in the human superior parietal cortex: Relations to visual and somatosensory regions. *Neuroimage*, **28**, 362–379.

Schleicher, A., Amunts, K., Geyer, S., Morosan, P. and Zilles, K. (1999). Observer-independent method for microstructural parcellation of cerebral cortex: a quantitative approach to cytoarchitecture. *Neuroimage.* **9**, 165–177.

Schluter, N. D., Rushworth, M. F. S., Passingham, R. E. and **Mills, K. R.** (1998). Temporary inactivation of human lateral premotor cortex suggests dominance for the selection of movements: a study using transcranial magnetic stimulation. *Brain.* **121**, 785–799.

Schluter, N. D., Krams, M., Rushworth, M. F. and **Passingham, R. E.** (2001). Cerebral dominance for action in the human brain: the selection of actions. *Neuropsychologia.* **39**, 105–113.

Schmahmann, J. D. and **Pandya, D. N.** (1997). The cerebrocerellar system. In: Schmahmann, J. D. (ed.), *The Cerebellum and Cognition.* Academic Press, San Diego, pp. 31–60.

Schmahmann, J. D., Pandya, D. N., Wang, R., Dai, G., D'Arceuil, H. E., de Crespigny, A. J. and **Wedeen, V. J.** (2007). Association fibre pathways of the brain: parallel observations from diffusion spectrum imaging and autoradiography. *Brain.* **130**, 630–653.

Schoen, J. H. (1964). Comparative Aspects of the Descending Fibre Systems in the Spinal Cord. *Prog Brain Res.* **11**, 203–222.

Schoenemann, P. T., Sheehan, M. J. and **Glotzer, L. D.** (2005). Prefrontal white matter volume is disproportionately larger in humans than in other primates. *Nat Neurosci.* **8**, 242–252.

Schrier, A. M., R., A. and **Povar, M. L.** (1984). Studies of concept formation by stumptailed monkeys: concepts humans, monkeys and letter A. *Animal Behaviour Processes.* **13**, 564–584.

Schultz, W., Tremblay, L. and **Hollerman, J. R.** (2000). Reward processing in primate orbitofrontal cortex and basal ganglia. *Cerebral Cortex.* **10**, 272–284.

Schwartz, E. L., Desimone, R., Albright, T. D. and **Gross, C. G.** (1983). Shape recognition and inferior temporal neurons. *Proc Natl Acad Sci USA.* **80**, 5776–5778.

Scott, S. K., Blank, C. C., Rosen, S. and **Wise, R. J.** (2000). Identification of a pathway for intelligible speech in the left temporal lobe. *Brain.* **123**, (Pt 12), 2400–2406.

Searle, J. (2007). *Freedom and Neurobiology.* Columbia University Press, New York.

Seldon, H. L. (1985). The anatomy of speech perception: human auditory cortex. In: Peters, A. and Jones, E. G. (ed.), *Cerebral Cortex*, vol.4. Plenum, New York, pp. 273–328.

Seltzer, B. and **Pandya, D. N.** (1994). Parietal, temporal, and occipital projections to cortex of the superior temporal sulcus in the rhesus monkey: a retrograde tracer study. *J Comp Neurol.* **343**, 445–463.

Semendeferi, K. and **Damasio, H.** (2000). The brain and its main anatomical subdivisions in living hominoids using magnetic resonance imaging. *J Hum Evol.* **38**, 317–332.

Semendeferi, K., Armstrong, E., Schleicher, A., Zilles, K. and **Van Hoesen, G. W.** (2001). Prefrontal cortex in humans and apes: a comparative study of area 10. *Am J Phys Anthropol.* **114**, 224–241.

Semendeferi, K., Lu, A., Schenker, N. and Damasio, H. (2002). Humans and great apes share a large frontal cortex. *Nat Neurosci.* **5**, 272–276.

Sereno, M. I. and Tootell, R. B. (2005). From monkeys to humans: what do we now know about brain homologies? *Curr Opin Neurobiol.* **15**, 135–144.

Sereno, M. I., Dale, A. M., Reppas, J. B., Kwong, K. K., Belliveau, J. W., Brady, T. J., Rosen, B. R. and Tootell, R. B. H. (1995). Borders of multiple visual areas in humans revealed by functional magnetic resonance imaging. *Science.* **268**, 889–893.

Sereno, M. I., Pitzalis, S. and Martinez, A. (2001). Mapping of contralateral space in retinotopic coordinates by a parietal cortical area in humans. *Science.* **294**, 1350–1354.

Shallice, T. (1982). Specific impairments of planning. *Phil Trans Roy Soc London, series B.* **298**, 199–209.

Shallice, T. and Burgess, P. (1998). The domain of supervisory processes and the temporal organization of behaviour. In: Roberts, A. C. *et al.* (ed.), *The Prefrontal Cortex.* Oxford University Press, Oxford, pp. 22–35.

Shapiro, K. A., Pascual-Leone, A., Mottaghy, F. M., Gangitano, M. and Caramazza, A. (2001). Grammatical distinctions in the left frontal cortex. *J Cogn Neurosci.* **13**, 713–720.

Shariff, G. A. (1953). Cell counts in the primate cerebral cortex. *J Comp Neurol.* **98**, 381–400.

Sheinberg, D. L. and Logothetis, N. K. (1997). The role of temporal cortical areas in perceptual organization. *Proc Natl Acad Sci USA.* **94**, 3408–3413.

Shergill, S. S., Brammer, M. J., Fukuda, R., Bullmore, E., Amaro, E., Jr., Murray, R. M. and McGuire, P. K. (2002). Modulation of activity in temporal cortex during generation of inner speech. *Hum Brain Mapp.* **16**, 219–227.

Shergill, S. S., Brammer, M. J., Amaro, E., Williams, S. C., Murray, R. M. and McGuire, P. K. (2004). Temporal course of auditory hallucinations. *British Journal of Psychiatry.* **185**, 516–517.

Sherwood, C. C. and Hof, P. R. (2007). The evolution of neuron types and cortical histology in apes and humans. In: Kaas, J. and Preuss, T. M. (ed.), *Evolution of Nervous Systems: a Comprehensive Reference*, vol.4. Elsevier, New York, pp. 355–378.

Sherwood, C. C., Broadfield, D. C., Holloway, R. L., Gannon, P. J. and Hof, P. R. (2003). Variability of Broca's area homologue in African great apes: implications for language evolution. *Anat Rec.* **271A**, 276–285.

Sherwood, C. C., Hof, P. R., Holloway, R. L., Semendeferi, K., Gannon, P. J., Frahm, H. D. and Zilles, K. (2005a). Evolution of the brainstem orofacial motor system in primates: a comparative study of trigeminal, facial, and hypoglossal nuclei. *J Hum Evol.* **48**, 45–84.

Sherwood, C. C., Holloway, R. L., Semendeferi, K. and Hof, P. R. (2005b). Is prefrontal white matter enlargement a human evolutionary specialization? *Nat Neurosci.* **8**, 537–538; author's reply 538.

Shima, K. and **Tanji, J.** (1998). Role for cingulate motor area cells in voluntary movement selection based on reward. *Science.* **282**, 1335–1338.

Shipp, S., Blanton, M. and **Zeki, S.** (1998). A visuo-somatomotor pathway through superior parietal cortex in the macaque monkey: cortical connections of areas V6 and V6A. *EurJ Neurosci.* **10**, 3171–3193.

Simon, O., Mangin, J. F., Cohen, L., Le Bihan, D. and **Dehaene, S.** (2002). Topographical layout of hand, eye, calculation, and language-related areas in the human parietal lobe. *Neuron.* **33**, 475–487.

Simon, O., Kherif, F., Flandin, G., Poline, J. B., Riviere, D., Mangin, J. F., Le Bihan, D. and **Dehaene, S.** (2004). Automatized clustering and functional geometry of human parietofrontal networks for language, space, and number. *Neuroimage.* **23**, 1192–1202.

Simonyan, K. and **Jurgens, U.** (2002). Cortico-cortical projections of the motorcortical larynx area in the rhesus monkey. *Brain Res.* **949**, 23–31.

Simonyan, K. and **Jurgens, U.** (2003). Efferent subcortical projections of the laryngeal motorcortex in the rhesus monkey. *Brain Res.* **974**, 43–59.

Simonyan, K. and **Jurgens, U.** (2005). Afferent cortical connections of the motor cortical larynx area in the rhesus monkey. *Neuroscience.* **130**, 133–149.

Singer, T., Kiebel, S. J., Winston, J. S., Dolan, R. J. and **Frith, C. D.** (2004*a*). Brain responses to the acquired moral status of faces. *Neuron.* **41**, 653–662.

Singer, T., Seymour, B., O'Doherty, J., Kaube, H., Dolan, R. J. and **Frith, C. D.** (2004*b*). Empathy for pain involves the affective but not sensory components of pain. *Science.* **303**, 1157–1162.

Singer, T., Seymour, B., O'Doherty, J. P., Stephan, K. E., Dolan, R. J. and **Frith, C. D.** (2006). Empathic neural responses are modulated by the perceived fairness of others. *Nature.* **439**, 466–469.

Snyder, L. H., Batista, A. P. and **Andersen, R. A.** (1997). Coding of intention in the posterior parietal cortex. *Nature.* **386**, 167–170.

Spelke, E. (1988). The origins of physical knowledge. In: Weiskrantz, L. (ed.), *Thought Without Language.* Oxford University Press, Oxford, pp. 168–184.

Spelke, E. S. (2003). What makes us smart? Core knowledge and natural language. In: Gentner, D. and Goldin-Meadow, S. (ed.), *Language in Mind.* MIT Press, Cambridge, pp. 277–312.

Spence, S. A. (1999). Towards a functional anatomy of volition. *Journal of Consciousness Studies.* **6**, 11–29.

Spence, S. A., Hirsch, S. R., Brooks, D. J. and **Grasby, P. M.** (1998). Prefrontal cortex activity in people with schizophrenia and control subjects. *J Psychiatry.* **172**, 1–8.

Spiers, H. J. and **Maguire, E. A.** (2006*a*). Spontaneous mentalizing during an interactive real world task: An fMRI study. *Neuropsychologia.* **44**, 1674–1682.

Spiers, H. J. and **Maguire, E. A.** (2006*b*). Thoughts, behaviour, and brain dynamics during navigation in the real world. *Neuroimage.* **31**, 1826–1840.

Springer, J. A., Binder, J. R., Hammeke, T. A., Swanson, S. J., Frost, J. A., Bellgowan, P. S., Brewer, C. C., Perry, H. M., Morris, G. L. and **Mueller, W. M.** (1999). Language dominance in neurologically normal and epilepsy subjects: a functional MRI study. *Brain.* **122**, (Pt 11), 2033–2046.

Stebbins, W. C. (1978. Hearing of the primates. In: Chivers, D. J. and Herbert, J. (ed.), *Recent Advances in Primatology.* Academic Press, London, pp. 705–720.

Steinschneider, M., Schroeder, C. E., Arezzo, J. C. and **Vaughan, H. G., Jr.** (1995. Physiologic correlates of the voice onset time boundary in primary auditory cortex (A1) of the awake monkey: temporal response patterns. *Brain Lang.* **48**, 326–340.

Steinvorth, S., Corkin, S. and **Halgren, E.** (2006). Ecphory of autobiographical memories: an fMRI study of recent and remote memory retrieval. *Neuroimage.* **30**, 285–298.

Stephan, H., Bauchot, R. and **Andy, A. J.** (1970). Data on size of the brain and of various brain parts in insectivores and primates. In: Noback, C. R. and Montagna, W. (ed.), *The Primate Brain.* Appleton–Century–Crofts, New York, pp. 289–297.

Stephan, H., Frahm, H. and **Baron, G.** (1981). New and revised data on volumes of brain structures in insectivores and primates. *Folia Primatol.* **35**, 1–29.

Stephan, K. M., Binkofski, F., Posse, S., Seitz, R. J. and **Freund, H. J.** (1999). Cerebral midline structures in bimanual coordination. *Exp Brain Res.* **128**, 243–249.

Stephan, K. E., Marshall, J. C., Friston, K., Rowe, J. B., Ritzl, A., Zilles, K. and **Fink, G.** (2003). Lateralized cognitive processes and lateralized task control in the human brain. *Science*, **301**, 384–386.

Stevens, J. A., Fonlupt, P., Shiffrar, M. and **Decety, J.** (2000). New aspects of motion perception: selective neural encoding of apparent human movements. *Neuroreport.* **11**, 109–115.

Stoerig, P., Zontanou, A. and **Cowey, A.** (2002). Aware or unaware: assessment of cortical blindness in four men and a monkey. *Cerebral Cortex.* **12**, 565–574.

Stout, D. and **Chaminade, T.** (2007). The evolutionary neuroscience of tool making. *Neuropsychologia.* **45**, 1091–1100.

Subiaul, F., Cantlon, J. F., Holloway, R. L. and **Terrace, H. S.** (2004). Cognitive imitation in rhesus macaques. *Science.* **305**, 407–410.

Subiaul, F., Barth, J., Okamoto-Barth, S. and **Povinelli, D. J.** (2007). Human Cognitive Specializations. In: Kaas, J. and Preuss, T. M. (ed.), *Evolution of Nervous Systems: a Comprehensive Reference*, vol.4. Elsevier, New York, pp. 509–528.

Suddendorf, T. and **Busby, J.** (2003). Mental time travel in animals? *Trends Cogn Sci.* **7**, 391–396.

Sulkowski, G. M. and **Hauser, M. D.** (2001). Can rhesus monkeys spontaneously subtract? *Cognition.* **79**, 239–262.

Sullivan, K. and **Winner, E.** (1993. Three-year-olds' understanding of mental states: the influence of trickery. *J Exp Child Psychol.* **56**, 135–148.

Sutton, D., Larson, C. and **Lindeman, R. C.** (1974). Neocortical and limbic lesion effects on primate phonation. *Brain Research.* **71**, 61–75.

Sutton, D., Herman, H. and Larson, C. R. (1978. Brain mechanisms in learned phonation of (*Macaca mulatta*). In: Chivers, D. J. and Herbert, J. (ed.), *Recent Advances in Primatology*, vol.1. Academic Press, New York, pp. 769–784.

Suzuki, K. and Sakai, K. L. (2003). An event-related fMRI study of explicit syntactic processing of normal/anomalous sentences in contrast to implicit syntactic processing. *Cerebral Cortex.* **13**, 517–526.

Sweet, R. A., Dorph-Petersen, K. A. and Lewis, D. A. (2005). Mapping auditory core, lateral belt, and parabelt cortices in the human superior temporal gyrus. *J Comp Neurol.* **491**, 270–289.

Swisher, J. D., Halko, M. A., Merabet, L. B., McMains, S. A. and Somers, D. C. (2007). Visual topography of human intraparietal sulcus. *J Neurosci.* **27**, 5326–5337.

Takeda, K. and Funahashi, S. (2002). Prefrontal task-related activity representing visual cue location or saccade direction in spatial working memory tasks. *J Neurophysiol.* **87**, 567–588.

Takeda, K. and Funahashi, S. (2004). Population vector analysis of primate prefrontal activity during spatial working memory. *Cerebral Cortex.* **14**, 1328–1339.

Takada, M., Nambu, A., Hatanaka, N., Tachibana, Y., Miyachi, S., Taira, M. and Inase, M. (2004). Organization of prefrontal outflow toward frontal motor-related areas in macaque monkeys. *EurJ Neurosci.* **19**, 3328–3342.

Tardif, E. and Clarke, S. (2001). Intrinsic connectivity of human auditory areas: a tracing study with DiI. *EurJ Neurosci.* **13**, 1045–1050.

Tchernichovski, O., Mitra, P. P., Lints, T. and Nottebohm, F. (2001). Dynamics of the vocal imitation process: how a zebra finch learns its song. *Science.* **291**, 2564–2569.

Teramitsu, I., Kudo, L. C., London, S. E., Geschwind, D. H. and White, S. A. (2004). Parallel FoxP1 and FoxP2 expression in songbird and human brain predicts functional interaction. *J Neurosci.* **24**, 3152–3163.

Terrace, H. S., Pettito, L. A., Saunders, R. J. and Bever, T. G. (1979). Can an ape create a sentence? *Science.* **256**, 891–902.

Thaler, D., Chen, Y.-C., Nixon, P. D., Stern, C. and Passingham, R. E. (1995). The functions of the medial premotor cortex (SMA). I. Simple learned movements. *Experimental Brain Research.* **102**, 445–460.

Thompson, P. M., Cannon, T. D., Narr, K. L., van Erp, T., Poutanen, V., Huttenen, M., Lonnquvist, J., Standerstjold-Nordenstaum, C., Kaprio, J., Khadeley, M., Dail, R., Zoumalan, C. I. and Toga, A. W. (2001). Genetic influence on brain structure. *Nat Neurosci.* **4**, 1253–1258.

Todd, R. D. (2005). Genetic advances in autism hinge on the method of measuring symptoms. Curr Psychiatry Rep. **7**, 133–137.

Tomaiuolo, F., MacDonald, J. D., Caramonos, Z., Posner, G., Chiavaras, M., Evans, A. C. and Petrides, M. (1999). Morphology, morphometry and probability mapping of the pars opercularis of the inferior frontal gyrus: an in vivo MRI analysis. *Eur J Neurosci.* **11**, 3033–3046.

Tomasello, M. (1999). *The Cultural Origins of Human Cognition*. Harvard, Cambridge.

Tomasello, M. (2003). *Constructing a Language*. Harvard, Cambridge.

Tomasello, M. and **Call, J.** (1997). *Primate Cognition*. Oxford University Press, Oxford.

Tomasello, M. and **Call, J.** (2006). Do chimpanzees know what others see—or only what they are looking at? In: Hurley, S. and Nudds, M. (ed.), *Rational Animals*. Oxford University Press, Oxford, pp. 371–384.

Tomasello, M. and **Carpenter, M.** (2005). The emergence of social cognition in three young chimpanzees. *Monogr Soc Res Child Development*. **70**, vii-132.

Tomasello, M. and **Carpenter, M.** (2007). Shared intentionality. *Dev Sci*. **10**, 121–125.

Tomasello, M., Hare, B. and **Agnetta, B.** (1999). Chimpanzees, *Pan troglodytes*, follow gaze direction geometrically. *Animal Behaviour*. **58**, 769–777.

Tomita, H., Ohbayashi, M., Nakahara, K., Hasegawa, I. and **Miyashita, Y.** (1999). Top-down signal from prefrontal cortex in executive control of memory retrieval. *Nature*. **401**, 699–703.

Tong, F., Nakayama, K., Vaughan, J. T. and **Kanwisher, N.** (1998). Binocular rivalry and visual awareness in human extrastriate cortex. *Neuron*. **21**, 753–759.

Tong, F., Meng, M. and **Blake, R.** (2006). Neural bases of binocular rivalry. *Trends Cogn Sci*. **10**, 502–511.

Toni, I., Krams, M., Turner, R. and **Passingham, R. E.** (1998*a*). The time-course of changes during motor sequence learning: a whole-brain fMRI study. *Neuroimage*. **8**, 50–61.

Toni, I., Krams, M., Turner, R. and **Passingham, R. E.** (1998*b*). The time course of changes during motor sequence learning: a whole-brain fMRI study. *Neuroimage*. **8**, 50–61.

Toni, I., Schluter, N. D., Josephs, O., Friston, K. and **Passingham, R. E.** (1999). Signal-, set- and movement-related activity in the human brain: an event-related fMRI study. *Cer. Cort*. **9**, 35–49.

Toni, I., Ramnani, N., Josephs, O., Ashburner, J. and **Passingham, R. E.** (2001). Learning arbitrary visuomotor associations: temporal dynamic of brain activity. *Neuroimage*. **14**, 1048–1057.

Toni, I., Shah, N. J., Fink, G. R., Thoenissen, D., Passingham, R. E. and **Zilles, K.** (2002). Multiple movement representations in the human brain: an event-related fMRI study. *J Cogn Neurosci*. **14**, 769–784.

Tootell, R. B. and **Hadjikhani, N.** (2001). Where is 'dorsal V4' in human visual cortex? Retinotopic, topographic and functional evidence. *Cerebral Cortex*. **11**, 298–311.

Tootell, R. B., Reppas, J. B., Dale, A. M., Look, R. B., Sereno, M. I., Malach, R., Brady, T. J. and **Rosen, B. R.** (1995). Visual motion aftereffect in human cortical area MT revealed by functional magnetic resonance imaging. *Nature*. **375**, 139–141.

Tootell, R. B., Dale, A. M., Sereno, M. I. and **Malach, R.** (1996). New images from human visual cortex. *Trends Neurosci*. **19**, 481–489.

Tootell, R. B. H., Hadjikhani, N. K., Mendola, J. D., Marrett, S. and **Dale, A. M.** (1998). From retinotopy to recognition: fMRI in human visual cortex. *Trends in Cognitive Sciences*. **2**, 174–183.

Tootell, R. B., Nelissen, K., Vanduffel, W. and **Orban, G. A.** (2004). Search for color 'center(s)' in macaque visual cortex. *Cerebral Cortex*. **14**, 353–363.

Tremblay, L. and **Schultz, W.** (1999). Relative reward preference in primate orbitofrontal cortex. *Nature*. **398**, 704–708.

Tsao, D. Y., Freiwald, W. A., Knutsen, T. A., Mandeville, J. B. and **Tootell, R. B.** (2003). Faces and objects in macaque cerebral cortex. *Nat Neurosci*. **6**, 989–995.

Tulving, E. (1983). *Elements of Episodic Memory*. Oxford University Press, Oxford.

Tulving, E. (2001). Episodic memory and common sense: how far apart? *Phil Trans Roy Soc Lond B Biol Sci*. **356**, 1505–1515.

Tulving, E. (2005). Episodic memory and autonoesis: uniquely human? In: **Terrace, H. S.** and **Metcalfe, J.** (ed.), *The Missing Link in Cognition*. Oxford University Press, Oxford, pp. 3–56.

Turner, D. C., Aitken, M. R., Shanks, D. R., Sahakian, B. J., Robbins, T. W., Schwarzbauer, C. and **Fletcher, P. C.** (2004). The role of the lateral frontal cortex in causal associative learning: exploring preventative and super-learning. *Cerebral Cortex*. **14**, 872–880.

Ungerleider, G. and **Desimone, R.** (1986). Cortical connections of visual area MT in the macaque. *J Comp Neurol*. **248**, 190–222.

Ungerleider, L. G. and **Mishkin, M.** (1982. Two cortical visual systems. In: Ingle, D. J. *et al.* (ed.), *Advances in the Analysis of Visual Behavior*. MIT Press, Cambridge, pp. 549–586.

Unterrainer, J. M., Rahm, B., Kaller, C. P., Ruff, C. C., Spreer, J., Krause, B. J., Schwarzwald, R., Hautzel, H. and **Halsband, U.** (2004). When planning fails: individual differences and error-related brain activity in problem solving. *Cerebral Cortex*. **14**, 1390–1397.

Unterrainer, J. M., Ruff, C. C., Rahm, B., Kaller, C. P., Spreer, J., Schwarzwald, R. and **Halsband, U.** (2005). The influence of sex differences and individual task performance on brain activation during planning. *Neuroimage*. **24**, 586–590.

Vandenberghe, R., Price, C., Wise, R., Josephs, O. and **Frackowiak, R. S. J.** (1996). Functional anatomy of a common semantic system for words and pictures. *Nature*. **383**, 254–256.

Vanduffel, W., Fize, D., Peuskens, H., Denys, K., Sunaert, S., Todd, J. T. and **Orban, G. A.** (2002). Extracting 3D from motion: differences in human and monkey intraparietal cortex. *Science*. **298**, 413–415.

Van Essen, D. and **DeYoe, E. A.** (1995). Concurrent processing in the primate visual cortex. In: Gazzaniga, M. S. (ed.), *The Cognitive Neurosciences*. MIT Press, Cambridge, pp. 383–400.

Van Essen, D. C., Lewis, J. W., Drury, H. A., Hadjikhani, N., Tootell, R. B., Bakircioglu, M. and **Miller, M. I.** (2001). Mapping visual cortex in monkeys and humans using surface-based atlases. *Vision Res*. **41**, 1359–1378.

Van Lawick-Goodall, J. (1968). The behavior of free-living chimpanzees in the Gombe Stream Reserve. *Anim Behav* Mon. **1**, 161–311.

Van Schaik, C. P., Ancrenaz, M., Borgen, G., Galdikas, B., Knott, C. D., Singleton, I., Suzuki, A., Utami, S. S. and Merrill, M. (2003). Orangutan cultures and the evolution of material culture. *Science*. **299**, 102–105.

Vargha-Khadem, F., Watkins, K., Alcock, K., Fletcher, P. and Passingham, R. (1995). Praxic and nonverbal cognitive deficits in a large family with a genetically transmitted speech and language disorder. *Proc Natl Acad Sci USA*. **92**, 930–933.

Vargha-Khadem, F., Gadian, D. G. and Mishkin, M. (2001). Dissociations in cognitive memory: the syndrome of developmental amnesia. *Phil Trans Roy Soc Lond B Biol Sci*. **356**, 1435–1440.

Velmans, M. (1991. Is human information processing conscious? *Behavioural and Brain Sciences*. **14**, 651–726.

Vigneau, M., Beaucousin, V., Herve, P. Y., Duffau, H., Crivello, F., Houde, O., Mazoyer, B. and Tzourio-Mazoyer, N. (2006). Meta-analyzing left hemisphere language areas: phonology, semantics, and sentence processing. *Neuroimage*. **30**, 1414–1432.

Vincent, J. L., Patel, G. H., Fox, M. D., Snyder, A. Z., Baker, J. T., Van Essen, D. C., Zempel, J. M., Snyder, L. H., Corbetta, M. and Raichle, M. E. (2007). Intrinsic functional architecture in the anaesthetized monkey brain. *Nature*. **447**, 83–86.

Vogeley, K., Bussfeld, P., Newen, A., Herrmann, S., Happe, F., Falkai, P., Maier, W., Shah, N. J., Fink, G. R. and Zilles, K. (2001). Mind reading: neural mechanisms of theory of mind and self-perspective. *Neuroimage*. **14**, 170–181.

Vogt, B. A., Nimchinsky, E. A., Vogt, L. J. and Hof, P. R. (1995). Human cingulate cortex: surface features, flat maps, and cytoarchitecture. *J Comparative Neurology*. **359**, 490–506.

Vogt, B. A., Vogt, L. J., Farber, N. B. and Bush, G. (2005). Architecture and neurocytology of monkey cingulate gyrus. *J Comp Neurol*. **485**, 218–239.

Von Bonin, G. and Bailey, P. (1947). *The Neocortex of Macaca Mulatta*. University of Illinois Press, Urbana.

Von Economo, C. (1926). Eine neure art spezialzellen des lobus cinguli und lobus insulae. *Z Ges Neurol Psychiatr*. **100**, 706–712.

Vuilleumier, P. O. and Rafal, R. D. (2000). A systematic study of visual extinction. Between- and within-field deficits of attention in hemispatial neglect. *Brain*. **123**, (Pt 6), 1263–1279.

Vuilleumier, P., Henson, R. N., Driver, J. and Dolan, R. J. (2002). Multiple levels of visual object constancy revealed by event-related fMRI of repetition priming. *Nat Neurosci*. **5**, 491–499.

Waiter, G. D., Williams, J. H., Murray, A. D., Gilchrist, A., Perrett, D. I. and Whiten, A. (2004). A voxel-based investigation of brain structure in male adolescents with autistic spectrum disorder. *Neuroimage*. **22**, 619–625.

Wakabayashi, A., Baron-Cohen, S., Uchiyama, T., Yoshida, Y., Kuroda, M. and Wheelwright, S. (2007). Empathizing and systemizing in adults with and without autism spectrum conditions: cross-cultural stability. *J Autism Dev Disord.* **37**, 1823–1832.

Walker, E. A. (1940). A cytoarchitectural study of the prefrontal area of the macaque monkey. *J Comparative Neurology.* **73**, 59–86.

Wallis, J. D. and **Miller, E. K.** (2003). *Neuronal* activity in primate dorsolateral and orbital prefrontal cortex during performance of a reward preference task. *EurJ Neurosci.* **18**, 2069–2081.

Wallis, J. D., Anderson, K. C. and **Miller, E. K.** (2001). Single neurons in prefrontal cortex encode abstract rules. *Nature.* **411**, 953–956.

Walters, N. B., Eickhoff, S. B., Schleicher, A., Zilles, K., Amunts, K., Egan, G. F. and **Watson, J. D.** (2007). Observer-independent analysis of high-resolution MR images of the human cerebral cortex: in vivo delineation of cortical areas. *Hum Brain Mapp.* **28**, 1–8.

Wang, M., Zhang, H. and **Li, B. M.** (2000). Deficit in conditional visuomotor learning by local infusion of bicuculline into the ventral prefrontal cortex in monkeys. *EurJ Neurosci.* **12**, 3787–3796.

Warburton, E., Wise, R. J., Price, C. J., Weiller, C., Hadar, U., Ramsay, S. and **Frackowiak, R. S.** (1996). Noun and verb retrieval by normal subjects. Studies with PET. *Brain.* **119**, (Pt 1), 159–179.

Wardak, C., Olivier, E. and **Duhamel, J. R.** (2002). Saccadic target selection deficits after lateral intraparietal area inactivation in monkeys. *J Neurosci.* **22**, 9877–9884.

Warneken, F., Chen, F. and **Tomasello, M.** (2006). Cooperative activities in young children and chimpanzees. *Child Development.* **77**, 640–663.

Warrington, E. K. (1982). *Neuropsycholo*gical studies of object recognition. *Phil Trans Roy Soc Lond* B. **298**, 15–34.

Warrington, E. K. and **James, M.** (1988). Visual apperceptive agnosia: a clinico-anatomical study of three cases. *Cortex.* **24**, 13–32.

Watkins, K. and **Paus, T.** (2004). Modulation of motor excitability during speech perception: the role of Broca's area. *J Cogn Neurosci.* **16**, 978–987.

Watkins, K. E., Paus, T., Lerch, J. P., Zijdenbos, A., Collins, D. L., Neelin, P., Taylor, J., Worsley, K. J. and **Evans, A. C.** (2001). Structural asymmetries in the human brain: a voxel-based statistical analysis of 142 MRI scans. *Cerebral Cortex.* **11**, 868–877.

Watkins, K. E., Dronkers, N. F. and **Vargha-Khadem, F.** (2002*a*). Behavioural analysis of an inherited speech and language disorder: comparison with acquired aphasia. *Brain.* **125**, 452–464.

Watkins, K. E., Vargha-Khadem, F., Ashburner, J., Passingham, R. E., Connelly, A., Friston, K. J., Frackowiak, R. S., Mishkin, M. and **Gadian, D. G.** (2002*b*). MRI analysis of an inherited speech and language disorder: structural brain abnormalities. *Brain.* **125**, 465–478.

Watson, J. D. G., Frackowiak, R. S. J. and **Zeki, S.** (1993. Functional separation of colour and motion centres in human visual cortex. In: Roland, P. E. and Gulyas, B. (ed.), *The Functional Organization of Human Visual Cortex.* Pergamon, Oxford, pp. 317–327.

Watson, K. K. and **Allman, J. M.** (2007). Role of spindle cells in the social cognition of apes and humans. In: Kaas, J. and Preuss, T. M. (ed.), *Evolution of Nervous Systems: a Comprehensive Reference*, vol.IV. Academic Press, New York, pp. 479–484.

Webb, D. M. and **Zhang, J.** (2005). FoxP2 in song-learning birds and vocal-learning mammals. *J Hered*. **96**, 212–216.

Wegner, D. M. (2002). *The Illusion of Conscious Will*. MIT Press, Cambridge.

Wegner, D. M. (2003). The mind's best trick: how we experience conscious will. *Trends Cogn Sci*. **7**, 65–69.

Weiskrantz, L. (1986). *Blindsight: a Case Study and Implications*. Oxford University Press, Oxford.

Weiskrantz, L. (1997). Consciousness Lost and Found. Oxford University Press, Oxford.

Weiskrantz, L. and **Saunders, R. C.** (1984). Impairments of visual object transforms in monkeys. *Brain*. **107**, 1033–1072.

Weiskrantz, L., Cowey, A. and **Passingham, C.** (1977). Spatial responses to brief stimuli by monkeys with striate cortex ablations. *Brain*. **100**, 655–670.

Wernicke, K. (1874). *Der Aphasische Symptomcomplex. Eine Psychologische Studie auf Anatomischer Basis*. Crohn and Weigert, Breslau.

Westbury, C. F., Zatorre, R. J. and **Evans, A. C.** (1999). Quantifying variability in the planum temporale: a probability map. *Cerebral Cortex*. **9**, 392–405.

Wheatley, T., Milleville, S. C. and **Martin, A.** (2007). Understanding animate agents: distinct roles for the social network and mirror system. *Psychol Sci*. **18**, 469–474.

Wheeler, M. E., Petersen, S. E. and **Buckner, R. L.** (2000). Memory's echo: vivid remembering reactivates sensory-specific cortex. *Proc Natl Acad Sci USA*. **97**, 11125–11129.

Whiten, A. (2000). Primate culture and social learning. Cognitive *Science*. **24**, 477–508.

Whiten, A. (2005). The second inheritance system of chimpanzees and humans. *Nature*. **437**, 52–55.

Whiten, A., Custance, D. M., Gomez, J. C., Teixidor, P. and **Bard, K. A.** (1996). Imitative learning of artificial fruit processing in children (*Homo sapiens*) and chimpanzees (*Pan troglodytes*). *J Comp Psychol*. **110**, 3–14.

Whiten, A., Goodall, J., McGrew, W. C., Nishida, T., Reynolds, V., Sugiyama, Y., Tutin, C. E., Wrangham, R. W. and **Boesch, C.** (1999). Cultures in chimpanzees. *Nature*. **399**, 682–685.

Whiten, A., Horner, V. and **de Waal, F. B.** (2005). Conformity to cultural norms of tool use in chimpanzees. *Nature*. **437**, 737–740.

Wicker, B., Keysers, C., Plailly, J., Royet, J. P., Gallese, V. and **Rizzolatti, G.** (2003). Both of us disgusted in My insula: the common neural basis of seeing and feeling disgust. *Neuron*. **40**, 655–664.

Wilbrecht, L. and **Nottebohm, F.** (2003). Vocal learning in birds and humans. *Ment Retard Dev Disabil Res Rev*. **9**, 135–148.

Williams, Z. M., Bush, G., Rauch, S. L., Cosgrove, G. R. and **Eskandar, E. N.** (2004). Human anterior cingulate neurons and the integration of monetary reward with motor responses. *Nat Neurosci*. **7**, 1370–1375.

Wimmer, H. and **Perner, J.** (1983). Beliefs about beliefs: representation and constraining function of wrong beliefs in young children's understanding of deception. *Cognition.* **13**, 103–128.

Winston, J. S., O'Doherty, J. and **Dolan, R. J.** (2003). Common and distinct neural responses during direct and incidental processing of multiple facial emotions. *Neuroimage.* **20**, 84–97.

Wirth, F. P. and **O'Leary, J. L.** (1974. Locomotor behavior of decerebellated arboreal mammals–monkey and raccoon. *J Comp Neurol.* **157**, 53–85.

Wise, S. P. and **Mauritz, K.-H.** (1985). Set-related neuronal activity in the premotor cortex of rhesus monkeys: effects of change in motor set. *Proceeding of the Royal Society of London, series B.* **223**, 331–354.

Wise, S. P. and **Murray, E. A.** (2000). Arbitrary associations between antecedents and actions. *TINS.* **23**, 271–276.

Witelson, S. F. and **Pallie, W.** (1973). Left hemisphere specialization for language in the newborn. Neuroanatomical evidence of asymmetry. *Brain.* **96**, 641–646.

Wolpert, D. M., Goodbody, S. J. and **Husain, M.** (1998). Maintaining internal representations: the role of the human superior parietal lobe. *Nature Neuroscience.* **1**, 529–533.

Woodruff, G. and **Premack, D.** (1981). Primative mathematical concepts in the chimpanzee: proportionality and numerosity. *Nature.* **293**, 568–570.

Woolsey, C. N. (1958). Organization of somatic sensory and motor areas of the cerebral cortex. In: Harlow, H. F. and Woolsey, C. N. (ed.), *Biological and Biochemical Basis of Behaviour.* Wisconsin University Press, Wisconsin, pp. 63–81.

Yanez, I. B., Munoz, A., Contreras, J., Gonzalez, J., Rodriguez-Veiga, E. and **DeFelipe, J.** (2005). Double bouquet cell in the human cerebral cortex and a comparison with other mammals. *J Comp Neurol.* **486**, 344–360.

Yapici, Z. and **Eraksoy, M.** (2005). Non-progressive congenital ataxia with cerebellar hypoplasia in three families. *Acta Paediatr.* **94**, 248–253.

Yonelinas, A. P., Otten, L. J., Shaw, K. N. and **Rugg, M. D.** (2005). Separating the brain regions involved in recollection and familiarity in recognition memory. *J Neurosci.* **25**, 3002–3008.

Young, M. P. (1993). The organization of neural systems in the primate cerebral cortex. *Proceeding of the Royal Society of London, series B.* **252**, 13–18.

Yousry, T. A., Schmid, U. D., Alkadhi, H., Schmidt, D., Peraud, A., Buettner, A. and **Winkler, P.** (1997). Localization of the motor hand area to a knob on the precentral gyrus. A new landmark. *Brain.* **120**, (Pt 1), 141–157.

Zago, L., Pesenti, M., Mellet, E., Crivello, F., Mazoyer, B. and **Tzourio-Mazoyer, N.** (2001). Neural correlates of simple and complex mental calculation. *Neuroimage.* **13**, 314–327.

Zago, L. and **Tzourio-Mazoyer, N.** (2002). Distinguishing visuospatial working memory and complex mental calculation areas within the parietal lobes. *Neurosci Lett.* **331**, 45–49.

Zatorre, R. J., Evans, A. C., Meyer, E. and Gjedde, A. (1992. Lateralization of phonetic and pitch discrimination in speech processing. *Science*. **256**, 846–849.

Zeki, S. M. (1971). Convergent input from the striate cortex (area 17) to the cortex of the superior temporal sulcus in the rhesus monkey. *Brain Res*. **28**, 338–340.

Zeki, S. (1983). The distribution of wavelength and orientation selective cells in different areas of monkey visual cortex. *Proc Roy Soc Lond B Biol Sci*. **217**, 449–470.

Zeki, S. (1993). *A Vision of the Brain*. Blackwell, Oxford.

Zhang, J., Webb, D. M. and Podlaha, O. (2002). Accelerated Protein Evolution and Origins of Human-Specific Features. Foxp2 as an example. *Genetics*. **162**, 1825–1835.

Zhou, Y.-D. and Fuster, J. M. (2000). Visuo-tactile cross-modal associations in cortical somatosensory cells. *Proc Nat Acad Sci*. **97**, 9777–9782.

Zilles, K., Palomero-Gallagher, N., Grefkes, C., Scheperjans, F., Boy, C., Amunts, K. and Schleicher, A. (2002). Architectonics of the human cerebral cortex and transmitter receptor fingerprints: reconciling functional neuroanatomy and neurochemistry. *Eur Neuropsychopharmacol*. **12**, 587–599.

Index